SEAN MACLEOD is a r and author from Dublin, Ir writing songs, recording anc ....g for over 30 years. He has a keen interest in popular music and has written three books on its influence on modern culture. Sean also has a deep interest in philosophy and in particular the work of Rudolf Steiner, and has attempted to marry his interest in music, literature and the work of Steiner in both his writing and his music. Sean teaches film, music and media studies at the Limerick College of Further Education in Ireland and is currently finishing an Arts Practice PhD in Music at the University of Limerick. His PhD employs Steiner's phenomenological methods as a major research tool.

BEHIND THE
WALL OF ILLUSION

*The Religious, Esoteric and Occult Worlds
of the Beatles*

Sean MacLeod

CLAIRVIEW

Clairview Books Ltd.,
Russet, Sandy Lane,
West Hoathly,
W. Sussex RH19 4QQ

www.clairviewbooks.com

Published by Clairview Books 2023

A CIP catalogue record for this book is available from the British Library

ISBN 978 1 912992 46 1

Cover by Morgan Creative
Typeset by Symbiosys Technologies, Visakhapatnam, India
Printed and bound by 4Edge Ltd, Essex

Contents

Chapter 1

In the Beginning...
The Birth of the Beatles

Victory Day

On 7 May 1945, a great euphoria spread over Britain as World War Two came to an end and the country celebrated their victory over a fascist regime that was considered a major threat to mainland Europe. The end of the War meant that normal life could resume, while the sense of camaraderie that had emerged throughout the War remained, despite government imposed policies of austerity. The government had enforced strict rationings along with slogans like 'make and do' to encourage the population to 'do their duty', and pull together in an effort to restore the country to its former glory. Popular ditties like the following were also used to cajole the people to conform to the government's post-war policies:

> Those who have a will to win
> cook potatoes in their skin
> knowing that the sight of peelings
> deeply hurts his majesty's feelings.

Old fashioned values, almost Dickensian, of Britishness were instilled after the War, while children were encouraged to conform through mottos, like that at Paul McCartney's school — 'NON NOBIS SOLUM, SED TOTI MUNDO NATI' ('we're not born for ourselves, but for the good of the world') — or through corporal punishment,[1] dished out regularly at John Lennon's Quarry Bank School by headmaster, E. R. Taylor, a lay preacher who instilled high 'Christian' morality into his pupils with the aid of his cane.[2] The motto of the Quarry Bank School was 'from this quarry, virtue is forged', while the school anthem, which every school boy at Quarry

Bank was expected to know by heart and sing at the beginning of every school term, with 'vigoroso', went something like:

> Quarry men old before our birth
> Straining each muscle and sinew.
> Toiling together, Mother Earth
> Conquered the Rock that was in you.[3]

Ironic in a way, since the school's most famous pupil of the post-war Fifties did just that (conquer 'the Rock' that was in him) but in a manner totally unintended by headmaster Taylor and all the other Quarry Bank teachers who 'toiled' to 'forge' the virtue in each of their pupils. Lennon – never too enthusiastic to forge any kind of 'virtue' while a pupil of the school, and more intent on causing trouble – with his group The Quarrymen, would play one of his first public performances, at the annual Woolton Parish Church Garden Fete, where he first met Paul McCartney, under the 'benign eye' of Reverend Morris Pryce-Jones and his committee, while 'smiling church ladies poured tea'.

After the War, Liverpool was a virtual bombsite with little prospects for the city's young talent, and the outdated Victorian values still attempted to keep the populace in its place. Liverpool, like much of the rest of British society and culture, was full of secrecy and hypocrisy (culminating in the Profumo scandal, in which the Secretary of State for War had an extramarital affair with a 19-year-old call girl) that imbued the post-war atmosphere, which many of the post-war generation were aware of to some extent.[4] 'Was it any wonder', Lennon would later observe 'we all went raving mad in the Sixties'.[5]

Growing up in Britain during and immediately after the War, as all the Beatles had, was, for most young boys, probably both exhilarating and frightening. Air-raids, curfews and bomb shelters, mixed with stories of bravery and trepidation by British soldiers, painted an exciting image of war, while newsreels and films of British heroism, like The Wooden Horse (1952) and the Dam Busters (1954) — 'were a comforting reminder of the reasons the British had for feeling proud of themselves – and self-sufficient... they cultivated the myth of Britain's War, paying special attention to the importance of comradeship across class and occupation'.[6]

Despite the austerity and the expectation for everyone cheerfully to weather the hardship, the country still willingly supported the same group of politicians who had not only imposed the austerity but who had also led the country to war in the first place. Such figures included Winston Churchill, who had replaced Neville Chamberlain just after the outbreak of World War Two. Churchill was considered the 'great' leader who, with the determination of a British bulldog, guided the nation safely through the War to victory. Families, just like that of George Harrison's, would gather around the radio eagerly listening as their Prime Minister exhorted the people to be brave in the face of Hitler and the buzz bombs of the Luftwaffe. John Lennon was even given the middle name Winston in honour of the War leader, while his aunt Mimi, who became John's primary guardian and with whom he lived from about the age of five, proudly displayed *The Complete Works of Churchill* on the family bookshelf.

Churchill came to represent the idea of British determination, strength and sturdiness. To those living through the War, the sense of the old British values, with its traditions, institutions and modest way of life, were celebrated and cherished. After all, it was to preserve this way of life, this sense of 'liberty, fraternity and democracy' against the tyranny of the Nazis, that many young British men had given their lives.

Immediately after the War, due to the feeling of national pride, most people in Liverpool continued to conform to traditional British values, and on 2 June 1953 they, like the rest of the country, happily celebrated the Coronation of their new Queen, Elizabeth II, every aspect of which they could observe closely on their new television sets. The Coronation was a day when a sense of monarchy and Empire were firmly inculcated in the people of the nation, but also one when austerity finally ended for Britain and a consumer culture, coming from America, mainly through the medium of television, began to find its way into modern British society. The arrival of American soldiers also had a profound influence on British culture, as they brought with them a sense of wonder, newness and excitement that filled the decimated and drab world of post-war Britain with colour.

Though America had also suffered in the aftermath of the War, the country was able, largely due to industry, to create a flourishing economy based mostly on the production of domestic products that encouraged a new consumer culture. The American youth saw the old traditions and attitudes being wiped away after the War and replaced by a whole different attitude. One commentator observed that, 'It wasn't long after World War Two, from which America emerged victorious, that things began to change quite dramatically at home. All sorts of forces were at work to make the Fifties and then the Sixties a time of enormous social upheaval.'[7] By the mid-Fifties, these attitudes began to make their way across the Atlantic, while American loans helped to restore the economies of Britain and Europe.

Angry Young Men

Since Liverpool was Britain's principal port for bringing in supplies from the Irish Sea, as well as a major manufacturing centre for armaments, Hitler's tactic was to starve Britain into submission by bombing the supply lines, and as a result the city became a prime target for Hermann Goering's Luftwaffe. After London, Liverpool was the hardest hit city during the war[8] with almost 27,000 inhabitants evacuating the city to north Wales. By the end of the War much of the neoclassical city had been destroyed, while city planners' unimaginative restoration attempt more or less destroyed any last remaining beauty the city had, carelessly 'throwing up entire, prefabricated neighbourhoods on old bomb sites'. 'Clearance' was the word, and the result was drab, pitiful communities, 'full of fear and people smashing things up'.[9] One district typical of this type of planning was Speke, where all the Beatles except Lennon had spent some, if not all, of their childhoods growing up.[10]

Although Liverpool had incurred tremendous civilian casualties and architectural devastation,[11] the first few years following the War were probably the hardest of the twentieth century, and clothing coupons and food queues became a way of life. As the injured and broken soldiers returned home from the War and active bombs still lurked under the rubble where the children played, the long struggle that lay ahead and the massive debt that would have to be paid back in order to rebuild – not to mention the fact that the country was just beginning to heal itself from the devastation of the First World War only a generation earlier – people began to ask serious questions as to why these wars had started in the first place. Soon the feelings of victory and greatness in certain sectors of both British and American life began to fade, as despair and anger set in.

In America, those who questioned the War, primarily the beatniks and bohemians, saw a soullessness in the consumer culture that had become dominant in its wake. Black Americans (or 'Coloureds', as they were referred to then[12]) who had displayed their patriotism by risking their lives on the battlefields of Europe and Asia, were also discontent following the War and cried out for their equal rights in peacetime, considering they were treated equal enough to kill and be killed during wartime. The women who had served in the War also demanded equality on the same grounds, while the youth of the post-war generation, living in the shadow of the atomic bomb, were apprehensive about the type of world they would inherit. Many of these grievances found expression in art, music, literature and cinema.

Rock 'n' roll and jazz were a reaction to the establishment, while the beat poets and young American film-makers like László Benedek, *The Wild One* (1953) and Edward Dmytryk, *The Young Lions* (1958) – along with modern film stars like Marlon Brando and James Dean, with their 'What are you rebelling against? What have you got?' attitude – represented the individual, who struggled against the soullessness of the post-war consumerism in favour of 'authenticity'.[13]

Across Europe there was a similar reaction. Samuel Beckett's *Waiting for Godot* (1953), for example, created a whole new style of theatre, itself growing out of the emptiness and alienation of war. The so-called existentialist philosophies of Jean-Paul Sartre and Albert Camus, art movements and new musical forms from the avant-garde, like the Neo-Futurists, Fluxus (who emerged in the 1960s), John Cage and the Darmstadt School, decided the old forms had to be destroyed and that the world needed to start from year zero, destroying all values of pre-war attitudes and lifestyles, which they saw as responsible for the terrors that had been inflicted on humanity.

In Britain, there was possibly less reaction, but by the late Fifties there were certainly many who were angry about the War and the lies and deceit they had endured, not to mention the years of psychological, as well as physical, repair that the whole nation would need to undergo in order to get back to any sense of normality. A group of 'angry young men', playwriters and novelists, like Leslie Paul, *Angry Young Man* (1951), Kingsley Amis, *Lucky Jim* (1954) and John Osborne, *Look Back in Anger* (1956), expressed disdain at the old guard, while film-makers also reacted against the aimless and superficial films of the Forties and Fifties, and against the propaganda films that had emerged before, during and after the War.[14] The new playwrights and film-makers offered a new style of social realism — portraying not the happy-go-lucky, shiftless working class or the noble upper-class — but the realism of life as it actually was lived in Britain. These film-makers, such as Lindsay Anderson and Karel Reisz, whose film *Saturday Night Sunday Morning* (1960) was based on the novel by another 'angry young man', Alan Sillitoe, often expressed the discontent of many in Britain, usually working-class individuals who saw themselves as nothing more than servants and cannon-fodder for the ruling class.

In Britain, post-war recession produced groups of disenfranchised, young working-class men, like the Teddy Boys, who had reacted to the post-war poverty by adopting a flamboyant lifestyle and attitude in which they donned the most outrageous clothes dating back to the Edwardian era, which set them apart from post-war attitudes, 'fusing their own cultural heritage with American beats... pledging their undying visual devotion to American culture — as if by adopting the insignia of the prevailing post-war power, he might adopt some of its confidence for himself.'[15] These groups adopted an almost religious fanaticism to a lifestyle of extravagance, although bubbling beneath the exterior of a new kind of 'gentleman' was a disappointment and dissatisfaction with their working-class drudgery.

The Teds, as they were called, were often violent and anti-social because of their dissatisfaction and their sense of elitism. Like all British teenagers in the Fifties, Lennon, McCartney, Harrison and Starr all gravitated to the 'hard man' style of the Teddy Boys, wearing their hair, the obligatory greased back quiff, as a symbol of their rebellious attitudes to the British establishment and class system. Lennon was the local Ted, creating a tough image for himself to hide his insecurities. McCartney said: 'you saw Lennon before you met him'.[16] Lennon dropped out of education as soon as he could, devising his own programme of educational reading – by the age of ten he was reading Carroll, Richmal Crompton, Poe, Stevenson, Lear, Balzac – 'drawing and soaking up knowledge from the emergent pop culture of Liverpool and Britain in the 1950s'.[17]

Lennon would later use his song 'Working Class Hero' as an attempt to push back at the idea that hard work brings honour to a man, scoffing at the idea that it is the key to success and self-respect, and a form of heroism in and of itself. In the song he turns that cliché into a curse, the irony bent by experience: 'There's room at the top they are telling you still / but first you must learn how to smile as you kill.'[18] This would express Lennon's contempt for class hypocrisy,[19] which was already beginning to form in his early teens.

George Harrison would be as equally disenchanted with the manner in which his class and age group were institutionalized by a system that only prepared you for a life of bondage to full time employment, without any sense of personal satisfaction or self-respect. He had, from a young age, anti-authoritarian feelings and felt the education system set up in England was hell-bent on turning bright young minds into submissive drones.[20] He would later sum up his experience of state education at the Liverpool Institute in the following terms: 'The way they sent you out into the world was miserable.'[21] George rebelled, wearing a bright yellow coat, skin-tight pants, blue suede shoes and long slicked back hair. Teachers were outraged by his defiant look and attitude. He had, after all, been brought up to embrace conformity and stability.[22]

McCartney, though more often seen as the most obliging, conformist and diplomatic of the Beatles, also had a rebellious streak, which began to express itself more noticeably soon after the death of his mother, when he was just entering puberty. McCartney, having fallen in love with the non-conformist sentiments of rock 'n' roll, began to reject the steady, secure path that was being set out for him. One biographer noted that, 'Beyond the sorrow and self-reproach of the moment, the death of his mother was to become one of those pivotal events in McCartney's life, stirring ambitions and shaping decisions that might have been quite different had she lived'[23] – and he soon lost interest in the idea of being a teacher (a career path which his teachers had encouraged him towards) and threw himself into music. It was his mother's passing that made him do that.[24]

Ringo Starr, although the last to join the group, and who was not a childhood friend of the others, also rebelled against the norms of British society, particularly against the constraints that would be imposed by his typical working-class background. Having spent a large part of his school years in the TB ward at Heswall's Children's Hospital, when he was discharged Starr had decided that school was not for him and soon gravitated towards the new sound of rock 'n' roll with an ambition to be a professional drummer.[25]

By the mid-Fifties a massive cultural shift occurred, creating a split between those of the pre-war years with the generation that followed. The new generation no longer saw themselves as cheeky, loveable-though-lowly working-class figures. They looked to America for their role models and, particularly, to anti-authoritarian individuals like Elvis Presley and Marlon Brando. America was the place the post-war British teenager wanted to be, where the excitement of rock 'n' roll and Hollywood promised a world of colour and adventure; a stark contrast to, 'Britain's post-war austerity years, when the battle-exhausted, bankrupt nation seemed to have no warmth, no food, no fun, no colour'.[26] The Beatles and the rest of Liverpool experienced such a life on an extreme level, since it was there that 'felt like the austerity capital of the UK with its acres of shattered buildings and gaping craters'.[27]

The Rolling Stones manager, Andrew Oldham, described the British youths' disenchantment with its own country and admiration for all things American in his autobiography:

> Those of us punters not yet part of the new intelligentsia nurtured the hope that someday soon our lives would resemble the American movies we loved, we'd trade places with a miserable young James Dean in a flash. We had no perspective on Britain's glorious and unrecoverable past, so we lived in a make believe present time inspired by Hollywood and rock 'n' roll. ... Dreams were important because our elders had run out of them and therefore aspiration belonged to the young. Rock 'n' roll was ours because it was American and our parents didn't want it.[28]

Goodbye the Old Welcome the New

Though Liverpool did have a large and significant Catholic population, mostly the result of Irish immigrants to the city (George Harrison's family being a perfect example)[29] the dominant persuasion was more towards a secular Protestant liberalism, an ideology largely promoted in the mid-nineteenth century by groups like the British Association for the Advancement of Science and the Royal Society, who were in favour of a society that was informed by 'science, pure and free, untrammelled by religious dogma'.[30] Paul McCartney's father, Jim McCartney, whose family had converted from Catholicism to Protestantism, for example, was a non-believer. 'The world,' he was fond of saying, 'was a clock that God wound up and left to run down.'[31] The hypocrisy often witnessed in the Catholic Church didn't help the cause of religion either.[32]

Even though McCartney was baptised Catholic, resulting from his mother's pious Catholic background, later depicted in such terms in his Catholically-tinged hymn 'Let It Be', his religious education, at Stockton Road infants school, was 'exclusively Anglican'[33] while both Harrison and Lennon, who was also from a mixed Catholic/Protestant background (who had favoured their Protestant side for purely career advantages), attended the state-run, non-religious primary school of Dovedale.

The Protestant ethos of the country had rejected religious dogma for rationality and free-thinking, allowing one's own consciousness to determine behaviour and beliefs. Although laws were clearly there to maintain the public good and peace within communities, people's lifestyle choices and religious convictions were their own to choose and follow. Although the Beatles had grown up after the War in an atmosphere of austerity, by the 1960s a whole new attitude was beginning to emerge, and by November 1960 the Conservatives won a general election on the slogan 'You've never had it so good' and a policy of making Britain 'Great again'. The press spoke of consumer demand, while the young were encouraged – by the phasing out of national service – to enjoy their youth.

Like many teenagers of the Fifties, the Beatles found a certain free-spirited element influencing their view of the world, and all of the individual Beatles experienced a certain open-mindedness and loosening up of traditional ways through their immediate environment, signalling the change of attitude that the War had caused in some of the older generation. Paul McCartney found such an attitude in his father Jim, who even though he had tried to instil old fashioned values into both his sons and was unwelcoming to the Americanisms that had crept into British life – particularly through the language of rock 'n' roll – was encouraging towards Paul's interest in music, even tolerating his choice not to pursue a career as a teacher. Lennon, Harrison and Starr also had a liberating element within their lives. Lennon found it in his free-spirited mother, Julia, a stark contrast to his conservative and austere Aunt Mimi, and while Harrison's father was more traditional his mother, Louise, encouraged his individualism and fostered his interest in the guitar and rock 'n' roll — something Lennon's Aunt Mimi would barely tolerate — and Ringo seemed always encouraged by a single mother who was happy just to have her son healthy after many years of illness.

Though Britain had a tradition of 'tolerance' when it came to religious and spiritual beliefs, though this would often give way to bigotry when Catholics and Protestants clashed on 12 July – King Billy's Day, an important Protestant celebration – it would have looked patronisingly on other outlooks, particularly those of its crumbling Empire, which found their way into British society, along with an increasing number of immigrants during the 1950s. Though their traditions and practices were welcome by some, they were mostly treated as strange and often with suspicion. Non-British ways were often mocked, as McCartney's description of the Maharishi coming to Britain in the late Fifties ('a funny little man') indicates. Even significant cultural individuals like Gandhi were seen in the same way in 1950s' Britain. However, within a decade the Beatles, as well as a vast majority of British and American society, particularly those of the post-war generation, would happily embrace both figures and much of what India and many other non-western cultures had to offer in terms of art, philosophy and spiritual life.

While there had always been a keen interest in esoteric subjects among the British and American intellectual groups – such as the British Romantic poets, writers such as Charles Dickens, Arthur

Conan Doyle, and Mary Todd Lincoln, wife of America's sixteenth President – this was intensified following the First World War, primarily due to what the writer James Webb referred to as a 'flight from reason'.[34] A society stunned by the horrors of a war, into which the entire 'civilized' world had suddenly plummeted, sought meanings in the so-called 'irrational'.

In the aftermath of World War Two, however, there seemed to be a decline in esoteric and spiritual interests, as the consumer culture of the post-war era, as well as a more profoundly materialistic scientific outlook, held sway. For the most part, religion served only a superficial role which encouraged a conformity to a particular social ethos, influenced by consumerism and other materialistic outlooks, that had emerged after the War. For the vast majority, the established order was to be followed, and dissent only came after the War by the emerging youth groups, who tended to embrace a kind of nihilism that the figures of rock 'n' roll and the teen idols – like Dean, Brando and Elvis, at least their on-screen characters, embraced. These were existential characters trying to find their place in the consumerism of American post-war culture.

As the Beatles moved from virtual obscurity to worldwide fame, they became major cultural figures that significantly influenced and changed the world. The 1960s, the decade of the Beatles, underwent a tremendous transformation in relation to religion, esotericism and spirituality, both in personal terms and also in having a great influence on the world in these matters, at least in terms of popularizing and bringing to mainstream awareness issues regarding them.

The Beatles crossed the paths of many spiritual movements and ideologies, as well as religious groups, esoteric philosophies and occult and mystical teachings that acted on them and through them. This variety of ideas shaped their thinking, their music and their way of life, while at the same time influencing the overall consciousness of the culture in which they lived. Essentially the religious, philosophical and spiritual landscape of the western world, particularly in Britain and America, went through a tremendous shift during the 1960s, transforming the philosophical and spiritual thoughts of these two nations. The following chapters in this book aim to examine how pivotal the Beatles were to this cultural sea change.

Chapter 2

A Shot of Rhythm and Blues:
The New Religion of Rock 'n' Roll

A New Era: Teen Disciples

This difference between the pre-war and post-war generation was ultimately something more significant than just a generation gap. In fact, the War distinguished not just the generations, but a whole new consciousness, a whole new outlook on life and the human being's place within it. The War had unleashed certain forces, almost supernatural cosmic forces, that would transform the latter half of the century. The War had quashed the pre-war generation and left them far behind, but it meant little to the emerging generation of the mid-Fifties. The pop music journalist, Allison Taich, writes in her essay 'Beatlemania: The Defiance of a Generation':

> The idea of a grace period in life between childhood and adulthood was not recognised pre-World War Two. Suddenly there was an age where people did not identify with the helpless and dependent stages of childhood, nor with the pressures and responsibilities of adulthood. This middle ground of age and responsibility came into its own during the 1950s when it was no longer cool to share the same interests, mores or values of the previous generation. Attention was put more towards socialising with peers, while leisure and entertainment became increasing priorities. Popular music unleashed rock 'n' roll to the public, which catered to this new way of thinking and feeling.[35]

It was because of this, Taich suggests, that 'popular culture began to shift, and between the advertisement and entertainment industries a new breed was developing: the teenager'.[36]

Though other eras had had their rebellious elements, like the Flappers of the 1920s, following World War One, that generation underwent great changes, sowing many of the seeds that were halted by the Great Depression of the 1930s and then World War Two, but which would begin to flourish in the 1960s. The teenager was a totally new creation; it was something that had ultimately sprang up in America, particularly with the consumer culture that encouraged the fads and trends of the new generation, rejecting the stifling life of the pre-war generation of their parents, where conformity was expected.

As we have seen, this generation gap was effectively addressed, at least in Britain, through plays and films like John Osborne's *Look Back in Anger* (1956), as well as in the satirical commentary of TV programmes like *That Was the Week That Was* (1962) and *Beyond the Fringe* (1960), a stage revue, which included material from some of Britain's youngest comic talents, including Peter Cook and Dudley Moore, who were deeply critical of certain aspects of the pre-war generation. The cult of the individual, nurtured in the consumer culture of America, transferred itself strongly into the teenager, while American movies, particularly the rock 'n' roll 'exploitation' movies like *Rock Around the Clock* (1956), *The Girl Can't Help It* (1956) and *Jailhouse Rock* (1957), as well as its non-conformist music, brought the notion of the teenager alive, encouraging a youth culture never experienced before.

Rock 'n' Roll Prophets

While the War 'had made popular music a vital part of everyday life', in Britain and America this wartime music had appeal for the young.[37] The BBC's *Light Programme*, for example, was full of songs with a wartime sensibility but when rock 'n' roll hit in the mid-Fifties, with songs like 'Rocket 88' and 'Rock Around the Clock', the time was ripe for a new voice of teen America to express the feelings of the new generation. While most mainstream American radio was dismissive of it, favouring the music of singers like Bing

Crosby and Doris Day, and while Britain's 'puritanical' BBC excluded it completely,[38] some radio stations, like the pirate station Radio Luxemburg, and American DJs, like Alan Freed, understood rock 'n' roll's attraction to teenagers and championed it. Rock 'n' roll not only gave the new youth a sound to go with their new image and lifestyles, but introduced a whole new set of values by which the young could live their lives.

The first prophet of rock 'n' roll, Bill Haley, was introduced to Britain in 1955 through the teen movie *Blackboard Jungle* (1955), a film about the rising juvenile delinquency which was of concern to American society at the time and which caused frustrated Teddy Boys in Britain to rip up cinema seats when it was shown – an experience which the young Ringo Starr said impressed him deeply.[39] The War had not made Britain any less rigidly class-bound and the responses to rock 'n' roll awoke fears of a juvenile delinquency problem on the same scale as America, not to mention an older, darker fear of proletarian uprising.[40] For such reasons the Press and the Establishment hated it, making out that the lyrics were obscene and the rhythm jungle-like – a racist allusion to its black origins.[41] The clothes and hair were equally hated by parents, but the kids loved it and its non-acceptance made it even more enticing to teens. 'Rock radiated the fragrance of escape,' wrote McCartney's biographer, Christopher Sandford.

McCartney, like Lennon, had found escape in the new religion of rock 'n' roll after they both experienced a deep loss in their respective families. John had lost his stepfather, George Smith, and Paul had lost his mother, Mary McCartney. 'Paul,' wrote Sandford, 'had often stolen off to the Odeon to watch the adventures of Dick Barton or some similar action hero, whose exploits he excitedly re-enacted at the family tea table. He found Haley even more alluring.'[42] Rock 'n' roll offered Lennon and McCartney solace and belief that nothing else in their lives could give them.

Rock 'n' roll appealed to the deep feelings of sexual energy that the new youth were beginning to experience, and the new attitudes and freedoms that were also emerging at the time. It represented the life of a new economic class, both in Britain and America, as expertly captured in Colin MacInnes' novel *Absolute Beginners* (1959), which describes the new youth culture that had begun to emerge but which was very quickly hijacked by the business class (in America, this new economic class had, in 1956, a spending power of about seven billion dollars).

Where exactly this attitude came from is very hard to pinpoint, but was probably due to a combination of factors: the War itself; the destruction of countries and people; the post-war shock of a nation too numb to carry on in any real sense; a rejection of past values by the old as well as the young, who had no respect for a country and culture that could produce such a terrible thing as the atomic bomb; the relief that the end of the War brought and the realization that life must be lived and embraced, and that prosperity and happiness were all that really mattered. As well as all this, the post-war stress of the Cold War and of a potentially imminent nuclear war filled people with a sense of dread, which they attempted to distract themselves from with things like music, movies and consumerism.

The young, not always so worried about the future – though they were certainly aware of what the future could be like if war struck for a third time – made the most of the new consumer products. The consumerism and post-war industrializations of towns and cities brought more employment, which meant people could pre-occupy themselves with their work and, as a result of work, could be further distracted by spending their money and enjoying their free time.

Although rock 'n' roll was a fascination for American and British teenagers, on its first arrival to Britain it was too aggressive for many pubescent males who were trying to figure out their place in the world. George Harrison was a typical example of the younger teenagers who felt 'intimidated by the form ... and felt he was not grown up enough to be an active participant',[43] limiting his participation to just listening to the records. Rock 'n' roll was also too 'distant' and 'unattainable' for British youths to aspire to.[44] However, when the 'second prophet' of rock, Lonnie Donegan, arrived on the scene on 13 July 1954, just a week after Elvis recorded his first record for the Sun label, British teenage boys found a musical hero they could easily emulate. With his unique brand of music, known as skiffle – a form of American folk music which emerged following the Great Depression – Donegan inspired thousands of young British teenagers, 'poor whites, who couldn't afford conventional instruments', to form their own skiffle groups using makeshift instruments out of 'kitchen wash boards, jugs, and kazoos'.[45]

The vast number of skiffle groups that formed in Britain as a result of Donegan's success, like the Vipers, the Nomads, the Hobos, the Streamliners, and of course John Lennon's first group the Quarrymen, was, as one commentator noted, 'a way to release their violence. Instead of beating each other to death they beat a drum, and they didn't have to learn music. It was from the heart and a chance to break away from the poverty that surrounds you … a working class musical revolution.'[46]

In its British form, it was a mix of blues, country, folk, jazz and spirituals, of which most British teens knew nothing previously.[47] There was something 'primitive and overtly sexual in the music' that went hand-in-hand with the British adolescence entering puberty.[48] 'The effect,' suggested Philip Norman in his biography of Paul McCartney, 'was galvanising on bashful British boys with no previously musical leanings.'[49] 'Rock 'n' roll,' said Lennon's friend Eric Griffiths, 'was beyond our imagination, but skiffle was music we could play.'[50]

Every British teenager had read the story of how Donegan had taken half an hour to record his hit 'Rock Island Line', and his first quarter royalty cheque had been for TWENTY-SEVEN THOUSAND POUNDS (always in capitals), and the Beatles certainly wanted some of that.[51] It wasn't just money, however, that drew them to skiffle but the sense of belonging that the music gave them. While Lennon and McCartney found rock 'n' roll to be a welcome distraction from their personal pain, George, already disillusioned with established norms like formal education, channelled all his interests into learning the guitar,[52] while Ringo Starr had very early on developed a strong passion for the drums (as well as movies and girls). 'It was in my soul, I just wanted to be a drummer', he would declare.[53]

'The Messiah Has Arrived'

It was due to a mixture of this new sound and lifestyle coming from America that the Beatles, and groups like them, began to form. McCartney put it well when he described this new world, brought to life in technicolour on screen in the classic rock 'n' roll 'exploitation' movie *The Girl Can't Help It* (1956), as follows: 'The world had suddenly gone from black and white to technicolour.'[54] In their hometown of Liverpool, the influence of rock 'n' roll and skiffle was immense and the new groups, who were proficiently talented, created their own unique sound, which would later be called the 'Mersey Sound'. The sound became so popular that the BBC did a special report on it in the early Sixties, before anyone had ever heard of the Beatles. These groups were all richly talented, and apparently not any lesser than or deserving to be global superstars, in the way the Beatles would later be – but clearly something set the Beatles apart; some magical and mysterious ingredient that the other groups didn't appear to have.

Though Bill Haley and other rock 'n' roll pioneers were of tremendous importance in influencing the Fifties' teenagers, it wasn't until a young, handsome and extremely charismatic, 17-year-old from the backwaters of Tupelo, Mississippi, called Elvis Presley, came along, singing and dancing in a way never witnessed before by mainstream white culture, that a 'new religion', with its own 'Messianic' figure, was created virtually overnight. While the establishment were up in arms, Elvis pointed the way for the new generation, and the future seemed bright and positive – a strong contrast to the War and the early post-war years, particularly so in Britain.

While rock 'n' roll had a vast number of celebrities, such as Chuck Berry, Little Richard and Buddy Holly, all of whom were 'worshiped'[55] by the new generation, there was no doubt that Elvis was rock 'n' roll's central figure, and exerted more of an influence on his generation then all those other performers put together. As one commentator observed:

> Hair, hips, or feet to pound the old social order into dust. Before Elvis the Fifties culture was to conform. The post-war affluence encouraged people not to rock the boat but Elvis rocked the boat and the youth rebellion that transformed the nation owed a debt to rock 'n' roll and Elvis. Elvis emerged from Memphis to shock the sensibilities and transform modern culture.[56]

While Haley had appealed to the Teds, Presley's effect on females was uncanny. Females, noted Beatles' biographer Philip Norman, 'rousing previously decorous, tight-corseted Fifties' young womanhood to hysterical screams, reciprocal bodily writhings and an apparent compulsion to tear the singer's clothes from his back'.[57] Branded the 'disciple of the devil' by orthodox elements of society, with his swivelling hips some thought Elvis was a black conspiracy, 'n***er animalistic behaviour' – which caused youth culture, as well as African-American communities, to support him even more. The 'innocent rebellious leader', he told young girls that it was OK to have sexual impulses. Elvis unleashed forces beyond his control. He made girls cry, reaching deep emotions within them. For young men, Elvis, the James Dean of popular music, became a symbol for all those that felt disenfranchised.

In America, for these very reasons, many (like Ed Sullivan) didn't want Elvis appearing on national TV, but changed their tune when they saw the ratings he got. When Elvis did finally appear on *The Ed Sullivan Show*, it signified 'the minister of morality', (and the broader adult world) surrendering to the youth culture. Even though Elvis lost some of his 'revolutionary appeal' with youth culture through his appearance on the show, he had already 'harnessed the forces of sex, money, youth, music, technology, and race, transforming our culture, the country, and much of the rest of the western world'.[58]

Elvis became the instrument from which many became rich; an icon of teen rebellion but also of teen consumerism, and after he died – from exhaustion, drug abuse and mistreatment by those around him – he was virtually canonised by popular culture, becoming a 'saint' of modern consumerism and the celebrity culture that has taken a strong hold in our modern world. His home, Graceland, has become a place of pilgrimage of a solely consumeristic society.

In a strange sense, Elvis was a spiritual force, an icon and a 'Messiah' for a new era and was sadly sacrificed for it. His influence was so profound that Paul McCartney would claim: 'This was the guru we were waiting for. The Messiah has arrived.'[59] George Harrison, the Beatle often considered to be most concerned with 'authenticity', referred to Elvis as, 'the real one', who 'changed the course of his life',[60] while for John Lennon everything was 'unreal' except for Elvis, who was 'bigger than religion' to him.[61] Lennon would make clear the huge impact Elvis had on both him and on modern culture when he stated that 'before Elvis, there was nothing',[62] almost echoing the notion that, 'In the beginning was the Word.'

The Four Evangelists

Rock 'n' roll and the idea of stardom attracted the four young Beatles to a life of music and entertainment. Harrison, Lennon and McCartney were drawn to the gigging circuit in Hamburg after a short stint in Liverpool, while Starr, who would eventually become friends with the other Beatles, found his way to Hamburg after playing in the national holiday camps of Butlin's. It was, however, the power of the music, the love affair with rock 'n' roll as a meaningful and 'authentic' teenage voice of expression, that appealed to the Beatles – not just the trappings of fame or wealth. Even though the band would claim on their second album that 'money' was what they really wanted, there was a devout integrity to their music, a sincere connection with its emotional and spiritual roots that really drove them. There was also the notion that they were destined to do something special, not just for their country or their class or their generation, but something that would open up a channel of a new age and era; something that would transform culture and music for the next half a century.

This was clearly shown by the way in which they had presented themselves to their Liverpool public, later then to their A&R man and producer George Martin, their manager Brian Epstein, and ultimately to their record company. They presented themselves as working-class, Liverpool boys, who insisted on offering their music as it was, not content on superficial and insincere tunes that would make them a success. The group had been irreverent towards Martin when they first met, Harrison apparently exclaiming that he didn't like Martin's tie, while they were respectful but mildly defiant towards both Epstein and Martin throughout their career. They had refused to record 'How Do You Do It' when Martin had procured the song as their first potential No. 1 from local songwriter Mitch Murray. They wouldn't cover it, feeling it was not a true representation of their sound and style. Lennon would give a less than committed performance when they demoed the track, possibly to appease Martin, but at the same time to let him know that they weren't going to be music industry puppets for Martin to do with them as he pleased.

They would also defy their record company's expectations of their artists, as well as the media establishment, particularly in Britain, who would usually attempt to refine their artists' accents and manners to fit in to the established notions of middle-class entertainment. Granted, they got rid of their leather and donned suits as a theatrical move, designed by their manager Brian Epstein, to make them more accessible, but it was probably – as McCartney and Lennon would later admit – a change that they realized was necessary themselves, the hardcore leather look at this stage being somewhat cliched.[63] As well as that, their mop-top hairstyles set them apart from other groups, while their Italian suits and

Spanish-heeled boots, later known as Beatle boots, made them seem more cosmopolitan. They were simultaneously commercial and artsy but most of all they had an authenticity that appealed to a younger generation fed up with the phoneyness of the social and class structures of the pre-war era.

The Beatles, like Elvis, had more or less created their own 'religious' fanaticism and cult worship, but while Elvis had become a symbolic representation of the new youth movement on a 'superficial' level, i.e. through his image and performance, as well as on a primitive level, in which forces of a lower sexual nature sprang forth to awake the sexual instincts of the new generation, the Beatles were something uniquely different. They expressed not just the overtly sexual emotions of the new generation, vented through the screaming and excitement produced by Beatlemania, but also the inner world of the next generation that came to focus their attention not solely on sexual attitudes but on imagination, philosophy and in their intellectual and political concerns. As well as this expression of an inner self, the Beatles, in their presentation as a tightly knit, creative unit, also represented the democratization of youth culture.

The music of Elvis fused the church music of his own culture with the black gospel and blues music from the communities in which he lived. His movements were encouraged by the movements of black dancers, and the shakes and gyrations would emulate the secular music, which inspired the primal forces within the individual. The pelvic movements of Elvis expressed the overtly-sexual tensions that were evident within some communities but which had been deeply suppressed within white culture, at least until they were unleashed for the new white youth groups that were ready to express themselves sexually.

The songs that many white artists recorded were written by Jewish songsmiths, often referred to as the Brill Building songwriters in New York, like Lieber and Stoller or Goffin and King, and were produced by Jewish or black producers, like Phil Spector or Robert

'Bumps' Blackwell. This merging of cultures and race created a kind of collective consciousness, a working together of many different elements, although presented to the public through one individual. In this respect, Elvis had spawned the next generation of artists and the new cultural era that pointed in the direction of 'the self ', although this was itself a collective consciousness.

Although they had emerged from a collective consciousness, of the pop music scene of the Fifties, the Beatles reinterpreted the music of girl groups, rock 'n' roll, country, and the deeply collaborative and collective approach of Motown and the Brill Building sound of New York. In many ways they reintroduced a lot of subcultural American music to mainstream American audiences, as well as their own British hybrid of skiffle and music hall. Their music would later come to express their own unique style and personal feelings and thoughts, although often mixed with an eclectic sound that would incorporate a huge amount of western musical styles, from classical to folk, rock and pop, music hall, as well as avant-garde and eastern styles.

In other words, Elvis and rock 'n' roll represented a naive and primitive culture that was still focused in communities, and which figures like Elvis represented; individuals who led the new youth towards their promised land of self-expression. The Beatles, although a collective group from the outside, particularly in their early days, first mirrored the collective consciousness of the new youth but also represented the democratization of the new form in which anyone, anywhere, of any age or class, could become a worldwide success.

Elvis was beyond the grasp of most young people's talents; they couldn't sing like him, move like him or look like him. Incidentally, Lennon would mention this very idea when saying that he and Paul needed each other to compensate for their shortcomings in being the Sixties' answer to Elvis. The Beatles were ordinary working-class boys, not too unlike the average boy, and so showed how possible it was for anyone to be successful. Artistically though, they were further ahead of the average person and inwardly expressed what many couldn't, essentially the feelings of a new-found self. The Beatles in essence were a contradiction, familiar yet unfamiliar, the sum of everything that had been, while unlike anything ever seen before. They could be accepted by those who recognized elements of the past and embraced by those who sought a new voice. They represented hope, optimism and wit, and a symbol that anyone can be a success, provided that they had a will to do it. Their capacity for survival impressed people – they just seemed unstoppable. Without anyone getting hurt or dying, it was the longest running story since the Second World War.[64]

Their days in Hamburg had signified the beginnings of a reconciliation between Britain and Germany and their success at home and abroad – particularly in Germany, Sweden and France and later in America, and finally in Australia and Japan – had, more than any other event since the War, brought much of the world together, which only two decades previously was intent on destroying itself. The young would soon recognize the differences between themselves and the older generation, a generation intent on destruction, while theirs would be a generation that would embrace 'the other' with all their differences.

The Beatles were more than just a rock 'n' roll group, and although the groups' members were proudly working-class, they were the first truly global and classless, as well as generation-less, event that had sprung up after the War – right through the negativity of the Cold War era.

By the Sixties, both teenage culture and rock music were in the phase of their second coming. For teens, there was a heightened sense of awareness of their position in life. For popular music, sounds got increasingly louder, amplified, raw and electrifying; recording technology began to adapt, opening the doors for more audio possibilities, and lyrics started to lose their innocence. Suddenly, rock music began to influence girls in strange and odd ways: females began to form mobs, grow hysterical over boys, disregard the law, physically abuse themselves by yanking on their hair, and sobbing until exhausted.

The question was, what were they so hysterical about? Was the progression of time and culture too much pressure to handle? Did the devil's music, i.e. rock 'n' roll, infiltrate their innocent bodies, minds and emotions? Or was it a reaction to the Sixties and the sounds of four charismatic lads from Liverpool?[65]

The Flight to Hamburg

Hamburg was a period of spiritual incubation for the group. They would learn their craft, while also be thrown into a world of danger – sex, drugs and the darker side of the human psyche. They would consort with prostitutes, sailors, pimps and those that lived during the night – outcasts from German society. It was here they would have experiences not to be found at home, experiences that allowed them to break free from the restraints of English life, of class consciousness and of the pre-war values that still conducted life at home. 'In Hamburg,' said, their first manager Alan Williams, 'we were there at the right time in the right place, people were hungry for this new rawer sound.'[66]

It was in Hamburg that they learned about the so-called 'enemy', the people they were supposed to hate. They became friends with their enemies. They even formed deep bonds with them, bonds that would last throughout their entire careers, physically, artistically and spiritually. The group of artists that they befriended in Hamburg – the Exis (named so after the European Existential philosophers who inspired them), led by the otherworldly Astrid Kirchherr – gave them an artistic slant to their rock 'n' roll ,'and in its own way,' said Tony Sheridan, a fellow musician and friend of the Beatles while in Hamburg, 'the music helped to heal the rift that had opened up between British and German people in the Second World War.' Sheridan had no doubt that the shows they did were about 'helping people with reconciliation'.[67]

They came to look like their enemies, mop-tops and polo necks; the uniform of the Exis. Astrid was a mother figure to the Liverpool groups that came to Hamburg, and particularly to the Beatles, on whom she also impressed her unique artistic sensibility. She helped reinvent the group, before Epstein added the last touches, that the world would soon come to know and love. She presented them to the world as something totally new, cutting their hair in the style of the Exis, which would later become known as the Beatle haircut, their trade mark, distinguishing feature. According to Tony Sheridan: 'She also had an artistic vision... and had an immense influence on the Beatles. The rough edges disappeared. Without her the Beatles would have been a different group.'[68] Klaus Voorman, their Hamburg friend, would contribute to their artistic output when he designed their majorly influential album cover *Revolver* and later played on Lennon's and Harrison's solo albums. Stuart Sutcliffe, one of the so-called fifth Beatles, would even opt to stay behind in Hamburg and live with his beloved Astrid, after the group returned to Liverpool.

If Liverpool had instilled them with certain English and working-class values, as well as being responsible for bringing the main body of the group together in the form of Lennon, McCartney and Harrison, Hamburg was a spiritual and artistic birthplace for the band, as well as for the individual members themselves. After Hamburg, the group was finally complete and ready to fulfil their role on the global stage of 1960s' culture, cutting away the superfluous elements that could no longer continue the journey – specifically, Pete Best, who had never quite fitted-in with the others, and Stu Sutcliffe, who felt his talents lay in another direction – and bringing instead the missing piece that gelled them together with the distinct and balancing personality of Ringo Starr.

Since the first stirrings of Beatlemania, a quasi-religion had sprung up around the group, side by side with the other semi-religious phenomena that began to manifest through the era, like the adoration of youth and beauty, the religion of mass consumerism and the gospel-like effect that the new telecommunications and mass media industry had produced, (particularly true in the case of television). Another was the fascination of rock 'n' roll with modern-day 'prophets', like Elvis and Buddy Holly, as well as cinema, which was a virtual 'church' for American and British teenagers in the 1950s, and movie stars that expressed the attitudes of the modern youth, like James Dean and Marlon Brando. These produced an illusion of religious fervour and a sense of mystery, of newness, that broke with traditional streams. This 'new religion' promised to produce a saviour (or saviours) for the post-war generation, which is why Sixties' cultural guru Timothy Leary called the Beatles 'poet philosophers of the new religion'[69] – but they were also the product of materialism, in which the disassociation with supersensible worlds had allowed for a saviour to be seen in completely material terms.

By the mid-Sixties these notions had become more enhanced, and with groups like the Beatles and the Rolling Stones, the youth of the 1960s saw itself as completely separate from the older pre-war generation, and as such they had their own religion and religious figures. For a moment, rock 'n' roll looked as if it was going to inherit the earth. The Rolling Stones (conceived as a virtual antithesis to the Beatles) would take advantage of this idea by proclaiming themselves in sympathy with darker and more devilish forces, while the Beatles were to marry themselves to a 'religion' of 'Love' and 'Light', as displayed in anthems like 'All You Need Is Love', and 'Give Peace a Chance'.

Chapter 3

Yeah, Yeah, Yeah:
Beatlemania and the Cult of Dionysus

In his book *The Birth of Tragedy*, the German philosopher, Friedrich Nietzsche proposes that modern western culture had become anaemic due to its one-sided rationalistic view of the world. Such rationalism, resulting, Nietzsche proclaims, from the Socratic/ Platonic tradition, associated with the Apollonian element of beautiful dreaming, intellect and 'identification of the individual', disconnects humanity from life and all its horrific and absurd messiness. Dionysus (or Bacchus) the god of revelry and intoxication, of ecstatic dance and song, is, on the other hand, concerned with irrational exuberance and with a 'deintellectualization' of the self.[70] Dionysus, the polar opposite of Apollo, symbolizes a return to a primordial unity and the reconciliation of humanity with itself and the 'innermost depths of nature'.

As Nietzsche had called for the reawakening of the Dionysian in western society, one might argue that the Beatles, and the 1960s in general, was a moment in western culture that experienced a reaffirming of the Dionysian, and a reintegration of the Apollonian and Dionysian duality, necessary for what Nietzsche considered would be a healthy social organism.

The musicologist Ruth Padel observes that tragedy, the beginning of western theatre, of which rock 'n' roll, as a live performance, was part of, was written for Dionysus' festival, and that 'drink, drugs, ecstatic loss of self in illusion of every kind (especially drink and madness); violent dance, crowds, theatrical spectacle and violence' were as much a part of 1960s' culture as they were the ancient, pre-Socratic Greek Cult of Dionysus. 'As a summary of Sixties rock,' writes Padel, 'Dionysus couldn't be bettered … in the Sixties, popular culture made him the figurehead for the male rock god.'[71]

Beatlemania and the Cultural Zeitgeist

At the height of their success, the Beatles had stirred the emotions of British and American youth to such a level of frenzy never before experienced. Girls would scream and pull their hair, lose control of their bodily functions, urinating over the seats at their concerts. Riots would break out in towns when the Beatles arrived to perform. The Press came to dub this phenomenon 'Beatlemania'.

'It is impossible to exaggerate Beatlemania because it was itself an exaggeration',[72] wrote Hunter Davies in his biography of the Beatles.[73] Beatlemania was the result of a youth culture, of rock 'n' roll, and of a diversion from the pessimism of war and nihilism; it was the product of consumerism and a distraction from its emptiness; it was a release of sexual emotions and feelings, a mask for the psychosis of modern life and the beginnings of a social expression, as well as the coming together, of a group of people who felt these things and collectively experienced them through the Beatles. Beatlemania was above all a mirror of both Britain's and America's changing attitudes and values, a release of the pressures that past traditions had confined them to. Uncontrollable, frenzied and beyond any proper intelligent explanation, Beatlemania was, above all, a Dionysian emotional and irrational response to something of a non-material, almost supersensible, nature.

Spiritually, the Beatles brought something hopeful after the horrors of two world wars, political scandals and the death of a president. In this sense Beatlemania was a remedy, a cure and a resurrection.

The journalist Ross Langager suggests that:

> The Beatles were consistently constructed as symbolic avatars for the social and cultural shifts of their time and place, even while they were still in the midst of that time and place. Their 1964 descent on America came mere weeks after the young, hopeful King-Arthur-Proxy-in-Chief was gunned down by shadowy forces in a sunny plaza in Dallas. Their giddy pop songs were derived from the ghettoized music of the same Black America that was

marching for its civil rights across the South, and their shaggy haircuts and dismissive wit spoke to an impetuous rejection of fossilized mores and codes whose breakdown was the fuel for Swinging London. Their very being seemed to presage a burst of mass enlightenment, a collective epiphany for the messy cannibalistic social and cultural superstructure of the western democracies that never quite came.[74]

The Beatles triggered a mania so intense, unlike any mass popularity the world had seen before, setting a standard and image of the pop star that has remained ever since. They opened the floodgates for a host of other talented British groups, like the Rolling Stones, into America, while also re-establishing the British Empire as a modern force. 'The pundits,' said one commentator, 'decided the Beatles were of social significance, symbolizing all the frustrations and ambitions of the new emergent, shadow of the bomb, classless, unmaterialistic, unphoney teenagers...'.[75] The Beatles would also exert a profound effect on America's new arch-enemy, Russia, and for many played a significant role in the fall of Communism as 'Lenin was traded for Lennon'.[76]

While many were impressed with the Beatles, there was a portion of society that was horrified by them and their cultural influence. Paul Johnson, a journalist for the political magazine *New Statesman*, saw the Beatles as an 'electorally valuable property', but ultimately thought them the epitome of a declining culture: 'the growing public approval of anti-culture is itself, I think, a reflection of the new cult of youth... a collective grovelling to gods who are themselves blind and empty'.[77] Johnson bemoaned the lack of interest by Sixties' youth in cultural heroes, like Wagner, Proust and El Greco, but these figures, some of whom lived over four hundred years ago, could not be a reflection of the 1960s social, political and cultural thoughts and feelings, and from that point of view were irrelevant. The Beatles, on the other hand, perfectly reflected the soul of the new society, at least as it was experienced by those growing up in it. It was not the past-present-future linear consciousness of Apollonian rationalism that concerned the post-war generation, but the Dionysian loss-of-self in the oneness of life, in the 'NOW'.[78]

Gods of Epiphany

In some cults, Dionysus arrives from the East, as an Asiatic foreigner, whilst in others from Ethiopia in the South. He is a 'god of epiphany', 'the god that comes', and his 'foreignness' as an arriving outsider-god may be inherent and essential to his cults. Thus, the Beatles 'arriving' in America in 1964 and 'returning' to Britain, following the media hype of their American tour, might be seen as an expression of the Dionysian myth of the god of epiphany. The Beatles arrived in both Britain and America at a time of great social, political and emotional upheaval, healing and transforming both nations, but it was society itself that went through its own grieving process, followed by a deep social and spiritual transformation. The Beatles (and the 1960s in general) were more so a vehicle through which this process could happen.

With the coming of rock 'n' roll's 'messiah', Elvis Presley, a fuse was lit that prepared the way for greater cultural forces to emerge, but with the death of Kennedy a vacuum was created to allow for such cultural forces to penetrate deeper into American (and British) society. So horrific was Kennedy's assassination that the country went into mourning for the entire winter of 1963/64. The media propaganda surrounding Kennedy's assassination created in the minds of the American people a strong sense of paranoia, not to mention the claims that Kennedy's assassin was a supposed Communist, thus making the Cold War more justifiable, as well as making the threat of nuclear devastation more probable. With the earlier possibility of a nuclear war having just been diverted by the Cuban Missile Crisis, the assassination of Kennedy tore open the wound again, leaving people in a frozen state of fear regarding their future. Vietnam was also looming on the horizon, another 'Communist threat' that would need to be dealt with.

If the Beatles had arrived on the scene at the end of 1963, as opposed to the spring of 1964, things may have been entirely different. Not only did Kennedy's death leave a vacuum to be filled, a need for something to distract the nation from its loss, but also it demanded that something, preferably non-American – something more traditional and stable, something possibly English (considering the growing Anglo-American relations) – to give guidance to a relatively 'new' country momentarily losing its way, as well as something unusual and novel and unlike anything that the country had experienced before.

The Beatles, in the form of haircuts, accents, clothes and their unique fusion of rock 'n' roll, Motown, and homegrown music hall, arrived in an America that was still reeling from the trauma of the assassination of its president. Musicologist Paul Gambaccini would suggest as much, saying that a great trauma requires a great positivity to heal it.[79] It is also significant that Kennedy was murdered in the winter of 1963, the season of death and completion, while the Beatles would bring, like Dionysus, the god of spring and regeneration, a rejuvenating element when they arrived in the spring of 1964.

The Evangelist Billy Graham suggested that the Beatles were simply a passing phase of which 'all are symptoms of the uncertainty of the times and the confusion about us'.[80] He was right in some respects, although misunderstood the group's real cultural significance. In many ways, Beatlemania was a necessary 'religion', which would wipe away the hypocrisy of the old order. 'I only joined,' said their public relations officer Derek Taylor, 'because I wanted to be transported from the world I had always known.'[81] Taylor expressed what many young people of the time felt. They wanted to be transported from the emptiness of modern life, and the Beatles allowed them that escape.

The arrival of the Beatles in America marks the moment when the post-war 'baby boomers' claimed their time. William Deeds, a British Cabinet Minister during the early Sixties under Prime Minister Harold Macmillan, said of the Beatles:

They herald a cultural movement among the young which may become part of the history of our time... the young are rejecting some of the sloppy standards of their elders, by which far too much of our output has been governed in recent years... they have discerned dimly that in a world of automation, declining craftsmanship and increased leisure, something of this kind is essential to restore the human instinct to excel at something and the human faculty of discrimination.[82]

Pete Townshend of the Who would hit the nail on the head when he exclaimed to *Melody Maker*, the year after the Beatles' descent on America, that, 'the big social revolution that has taken place in the last five years is that youth, and not age, has become important'.[83] The Beatles themselves were fully aware of their role as youth's ambassadors. 'Youth,' they pronounced, 'is on our side, and it's youth that matters right now.'[84] In the words of their friend and actor Victor Spinetti, they were, 'the young speaking to the young'.[85]

The adolescent attraction towards music and intoxication, often through alcohol, is significant in the development of the teenager and is closely linked to the cult of Dionysus, the 'youthful god' and the god of intoxication and rapture. The myth and symbolism surrounding alcohol (particularly wine) is too great to deal with here, but the relationship with transcended consciousness seems to be strongly connected with the consumption of wine. In Christian symbolism, Jesus Christ identifies himself as the 'true vine',[86] and as the transformed, resurrected god. In this capacity, Christ can be closely identified with the myth of Dionysus, the god of wine, that encompasses life, death and rebirth. The trance induction central to the Dionysian cult involved not only chemo-gnosis, i.e. transformation, usually of consciousness, through chemical substances or alteration of bio-chemical substances in the human being, but also an 'invocation of spirit'.[87] In the Dionysian cult, this would be through communal dancing to music, while characteristic movements (such as the backward head flick found in all trance-inducing cults, such as Voodoo) were also part of the transforming effect. Interestingly, it was the famous head shake of the Beatles, equivalent to Elvis' pelvic thrust, that would have the girls screaming in frenzy.

The Beatles would, through music and dance, intoxicate their audience, as their appearance on *The Ed Sullivan Show* would indicate, with 73 million Americans enraptured for those fifteen minutes when the Beatles performed. It is in song and in dance, wrote Nietzsche that 'man expresses himself as a member of a higher community... supernatural sounds emanate from him... He is no longer an artist, he becomes a work of art: in these paroxysms of intoxication the artistic power of all nature reveals itself.'[88] Through their Dionysian energy, the Beatles transcended the individuating, separating nature of western society and brought it back into harmony with itself – even if only momentarily.

Dionysus, also called Eleutherios – 'the liberator' – through wine, music and ecstatic dance frees his followers from self-conscious fear and care and subverts the oppressive restraints of the powerful. Those who partake of his mysteries are possessed and empowered by the god himself. He is represented by city religions as the protector of those who do not belong to conventional society, such as slaves, outlaws and 'foreigners' – those who did not have 'access to implied rewards'.[89] All were equal in a cult that inverted their roles. The Dionysian Rite removed inhibitions and social constraints, liberating the individual to return to a natural state. The myth and rituals of Dionysus can be interpreted as a reconciling of the Apollonian individualization of humanity (through its separation from the Cosmic Soul) with primordial unity (the 'common soul of mankind').[90]

The Beatles were entirely democratic, as their accents and look, as well as their appreciation of other artists, including black artists and girl groups, certainly indicated. They were, as Bob Stanley observed,[91] 'cultural omnivores... their appetite for cultural newness and apparent fearlessness, seemed to speak a future language', and it was because of these 'north-western gods' that 'pop became respectable – indeed desirable – across all social barriers'.[92] Seeing the Beatles, remembered the comedienne Whoopie Goldberg, was a 'revelation' and she saw them as opening the door for individual freedom, despite class, race or sex.[93]

> The Beatles had songs for heartbreaks, troubles, loners, miscommunications, friendship and more. There were relatable and realistic themes in the lyrics containing a broader scope than their musical predecessors. The music spoke to the audience as if it were written for each individual on a personal level, which further bonded fans together as a community. At times, the music was playful, lively and full of high energy, while also being soft, soulful and reflective.[94]

All who wanted to be, were welcome into the world of the Beatles, just as the group of social outcasts were all welcome to the Dionysian Rites.

The Beatles and the 'Mad Women' of Dionysus

As well as being representatives of the new youth culture, the Beatles also encouraged the release of sexual tensions and explorations that had been suppressed during the post-war Anglo-American culture and, without doubt, as a response to changing attitudes towards women after the war. The music journalist Allison Taich expresses such a change in social attitudes:

> When the Beatles hit, females responded to their work with unpredicted emotional outbursts. At the time, sex was seen as taboo and full of consequences if performed out of wedlock. Due to the Beatles' comfortable and sensitive aura, sex became approachable and enjoyable as opposed to horrifying and full of penalties. Pent up energy and hormones surfaced in the form of rebellion and global lust and challenged the notion that women were to remain pure and domestic. The change in opinion and comfort levels furthered

the gap between the old-fashioned, conservative ideology from the new progressive thinking.[95]

The Beatles unleashed dormant sexual urges that manifested themselves like a Dionysian Rite, in which girls seemed to behave like Maenads – the priestesses who oversaw these rites. In Greek mythology, the Maenads, 'mad women' or 'raving ones', often portrayed with supernatural associations, were inspired by Dionysus into a state of ecstatic frenzy through a combination of dancing and intoxication. Dionysus, a catalyst of wild energy, was the link between new, raw sappy growth (in vines or young men), and crowd ecstasy and violence. He maddened his worshippers, the Maenads, who tore up live animals and expressed their suddenly abnormal consciousness in hallucinating and wild dance.

In January of 1964, a month before the Beatles first stepped foot on American soil, *Life* reported:

> A Beatle who ventures out unguarded into the streets runs the very real peril of being dismembered or crushed to death by his fans. When the Beatles officially arrived in the United States, a mere two months after the assassination of John F. Kennedy, thousands of fans, specifically young females, *enthusiastically*[96] greeted them by storming the Kennedy Airport in New York. Sure, there had been fan frenzies for musicians and celebrities in the past, but nothing to the extent of Beatlemania…[97]

The act of pulling at the Beatles, pulling their clothes or pulling at their own hair, seemed to reflect the activities at such rites in which the Maenads would pull apart the flesh of the resurrected Dionysus. The fact that the Beatles often barely got away with their lives when they were surrounded or pursued by hormonal teenage girls seemed also to parallel the activities of these 'raving ones', while Beatles' concerts were a direct manifestation of the Dionysian Rite, as Pedal keenly observes: 'an unearthly howl went up from thousands of possessed teenagers. Girls began pulling their hair out… pupils dilating, shaking uncontrollably… Clinical Dionysian mass hysteria was breaking out everywhere.'[98] The plays, which dealt with the myths of Dionysus, show how essential violence was to him, as someone is always torn to pieces – 'the gods of music and theatre', suggests Padel, 'are the two gods of violent dismembering.'[99] (It is significant to note that the Beatles were constantly surrounded by violence and tragic death, including the untimely deaths of John's and Paul's mothers, the tragic deaths of Stuart Sutcliffe and Brian Epstein, numerous death threats against the band, and most obviously, John's violent assassination.) The philologist Walter Otto, in trying to comprehend the Dionysian, suggests that, 'the rapture and terror of life are so profound because they are intoxicated with death', and that the more intense a participant's libido or life drives are, 'the worse one can fall towards motionless death and decay'. A participant in rites of Dionysus, or equally so in a Beatles' concert, may find an asylum from the 'traditional life-death power struggle'.[100]

The frenzy of Beatlemania was in a sense a dying and a rebirth, an orgy of ecstasy, in which young girls, particularly, would emerge – brought on by the social frenzy of Beatles' concerts – as women, losing their innocence with their first experience of 'sex'. One fan, Elizabeth Hess, accounted her experiences with feminism in relation to the Beatles: 'I was 12,' she wrote, 'just beginning to understand that sex was power: my first feminist epiphany. As the Sixties tore on, the crowd of girls, now women, was still moving together, marching against the war in Vietnam.'[101]

The Beatles, having a strong feminine quality to them (for example, their long hair and high singing registers), were both safe and dangerous at the same time, and at live shows girls could find a socially acceptable environment to allow their newly discovered sexuality to unravel, often in the form of hysterical communal screaming, which at times led to uncontrolled body functions and loss of consciousness. The girls could also form their own Beatle-focused social groups, in which one girl may like Paul, another John and a third Ringo, thus allowing the girls to have the same fantasies, or shared fantasies, without encroaching on the fantasies of the other. They could join their fantasies together, in which two girls of the same group could imagine they were married to a Beatle, touring together and possibly living together, as that was how the Beatles were perceived – especially in their films, *A Hard Day's Night* and *Help!* This would be typical, as Padel suggests, of pop music's ability to transpose the teenage mind into the theatre of Dionysus, in which these myths are played out. 'Like Greek myth,' Padel writes, 'pop song is about relationships, staged in the teenage mind rather than in the theatre of Dionysus... the whole project is focused on an intensely teenage search for identity through music. And the currency of its lyrics is relationship.'[102]

As well as filling a void left in the socio-political environment of America and Europe during the early Sixties, the Beatles also represented the changing attitudes in personal affairs. Hunter Davies presents the effects of Beatlemania in America through the eyes of one typical American teenage girl called Sandi Stewart, an ordinary Beatle fan, fifteen-years-old, growing up in New Hampshire. 'I became obsessed about John,' says Stewart:

> I dreamt about him all the time. We'd compare dreams at school. Tell each other what we did with our favourite Beatle... When absolutely nothing else was good, I'd go to my room and have the Beatles, especially my darling John. They all furnished something I desperately needed. The sort of rich community I lived in in New Hampshire gave me nothing. I didn't like school and I didn't like home. They gave me something to live for when everything was black and depressing.[103]

The English poet Philip Larkin would express such an idea when he wrote in his poem 'Annus Mirabilis': 'Sexual intercourse began / In nineteen sixty-three / (which was rather late for me) – / Between the end of the Chatterley ban / And the Beatles' first LP.' Of course, sexual intercourse had been around forever, but Larkin is referring to its sudden awakening in the human psyche as something very personal and emotional, not just a Darwinian matter of function and duty, which society had turned it into. The Beatles (and the birth control pill), Larkin is suggesting, were the catalyst for a whole generation awaking their sexual impulses, as well as their inner emotional life, independent of societal duties, concerns, repressions and taboos. The Beatles wiped these all away and freed the post-war baby boomers from such social constraints. Dustin Garlitz, in his essay on Nietzsche, points out that the Dionysian spirit, 'involves the scenario where a worshiper (a common mortal) is brought about by intoxicating methods to heightened inner awareness',[104] likewise the Beatles were an awakening for girls like Sandi Stewart; girls who were becoming aware of themselves, of their sexuality and of the 'insipid' world in which they lived.

In a more simplistic way, this corresponds to the philosopher Bertrand Russell's interpretation of the Dionysian/Bacchic ritual undertaken by the initiates on their journey to self-knowledge. Russell writes:

> In intoxication, physical or spiritual, the initiate recovers an intensity of feeling which prudence had destroyed; he finds the world full of delight and beauty, and his imagination is suddenly liberated from the prison of everyday preoccupations. The Bacchic ritual produced what was called 'enthusiasm', which means etymologically having the god enter the worshipper, who believed that he became one with the god.[105]

It would be inaccurate, however, to see the effect the Beatles had on teenage girls of the 1960s in only sexual terms. The Beatles were, in many respects, as Yoko Ono mentioned in one of her and John's final interviews in 1980, also a representation of the 'feminine side of society'.[106] The Beatles gave purpose and meaning to this new generation of lost souls, like Sandi Stewart. The sexual aspects of Beatlemania were not just something of a crude erotic nature but something life-affirming, an expression of the life force and of an element of the human being that was suppressed, damaged and unhealthily distorted by a prudish, overly unfeeling and cold society; a society controlled by intellect and reason; a society afraid of the emotional power of the feminine (what Russell suggests above as the 'intensity of feeling which prudence had destroyed'). In the culture of the 1960s, the Beatles seemed to bring a sense of enlightenment, a sense of realizing new things – things that were beyond the scope of comprehension to society as it had been before their arrival. This was a new consciousness, a new awakening, similar in some ways to what other prominent religious figures had brought with them at various times throughout history.

Androgyny and the New Adam

Dionysus is an androgynous god. The Beatles' admiration for the U.S. girl groups of the late 1950s and early 1960s has generally been taken by musicologists, like Barbara Bradby, to imply an 'androgynous' positioning on their part,[107] while cultural critics such as Simon Firth and Angela McRobbie suggest that the Beatles epitomized an interesting process of 'feminization' that rock underwent in the late 1950s early 1960s. 'The Beatles music,' wrote Firth and McRobbie, 'articulated simultaneously the conventions of feminine and masculine sexuality, and the Beatles' own image was ambiguous, neither boys-together aggressiveness nor boy-next-door pathos.'[108] After the Beatles' first performance on *The Ed Sullivan Show*, girls, as well as boys, began to form their own groups; groups such as the Bootles and the Pleasure Seekers. The girls began to occupy a space not before open to them.

Susan Douglas in her influential book *Where the Girls Are* gives an indication of how the Beatles allowed young girls to feel more comfortable with their newfound sexuality, while simultaneously allowing young boys an opportunity to explore their feminine side, without being railroaded into the traditional view or militaristic values of manhood, where self-expression was a taboo. Douglas saw the Beatles as a kind of interfusion of the girl groups of the early Sixties, which offered the teen and pre-teen girls of the time a mirror on which their own inner lives were made manifest, and in turn provided role models for these young girls.[109] The males of the time found the opposite to be so for them. They could emulate male-hood through the Beatles but at the same time express their emotions, often through music (for example the Four Preps' 'A Letter to the Beatles'), and their personal appearance — especially long hair.

The Beatles' image and likeness became a significant symbol of the 1960s, and their mop-top haircut came to represent youth, fun, optimism and hope. The mop-top symbolized a civilized and healthy disrespect and insolence rather than rebellion. Though it was acceptable, it was not conformist. Long hair has traditionally been connected to a notion of clairvoyance, which was cut out by the reasoning mind of the Enlightenment. As Danny, a character from the George Harrison-produced film *Withnail and I* enthuses: 'our hair is our aerials to the cosmos'. The Essenes, for example, kept their hair long in order to be able to witness the coming of the Messiah, and in ancient Israel hair was deeply associated with identity,[110] as one of the most famous of the Old Testament stories, Samson, suggests. Samson had felt the cosmic power rushing through him but was sapped of it once his hair was cut. Interestingly, Jesus has always been depicted with long hair, even though in conservative Christian countries long hair has come to be seen as anti-social and rebellious. 'What we call ancient clairvoyance,' exclaims the nineteenth century spiritual scientist Rudolf Steiner, 'this lighting up of the cosmic secrets within human souls, had to enter the soul somehow.'

> We have to picture this as streams flowing into human beings. The ancients did not perceive them, but when these streams occurred and lit up within them, people perceived them as their inspirations... In the distant past, these streams were purely spiritual, and clairvoyants could perceive them as purely astral-etheric streams. But later these purely spiritual streams dried up, as it were, and condensed to etheric-physical streams. What became of them? They developed into hair. Our hair is the result of these ancient streams. The hair on our body was formerly spiritual streams that flowed from outside into human beings. Our hair is nothing else but dried up astral-etheric streams.[111]

It is for this reason, Steiner explains, that in Hebrew the words for 'light' and 'hair' were virtually the same, as the Hebrews were conscious of the relationship between spiritual inspirations through 'light' streaming into the human being through the hair.

The artist, in order to identify with the younger generation, particularly during the Sixties, needed to have their hair long. 'Everyone,' remarked Byrds' vocalist Roger McGuinn, 'was trying to grow their hair long.'[112] Long hair seemed to naturally indicate something individual, anti-authoritarian and otherworldly. In reference to the Dionysian aspect of the Beatles, hair was significant in that the Satyrs, the followers of the god, still in old clairvoyant consciousness, were covered almost entirely in hair. For Nietzsche, the Satyr was sublime and divine, representing truth and nature in its most primordial form. The Satyr had the power to magically transform the Dionysian reveller into something transcendent. 'In this magic transformation,' suggests Nietzsche 'the Dionysian reveller sees himself as a Satyr, and as a Satyr, in turn he sees the god, which means that in his metamorphosis he beholds another vision outside himself, as the Apollonian complement of his own state.'[113]

Steiner interprets the biblical story of Jacob and Esau in a similar manner. In this story Jacob dresses himself in goat's skin to impersonate his slightly older twin brother, Esau, who was covered in bodily hair,[114] in order to receive the blessing of the firstborn from his father. From Steiner's perspective, this is the replacement of old clairvoyant, dreamlike consciousness (a kind of cosmic consciousness, in which we are not fully conscious and therefore not free) with 'sense-based reasoning', which, similar to Nietzsche's view, brings about a separation of humanity from its spiritual origins. For Steiner, this separation is a stage in humanity's evolution after which, in full consciousness and freedom, humanity must reunite with its spiritual origins,[115] i.e. the Dionysian primordial oneness.

While the Beatles' suits, boots and cheeky grins made their style and image acceptable across sex, race and generation, it was their hair that made them unique and progressive. The Beatles knew intuitively that their hair had given them a certain power. In their first ever television appearance, the interviewer asked them more about their hair style than he did about their music, and in their first press interview in America (on 7 February 1964) their hair style became a major talking point:

> Reporter: Do you feel like Samson? If you lost your hair, you'd lose what you had?
> Reporter: How many of you are bald if you have to wear those wigs?
> Lennon: We're all bald. And deaf and dumb too.

It was primarily through the hairstyle that a follower of these cultural icons could identify themselves, and possibly why Donna Lynn sang, 'My Boyfriend got a Beatles' Hair Cut' as a response to the groups' arrival in America in 1964.

What the Beatles were possibly achieving is the breaking down of barriers not only to class and race but also between the sexes. Paul McCartney would claim this fact, when he stated: 'short hair for men, long hair for women. We got rid of that convention for the Americans.'[116] The Beatles pointed to the androgynous nature of the human being, which if expressed in esoteric terms, is made up of a physical body and also a subtler body known as the etheric body – a spiritual aspect of the human being that is often the opposite sex to the physical body.[117] It might be argued that the Beatles allowed the etheric element of the teenage fan to find an expression in the personality of the physical being, and thus created a unified, androgynous, human individual – the 'new Adam', as the poet William Blake would name it. Here the human being was, in a non-sexual sense, balancing the yin and yang elements of masculine and feminine within them:

> The imagery of sexual warfare is central to the vision of apocalypse which Blake proclaims as his poetic mission. The political apocalypse of the earlier work, such as *The French Revolution*, fades as the spiritual gains prominence... by the time he was writing

Jerusalem the only apocalypse he could endorse was one in which the 'sexes must cease and vanish' in the psyche so that humanity can assume its spiritualized 'body'. It became clear to Blake that political reform of society could not be affected until an individual and spiritual redemption took place in every heart. To become androgynous, to overcome the flaws inherent in each sex, emerges as the central challenge for all Blake's characters.[118]

Blake insinuates that, after the apocalypse, young men will regain their polymorphous, perverse sexuality and live in a state of eternal bliss. Early Greek mirrors show paintings in which we see on the left Apollo as *ephebes*, a youth with the laurel, and on the right Dionysus, robed in a feminine *chiton*, a flowing robe. Thus the two gods together presented a complete representation of the human being in its androgynous state. For William Blake, this was the primordial state of the first human being, Adam. To a large degree this androgynous state was intuitively understood by the generation of the 1960s. The divine challenge in 'Know Thyself' was a coming together of the two gods in one harmonious state. The challenge to Know Thyself, 'was inscribed on the *pronaos* of the Delphic temple, sounded from the lips of Apollo and was taken up and fulfilled by Dionysus'.[119] It was also taken up by the culture of the 1960s. 'Know Thyself' was the essence of Sixties' 'flower power' and the psychedelic movement, with its desire to integrate the masculine and feminine energies of the human soul within, both the individual and in society in general.

Blake's prophetic poems were enormously popular and influential in the 1960s, while ideas of androgyny would become a major aspect of Sixties' cultural progression, particularly the latter half of it – the image, for example, of, 'sweet Loretta Martin' who 'thought she was a woman' but was in fact a man, in 'Get Back', expresses the androgynous culture of the latter half of the 1960s – but which by the 1970s, when it was highjacked for promotional reasons by pop stars like Marc Bolan and David Bowie, became a mostly commercial and sexual concern. In other words, the spiritual androgyny which Blake points to and which finds expression in the Beatles, becomes perverted into a purely sexual idea which many pop stars used to further their careers.

Beatlemania was a 'religious' experience that, in its Dionysian-like splendour, gave new energy to the dying forces of a world devastated by two world wars. It gave new hope to a post-war generation and allowed for a rebirth of consciousness and of society, spiritually, sexually, socially and economically. It cast away old ideas regarding race, class and gender and pointed towards a utopian vision of the future in which individuals were merging their male and female aspects, where the female intuition was given respect – balancing out the judgemental rationalism of the male energies and enabling the individual and community to live in harmony together.

While the figure of Dionysus would be consciously expressed in the latter half of the Sixties, mainly through figures like Mick Jagger, Jim Morrison – who gladly took on the identity of the god – and later by individuals like Iggy Pop and Bono (see his Fly and Macphisto characters), the Beatles' early live performance clearly captured a sense of the Dionysian Rites. The Beatles seemed to channel the energy of Dionysus unconsciously and as an intuitive reflection of Sixties' cultural evolution. The Beatles, in other words, were an authentic vehicle for both the frenetic impulses of the deity, which was completely outside their control, as well as the rejuvenating force of the same impulse that came through them, often in their early years, unconsciously. In fact, it is the very nature of Dionysus to be beyond conscious thought, out of control and 'puzzling to the core',[120] and many attempts by people (like Jim Morrison) to control it ultimately leads to their destruction.

Whether Beatlemania or the Beatles could ever have achieved such a utopian state, one such that William Blake hoped for, would be possibly too much to expect, but if anything, once the frenzy of Beatlemania quietened down, the Beatles (through their personalities, their image and their music) did manage to give to the world a brief feeling of what society could be like when in harmony with itself.

Chapter 4

Nothing is Real:
The Esoteric Beatles

*'We were talking about the space between us all
And the people who hide themselves behind a wall of illusion...'*
'Within You Without You' – George Harrison

The Beatles as One

The rock 'n' roll heroes of the 1950s were, more often than not, solo singers with a backup band, with whom the general public paid little, if any, attention. Such was the case with singers like Elvis, Buddy Holly and even British singer Cliff Richard. The Beatles never had this set up, although earlier attempts at a band formation would have followed this template, and evolved in such a way that they would have had to abandon it. It seems the Beatles were unique in this respect, which in many ways resulted from the group comradery that had formed during their childhood days in Liverpool.

At first Lennon, being the older and naturally the more inclined with leadership qualities, was the main focus and the band took names to reflect this, like Johnny and the Moondogs or Long John and the Silver Beatles, but it would soon become apparent that McCartney, with his natural musical gifts, drive and personable charm, was as equal to Lennon. When McCartney began to present his own songs, it became clear that Lennon realized he had heavy competition on his hands. George, always 'nine months younger' than McCartney, was never someone in the running for the group's leadership, but it would soon transpire that George brought something valuable to the group to make him an equal bandmember. Essentially, George brought his youthful energy, his guitar skills, his dry, self-deprecating humour and chiselled good looks, but most importantly he brought a sense of balance to the Lennon and McCartney competitiveness, creating a buffer zone that tempered these two polar opposite forces as well as acting as a kind of gelling agent between them.

The cool and detached personality of Stuart Sutcliffe, a friend of John Lennon when he attended the Liverpool College of Art, would add another dimension to the early set up of the band, as too would the sultry good looks of their original drummer Pete Best, who was a particular favourite with the girls – but neither of these two had the essential quality necessary to make the group complete. It was Ringo Starr, with his likeable personality and openness, that was able to fill this position, when he was asked to join the band shortly after they signed a contract with Parlophone, EMI. Ringo was the final piece to the jigsaw – lively, humorous, with a down-to-earth unpretentiousness, which seemed to be missing in the characters of Sutcliffe and Best and to some degree with the other three Beatles. While Lennon and McCartney were the driving force from a song-writing point of view and vocal prowess of the band – and Harrison fitted in as the 'quiet, serious one' that balanced out the polar characteristics of Lennon and McCartney – Starr, the everyday man, provided the group with an easygoingness. He grounded the group and made them 'loveable'.

With their initial success, these personality types were not so obvious, and the group simply came across as a unit with the personalities of each member, as well the musicality of each, simply merging into one being. In fact, it was often difficult for the public to identify one Beatle from the other; they simply existed as an undifferentiated unit, a kind of 'one mind' or as a 'Four Headed Monster', as Mick Jagger would perceive them.[121] Paul McCartney explained:

> The thing is, we're all really the same person. We're just four parts of the one, we're individuals, but we make up together The Mates,

which is one person. If one of us, one of the sides of the mates, leans over one way, we all go with him or we pull him back. We all add something different to the whole... Ringo he's got a sentimental thing. He likes soul music and always has, though we didn't see that scene for a long time, till he showed us... George he's very definite about things and dedicated when he's decided. It makes the four of us more definite about things, just because of George. We adapt what's in him to our own use. We all take out of each of us what we want or need... John he's got movement. He's a very fast mover. He sees new things happening and he's away... Me I'm conservative. I feel the need to check things... we still have the same basic roles, because that's what we are. But all of us will appear to be changing, just because we don't conform. It's this not conforming, wanting to be something different all the time, that keeps our music different.[122]

Even though the group would eventually splinter into four distinct personalities they managed to remain a single entity. Hunter Davies, in his biography of the group, would remark that each of the four individual Beatles always remained 'umbilically connected with the others', and although each of them would later draw on varying and differing music forms, they always managed to integrate these interests in such a way that they sounded like a complete unit. Brian Epstein, in the film *The Birth of the Beatles* (1979), put it best when he remarked to John Lennon that, 'no single one of you is the Beatles, each one is a part.' John, he says, is the mind, Paul the heart, George the soul, and Ringo the group's flesh and blood: 'If any one of you stops doing his part', he warns, 'the rest will die. You are all dependent on one another.' In effect, one might say that this representation of the Beatles parallels the esoteric representation of the human individual, which consists of ego or mind, astral body or heart, etheric body or soul, and the physical body or flesh and blood.[123]

The Beatles as Duality: Apollo and Dionysus

While the Beatles were a unit, consisting of four equal elements, they also had other numerical combinations, as two, three, four and five. The Beatles, like Elvis had seemed to channel the energy of Dionysus unconsciously and simply as a part of the Sixties' cultural evolution, but the Beatles would later move beyond simply the mere forces of Dionysian, unconscious regeneration and wild ecstasy. They would, by the mid-Sixties, become a conscious creative force, becoming more conscious of their artistic abilities, the poetic quality of their lyrics, and the effects both they themselves and their music was having on their culture. In this sense, the Beatles moved into the more controlled and consciously aware aspect of their art, which now began to express a more Apollonian nature.

As the musical landscape had changed from the carefree, teen-centric sound of the Fifties and early Sixties, so did the Beatles. The Vietnam conflict, the assassination of President John F. Kennedy and other sobering, faith-shaking factors, shifted popular music towards a more globally-conscious level, with folk and protest-laden acid rock marching towards the forefront. The Beatles stayed relevant by growing up alongside their audience, their music informed by current events and the new ventures that each Beatle found himself delving into.[124]

In Lennon's case, it led to his interest and belief in 'Love' and 'Peace', which began to take expression at the height of Beatlemania, mainly during the *Rubber Soul* period, and after the unconscious destructive and uncontrollable elements of Beatlemania became too much for him. He was drawn towards these ideas as a means to confront his personal pain, which he had, up to this point, masked by consumerism and hedonism, though inwardly he was screaming for 'Help!' Harrison would find his 'Apollonian' side in the form of spirituality and the search for God, best expressed in his songs 'Within You Without You', 'The Inner Light', 'Something', and his solo hit 'My Sweet Lord'. McCartney would seek it in both traditionalism, i.e. classical music, music hall and the mundanity of life, in which he tried to find beauty, as in songs like 'Eleanor Rigby' and 'Penny Lane.'

While the Beatles would push past the lower and unconscious elements of the Dionysian cult of rock 'n' roll and become a conscious force with their music, lyrics and personal interests, this move seemed to alienate those who had become so stuck in the notion that rock 'n' roll was simply about sex, drugs and 'Dionysian destruction'.[125] The Beatles were ultimately transcending the forces that brought them about and trying to operate on a more creatively conscious level. Others, who were unable to make it past the basic, unconscious forces that inspired them, collapsed once the initial fan frenzy wore away.[126]

However, a major split came in the culture of the youth — those wanting to move forward in a more conscious manner and those who remained stuck in the old, unconscious world of rock 'n' roll. Sitars, orchestras and the avant-garde, as well as studio-trickery and capability, was not part of rock 'n' roll, and neither was social commentary or philosophically-shaped lyrical content. Out of the conscious drive forward sprung the hippys, while out of the unconscious force arose Altamont (but this will be dealt with in another chapter).

This Dionysian/Apollonian duality, a preoccupation with the ancient Greeks in their search for perfection of the individual, also existed within the song-writing partnership of Lennon and McCartney; two songwriters both complementing while simultaneously competing with each other. In many ways, this was the essence of the Beatles, particularly from a musical point-of-view. 'John Lennon was the flipside of McCartney in that he played it fast and loose, carving out chunks of albums in scant hours, whereas Paul agonised over the smallest details. Each was a creative force in their own right, yet represented two sides of the same coin.'[127] Geoff Emerick, one of the group's sound engineers, commented on this Lennon-McCartney 'odd-couple' quality. 'Paul,' said Emerick:

> Was meticulous and organized: he always carried a notebook around with him, in which he methodically wrote down lyrics

and chord changes in his neat handwriting. In contrast, John seemed to live in chaos: he was constantly searching for scraps of paper that he'd hurriedly scribbled ideas on. Paul was a natural communicator; John couldn't articulate his ideas well. Paul was the diplomat; John was the agitator. Paul was soft-spoken and almost unfailingly polite; John could be a right loudmouth and quite rude. Paul was willing to put in long hours to get a part right; John was impatient, always ready to move on to the next thing. Paul usually knew exactly what he wanted and would often take offense at criticism; John was much more thick-skinned and was open to hearing what others had to say. In fact, unless he felt especially strongly about something, he was usually amenable to change.

It is the common view that Lennon and McCartney, after a very short collaborative period, began to write entirely alone. The 1960s' Radio Caroline DJ Johnnie Walker, among others, puts forward this very idea in the BBC's *The Nations Favourite Beatles Number One*. The writer Joshua Wolf Shenk, in challenging modern western cultures' adulation of the lone genius – the creative and often misunderstood talent that works in a vacuum, unable effectively to communicate their greatness to the masses – suggests that creativity is nearly always a group or collaborative effort. It is without doubt that, despite the individual talents of all the Beatles, they were ultimately a group of many different collaborators – and not just only of four but of a great number of individual people who had very specific skills that allowed the Beatles to exist in a cultural sense. They relied on their musical producer, George Martin, to realize their musical ideas, while their manager, Brian Epstein, had so much conviction in the group that he dedicated his money, time and energy to their cause, not to mention their indispensable sound engineers, Norman Smith and Geoff Emerick, and their personal assistants, Neil Aspinall and Mal Evans, who were totally devoted to the group. In relation to the song-writing partnership of Lennon and McCartney, the collaboration was essential not only to the Beatles and their sound, but also to Lennon and McCartney as individual songwriters. The extremely successful partnership of Lennon and McCartney demonstrates the brilliance of the creative pair, contradicting the myth of the lone genius. 'For centuries,' writes Wolf Shenk,

> the myth of the lone genius has towered over us, its shadow obscuring the way creative work really gets done. The attempts to pick apart the Lennon-McCartney partnership reveal just how misleading that myth can be, because John and Paul were so obviously more creative as a pair than as individuals, even if at times they appeared to work in opposition to each other. The lone-genius myth prevents us from grappling with a series of paradoxes about creative pairs: that distance doesn't impede intimacy, and is often a crucial ingredient of it; that competition and collaboration are often entwined.[128]

The relationship between Apollo and Dionysus is a very complex one, but in essence, they are seen as forming two contrasting but complementary sides of human nature. In modern material, neuroscientific terms, the Apollonian may be said to represent the left brain hemisphere, the rational part of man, compartmentalizing, logical and self-disciplined, while Dionysus represents the right brain, illogical, intuitive, spontaneous and emotional. From the perspective of spiritual science, the Apollonian and Dionysian stand for something much more significant and complex, however. Apollo was one of the 'upper gods' connected to cosmic forces, while Dionysus was related to the 'lower gods', that revealed themselves within the soul of man. Apollo worked through the head, Dionysus through the limbs. The day and the morning sun, rising in the east, was the realm of Apollo, but with the setting of the sun in the west, we are led into the Mysteries of Dionysus. The anthroposophist Friedrich Hiebel, in his book *The Gospel of Hellas, The Mission of Ancient Greece and the Advent of Christ*, points to the clear day-time consciousness of rational thought and control and the night-time consciousness of the inner life of emotions and intuition.[129] Hiebel explains that Apollo has its origins in the Greek Oracles, Dionysus in the Mysteries. He writes that:

> The oracles differed from the Mysteries in that they revealed the gods of the cosmos through the sense-world, in the rustling of the trees and the vapor of the earth, whereas the Mysteries had to do with the rites, cults and probations through which the soul could perceive the gods working within her realm. The seers, who received the message of the gods through the oracles, had to lower their consciousness in order that they might become mediums for them. The initiates of the Mysteries had to strengthen the faculties of their souls. This distinction leads us to the significant duality of the gods Apollo and Dionysus. The Apollonian way of clairvoyance and clairaudience reflected the wisdom of the past. The Dionysian way of initiation aimed at the future, at the goal (*telos*) of perfection; therefore those seeking initiation were called *Telestes*.[130]

Like Nietzsche, the philosopher Schopenhauer, who greatly influenced Nietzsche, argued against the dominance of the rational and logical over the intuitive, Dionysian aspect of the human being, as it resulted in the development of the human ego, which was represented by Apollo, causing the human individual to become separate, through rationalizing (i.e. extracting a portion or ratio from the whole) not just from their fellow human beings and society, but from nature, and from 'the mysterious primordial unity',[131] which could be reconnected with through the Mysteries (see Chapter 3). Apollo was, for Schopenhauer, the 'glorious divine image of the *principium individuationis*', the 'dream artist' for Nietzsche, in which serene thought can become separated from living experience and reality.

It is, however, the interaction of the Apollonian and the Dionysian that is the foundation of any creative work. Nietzsche observed that these two Greek gods of art, with their opposite and warring principles, co-existed in a dynamic state of tension.[132] Modern thinking, in the areas of philosophy, neuroscience, psychology, etc., have confirmed the importance of these dual principles in the creative process, establishing a very distinct relationship between 'breaking and making, challenging and refining, disrupting and organizing',[133] 'subjectivism and objectivism... chaos and cosmos'[134] (or even 'Chaos and Creation in the Backyard', to reference Paul McCartney's 2005 album).

The Greek city of Delphi, where the oracle of Apollo resided, was not only the centre of Apollo, but also of Dionysus, and as a result could become the true centre of Greek culture. 'The Apollonian clairvoyance,' states Hiebel, 'could become Dionysian initiation, and the Dionysian ecstasy was purified by the harmony of Apollo's music and meter.' In their spiritual manifestation, these two gods were one and the same; from the point-of-view of an earth-bound consciousness, they were separate, but for those with spiritual insight they were one divinity. 'It was at Delphi,' says Hiebel, 'that the oracles became mysteries and that therefore the revelation of the past could be transformed into a new insight.'[135]

The early music of the Beatles, in which Lennon and McCartney seemed to write together, brought a dual quality to the music; songs like 'I Wanna Hold Your Hand' began with an upbeat, energetic positivism that gives way to a downbeat section in a minor key, expressing a vulnerability contrasting with the frenetic energy of the song's main sections. This dualistic element would be noticeable in other songs like 'We Can Work It Out' or 'A Day in the Life', while their singles would often reflect this dualistic nature, with a particular song, like McCartney's 'Paperback Writer', offering up a more traditional and conventional single, while its double A-side, 'Rain', written by Lennon, would offer something contrasting. 'Rain' was an early psychedelic composition in which the 'trippy' soundscape, with processed instrumentation and backwards recordings, differed with the conventional approach of 'Paperback Writer'. The lyric to 'Rain' was more abstract and personal, compared to the straightforward narrative of McCartney's song, which was removed and distant from the composer and performer. McCartney's themes were much more universal in that they were concerned with the everyday, whilst Lennon's were more surreal and mysterious and stamped with his individualism.

'Penny Lane' and 'Strawberry Fields Forever' were probably the most obvious and celebrated example of this dualism, with the former drawing its inspiration from parochial Liverpool life, while the latter transported the listener to some otherworldly state of mind. Other prominent and extremely notable singles are 'Hello Goodbye' / 'I am the Walrus', 'Hey Jude'/ 'Revolution', 'I Wanna Hold Your Hand' / 'This Boy' (where the B-side shows off a much softer, ballad-type song contrasting with the fast pace of the A-side), and 'Can't Buy Me love' / 'You Can't Do That' (though both songs are upbeat tracks with a strong R&B flavour, the attitude of each is different). The A-side expresses McCartney's more romantic notion of love, while Lennon's B-side offers up a more pessimistic, controlling and jealous side of love.

Geoff Emerick, recognized from the outset that the two formed a single creative being. 'Even from the earliest days, I always felt that the artist was John Lennon and Paul McCartney, not the Beatles.'[136] The two songwriters would produce material that would resonate with the Apollonian/Dionysian elements of their listeners, those of a fiery, active, often rebellious nature finding something in the songs of Lennon, while those tending towards a passive nature, more romantic and easier-going in outlook were drawn towards McCartney's compositions. While McCartney's lyrics may often express the sunnier personality type of its composer, it might also suggest a conventional lyric that doesn't really consider the personality of its composer at all, drawing its themes from the conventions and generalities of pop songs as a type and genre. Lennon's lyrics in contrast are not so conventional and express a more authentic and personal element. George Martin said that, 'the tension between the two of them made for the bond'.

The Apollonian was purely Hellenic in character; the Dionysian Mysteries, in contrast to the parochialism of Hellenic/Greek life, were cosmopolitan, and thus both together combined the wisdom of the East with that of the West. 'The way from Apollo's oracles to Dionysus' Mysteries,' remarks Hiebel, 'led from polytheism to monotheism, or from the consciousness of tribal blood-ties to the individuality'.[137] The oracles inspired the people with awe and devotion to the heavenly gods, while the Mysteries brought the individual into their own being to search for the divine; they 'impelled the spirit of man to unfold the divine within the individuality, in other words to aim at becoming a god'.[138] Thus McCartney focused on multiple characters, as if all belonging to one large community, with a clearly parochial tinge; a world, 'beneath blue suburban skies',[139] that was visited by cosmic forces ('Mother Mary comes to me', 'Lady Madonna'). Lennon was not interested in drawing pictures of everyday people, of parochial characters, but instead explored his own inner life and world, attempting to 'unfold the divine within the individuality'.

It is not difficult, also, to see that McCartney liked to be in control. Always conscious and present, he shied away from mind-altering drugs, 'those devil drugs', as he referred to them,[140] and was always concerned about the direction in which he (and by extension the Beatles) was going and how he would get there. Lennon, abandoned as a child, threw himself with abandon into a world of hallucinogenic drugs, the subconscious and the surreal. His attitude was to live in the experience of the acid trip, to give up his ego (his *principium individuationis*) for some kind of primal cosmic experience, later substituting the LSD experience with Transcendental Meditation. The destruction of the ego was something many Sixties' rock singers, influenced by psychedelics, tried to do, but this usually ended with disastrous consequences.

The neophyte of the Ephesian Mysteries (those revealed to Saint Paul), explained Rudolf Steiner, had to develop a clear understanding of the Logos. 'This world-creating Word,' says Steiner:

> revealed itself concretely through its threefold intonation of the vowels: I-O-A. These three vowels were the objects of long meditations. The triad of I (Iota) in connection with A (Alpha) and O (Omega), the last letter of the alphabet, brought the disciple into contact with the Logos, that principle of life and spirit, which

later on was expressed in the Apocalypse of John: 'I Am Alpha and Omega'. In the pre-Christian era it was revealed through the name of the Ephesian Artemis as well as by the divine name of the Hebrews in I-eh- O-v-A.[141]

The teaching of the Logos at Ephesus became one of the most important influences in the life of Aristotle. It was he who transformed the teaching of the Logos into the principles of logic, and this was a major part of his instruction to Alexander the Great, who after his sojourn in Ephesus embarked upon his conquest of the Orient. This deed of Alexander, Heibel points out:

> Foreshadowed the final union between East and West which was sealed by Saint John when he became the bishop of the Christian community of Ephesus and wrote his Gospel, and connected its message with the teaching of the Logos: In the beginning was the Logos, and the Logos was with God and the Logos was a god.[142]

The early Greek philosopher Heraclitus taught, a century or so before Aristotle presented the idea in a formal manner, that 'the Logos dwells within the soul of him who augments himself'.[143] After the demise of Beatlemania in around 1965, at the point where Lennon is screaming for Help! as some kind of cathartic need to purge himself of the pressures of fame and fortune (catharsis is a process on the path of Dionysian initiation),[144] this notion of the Logos, expressed in the writings of Heraclitus and later Aristotle, became fundamental to the themes of many Beatles' songs. It is from this point on that Lennon and Harrison attempted to let go of their personal selves in some respects, and gave themselves over to a Universal Love or a search for a spiritual Truth. In essence, the young Dionysus dies in the process of initiation, and the mature and developed Dionysus, as the 'ugly old man', now the true 'brother of Apollo', takes his place. The initiate is no longer driven by unconscious drives, but works consciously, through their own individual freedom, for the betterment of the human race.

The Mysteries of Hellas in general and of Eleusis in particular taught the eternal presence of Dionysus. Exoterically, Dionysus was pictured as an old and ugly man. Within the Mysteries he was seen in his etheric form as a beautiful youth. The mystic neophyte could become 'a son of Dionysus'. In mentioning Dionysus as returning from Thrace – which in the Mysteries, as we have already seen, indicated the etheric world – the neophyte emphasized that in him the principle of individualization came from the spiritual world; that he returned to Delphi, becoming the true 'brother of Apollo' in revealing the profounder aspects of the Apollonian spirit; that he reached Eleusis and, finally, placed himself among the masks of Thespis in the theatre at Athens.

This Apollonian/Dionysian concept is not something that Lennon and Harrison, or the other Beatles for that matter, were necessarily aware of in any real sense, but the point made here is that a shift in consciousness seemed to take place in western culture during the mid-1960s which was reflected in the music of the Beatles and in their own personal developments. These forces seemed profoundly to affect the culture of the time, and thus the Beatles seemed to experience these social and cultural changes in a very intense way, possibly because they were in many ways conduits for these changes to take place within the social and cultural mainstream.

It was after the early days of Beatlemania in which the forces of the young Dionysus, 'the mystic neophyte', the 'son of Dionysus', were active. By the mid-Sixties, as each Beatle was becoming individuated, one could see the resurrection of the Dionysian as an 'old and ugly man', the 'brother of Apollo', revealing the profounder aspect of Apollo. It is interesting to note that Lennon focused on the Logos and its message in his song 'The Word'. This song would be the first of many by the group, and the Beatles as solo artists, that would explore the message of the Logos (or the Word), that is, that Christ's essence of Love was the meaning to our lives. In fact, nearly all of Harrison's and Lennon's songs after 1965 would deal with this theme. Songs like 'All You Need is Love', 'Across the Universe', 'Love', 'Mind Games', 'My Sweet Lord', 'Give Me Love' – and though it was expressed in simple and digestible forms through their form of popular song, it nonetheless carried within it the meaning of our lives here on earth, pointing those interested towards a deeper seeking of its message, mainly through the esoteric knowledge that was emerging through the culture of the 1960s.

The Beatles in their Apollo/Dionysian duality seem to have, like the yin and yang quality of the ancient Chinese wisdom, the seed of the one in the other; thus, the logical and rational of Apollo led to the individuation of the human being. Apollo, the god of the sun, was 'brought into relationship with the impulse of the human ego… Apollo appeared as the bringer and protector of man's selfhood',[145] cut off from the collective consciousness, yet at the same time he would hold together the Hellenic people.

Rudolf Steiner described Apollo as the Hellenic expression of a being whose mission was to restore the distorted harmony between thinking, feeling and will, and thus make the human being integral. This spiritual being was intimately linked with the impulse of Christ at the end of the epoch of Atlantis in a foreshadowing of the events of Palestine. Again, according to Hiebel, Apollo (derived from *appelazein*, 'hold together') indicated that this divinity held together the tribes of the Hellenes, through the harmony of his word, and he revealed his mission as the messenger and forerunner of Him who was to come as the 'Logos who was made flesh and dwelt among us'.[146]

In the later part of the Beatles' career and also as solo artists, Lennon and Harrison, in some capacity 'brothers of Apollo', would promote the raising of spiritual consciousness. Some would criticize both Harrison's and Lennon's search for spiritual Truth as a rejection of Christianity, instead unconsciously embracing and promoting a 'New Age' false religion. There may be some truth to this, in that they both became tenured to pre-Christian practices (such as Hinduism and Yoga), and Lennon would reject Jesus and all other idols, such as Buddha, Krishna, Elvis and even the Beatles in favour of his own inner self. In many ways, this was the rejection of all outside influences to search inside oneself, the essence of Dionysus, unfolding 'the divine within', as well as the message of Christ-Jesus who teaches that 'the kingdom of heaven is within'.[147] Steiner points out, in *The Philosophy of Freedom*, that the ethical individual acts freely out of his or her own moral intuition and not by dictates imposed by authority figures, regardless if those figures are the political state or some heavenly god. Love can only be activated through the free moral actions of the individual. Harrison was also, it seems, genuinely looking for the Truth and understood that humanity needed to make a conscious effort to 'see the light that has lighted the world' and that 'with our love we could save the world'.

From this dualistic approach, the Beatles were in effect their own antithesis, their very own Rolling Stones, so to speak. The group also had a dualistic nature by splitting the group into its pairings, Lennon and McCartney, Starr and Harrison, the creative two and the complementary two – the 'economy Beatles', as Harrison would refer to himself and Starr[148] – the major two and the supporting two, or the major and minor Beatles, to draw on a musical metaphor.

The Triumphant

Beatles' historian Mark Lewisohn states that, 'George joining also gave the relationships a whole new complexity', and although 'George had no one to lord it over, nor did he bother to jostle shoulder to shoulder with John and Paul on the front line, but he did expect to be considered an equal... and was.'[149] Klaus Voormann rightly observed that Harrison provided a bridge between McCartney and Lennon, often separating the two overpowering elements in order to bring balance, often pairing with one or the other when on stage, thus temporarily singling out the other as the main focus.[150] Harrison would act as a mirroring element through which McCartney would reflect Lennon and vice versa.

Harrison would physically stand between them on stage, while Lennon and McCartney – one right-handed, the other left-handed – would be on either side of the stage, at separate microphones, reflecting each other. Harrison would, as already mentioned, function as both a buffer and a gelling agent, while offering to the public another personality type for them to identify with, an alternative to choosing between Lennon and McCartney as their favourite Beatle.

The writer and scholar Matthew Schneider compares Harrison's positioning in the group to the Romantic poet Byron, as he stood in relation to the two other towering poets of British Romanticism – Wordsworth and Coleridge:

> As the overlooked genius standing between Lennon and McCartney, Harrison is the group's excluded middle, the aperture through which the titanic resentments aroused by the Beatles' unprecedented fame could be glimpsed and expressed. In addition, Harrison manifested psychic and philosophical in-between-ness by oscillating, as Byron did, between emotional extremes of disgust and delight, despair and transcendent faith, and by continually seeking to broaden the narrow range of thought and expression that the circumstances of his birth and his status as a member of the group – the English lower middle class, the Beatles, even the human race – made available to him.[151]

Harrison would complete the triumvirate of songwriters by the mid-Sixties, and this was often reflected in the Beatles' albums – probably best represented on the *Revolver* album, on which the first three songs, often considered to be the most impressive opening of all the Beatles' records, consists of one song from each of the three songwriters. Harrisons' songwriting style and approach would somewhat balance itself between Lennon and McCartney. Harrison, again as Lewisohn points out, though the youngest Beatle, 'often led their fashion moves'.[152] He was the first to adopt a Gene Vincent look, the first to introduce the others to Dylan, Indian culture and music, the first, with Lennon, to use psychedelics, the first to distance himself from his celebrity status and the first of the John, Paul, George trio to leave the group – and the first to have real success as a solo artist in his own right.

This triumvirate would also express itself with the Beatles personally, and in this respect reflected both the esoteric nature of the human being as thinking, feeling and will and the threefold social structure of economic, political and cultural realms, as suggested by Rudolf Steiner, based on the threefold nature of the human being.[153] While Lennon typically represented the mind and thinking aspect of the Beatles and McCartney the heart and feeling aspect, Harrison could be considered as the will.

The journalist Maureen Cleave, who had become very well acquainted with the group, had observed this aspect of Harrison. George, she said, in her profile on him, 'was strong-willed and uncompromising with a high regard for truth and rights'. She recognized his uniquely independent spirit, which strongly expressed itself not only in his songs like 'Don't Bother Me', 'Think for Yourself', and 'Within You Without You' – in which he often urges the listener to 'know where you're going to' and 'try and realise it's all within yourself. No one else can make you change' – but also in his commitment to spiritual movements and humanitarian causes, such as his Concert for Bangladesh. He was out-spoken against the Vietnam War and the fact that tax-payers' money was spent on such things, the disapproval of which he aired in the song 'Taxman'. He was also the first Beatle to voice disenchantment with pop star status and the whole illusion of not just celebrity, but of modern consumer culture, in which he understood the Beatles to be part.[154]

'In his in between-ness,' Schneider again remarks that, 'Harrison presented a striking alternative to the modes of ambitious selfhood modelled by Lennon and McCartney, and by doing so added another dimension to Rock Romanticism.'[155] For this reason, Schneider suggests: 'Harrison adds Byronic complexity and philosophical weight to Rock Romanticism', and not, he adds, by 'following the artistic path marked out by the founders of the movement to which [both] belonged, but by doing something that has come to be an archetypical Romantic gesture: scornfully rejecting the previous generation'.[156]

If we look at Lennon and McCartney in their dual aspects of Apollo and Dionysus, a third element is present. This is the figure of Orpheus, the revered poet and prophet of ancient Greece, who descended into the Underworld to retrieve his wife, Eurydice, but who was eventually torn to pieces by the Maenads of Dionysus, as he rejected the god in favour of Apollo. The figure of Orpheus stands between Apollo and Dionysus, and it was through him that the Greek initiation process led from Apollo to Dionysus.

Orpheus taught the law of reincarnation, that human beings are trapped in the prison of their own bodies and are subject to a cycle of earthly lives that is full of suffering unless their attitude to life and to the gods – and to Dionysus in particular, to whom Orpheus is closely related – changes. Or, one might say, until their spiritual consciousness changes. Orpheus brings a message of freedom; freedom from repeated earthly lives by the practice of asceticism, self-purification and self-realization.[157] Like Orpheus, standing between Apollo and Dionysus, Harrison, whose songs exhort the listener to change their attitude towards life, encouraging them to become more spiritually aware, stands between Lennon and McCartney. Harrison, through his connection and devotion to Indian culture, which he first became acquainted with in the mid-Sixties, brought the notion of reincarnation back into popular western consciousness.

This threefoldness is seen not just in the physical positioning of the three front men (Lennon on the right, McCartney on the left, and Harrison centred) but also through the vocal harmonies of bass, mid, and treble, as well as rhythm guitar, bass guitar, and lead — the three instruments and voices acting independently but together as the human beings' thinking, feeling and will elements should also act, and as society's three aspects of cultural, political and economic realms should also operate. If any one of these three dominates the others, then there is an imbalance in the individual or in society. The same applies in the vocal or instrumental working of these three Beatles. The inability of these three aspects to function together results in the collapse of society, or in this case the breakup of the group, which is of course what ultimately brought about the end of the Beatles, i.e. the inability of each of these three strong individuals to temper their personal needs and function together as a group.

The Beatles as Four

The Beatles were a unit of four and it was as four that they were most powerful or effective. Interestingly, people would often comment on how three Beatles in a room together was simply just three Beatles in a room together, but when the fourth was present, there was a transformation; a transformation that emitted an energy and force that was uncanny, mesmerizing and awesome. In effect, the four Beatles together brought a synergy that was greater than the sum of their parts. The Beatles, Lana Cooper would write in her perceptive essay, 'The Beatles As a Successful System of Archetypes':

> ... seemed to have created an archetype of their own, invoking 'Four as the Magic Number' comprising a single entity and laying the groundwork for other fabulous foursomes to emerge on both a musical scale and other realms of pop culture. Part of what made the Beatles so unique were the four distinct personality types that rounded out the group. In order for each member to have a shot at a certain level of recognition, there must be four. Four elements, four corners, four points on the compass – the Fab Four knew what it was all about. KISS. Gene Simmons himself once noted that his original concept for the band was to create a 'heavy metal Beatles.' Simmons also seems to recognise the importance of retaining (or at least retaining the illusion) of the original four members – or the band at their peak of popularity with the fans. The Beatles' 'Four as the Magical Mystery Number' formula can be applied to any of your favourite foursomes.[158]

Although the combination of personalities contributed to the enormous musical and social success of the Beatles, it was ultimately the reason for their final breakdown, as four strong personalities vied for creative control over their own lives and interests. It was evident that the Beatles' magic had begun to diminish by the time of the *White Album* in 1968 – though something fascinating in the band's disarray and emotional struggle for each to free himself from the constraints of Beatle life is greatly captured on this record. Cooper indicates as much:

> Although Yoko stands as the mythical catalyst that may or may not have splintered the Beatles, it's only natural that a band so prolific and innovative, made up of such distinctive personalities could only thrive as a single entity for so long. For one brief, shining moment, the Beatles were music's answer to Camelot. John, Paul, George, and Ringo were seated in a circle like their fellow, British knights of the Round Table. Fancy that, with no one component greater than the other, each one a necessary part of the wheel. In the short time that the Beatles had created music as a foursome, they left an indelible impression and laid the groundwork that countless bands would attempt to build upon and follow. It was this precise combination of personalities that helped to create such a being.[159]

In fact, like any group of people, the four individualities of the group would naturally fill positions in which they could all function as individuals with certain personality traits, and as individuals working cohesively as a unit, which is why Pete Best did not go on to be the Beatles' drummer. This is because he, as George Harrison pointed out, had not the right personality to fit in with the other three, while Ringo, as destiny shows, was a necessary element that allowed the quintessence of the Beatles to manifest.[160]

The Four Elements

In these personality types the basic elements of sanguine, choleric, phlegmatic and melancholic are very obvious, not only in their individual characters as they appear in the Beatles' movies – like a *Hard Day's Night, Help!, Yellow Submarine*, as well as in the Beatles' cartoon series – but also in interviews and in the public's perception in general. These personality types are also evident in their music.

McCartney's music tends to be more sanguine, romantic and upbeat in nature. The melodies are flowing and the harmonic developments are more traditional and less abrasive than both Harrison's and Lennon's styles. McCartney was the ultimate mimic, a strong trait of the sanguine personality, expertly emulating styles and genres, and tending more towards romantic ballads. It is primarily as a balladeer that McCartney is best known and most respected, with songs like 'All My Lovin'', 'Yesterday' and 'The Long and Winding Road' being probably some of his most considered compositions with the group. His sunny, sanguine nature is also expressed in his whimsical songs like 'Ob-La-Di Ob-La-Da', 'When I'm Sixty-Four', and of course the childlike favourite, 'Yellow Submarine'. McCartney, in typical sanguine manner, also expertly mimicked genres, such as the rock 'n' roll in songs like 'I Saw Her Standing There', showtunes like 'Your Mother Should Know', country in 'Rocky Racoon', light jazz in 'Honey Pie', and classical arrangements like 'Penny Lane', in which the piccolo trumpet solo was directly taken from J.S. Bach's second Brandenburg Concerto.

Lennon, on the other hand, was more aggressive and heavier in his style, with tracks like 'A Hard Day's Night', 'Help!', 'Ticket To Ride', and 'Revolution' having a sharp edge to them that the other Beatles never quite matched; even his first self-penned single, 'Please Please Me' had a rawness to it. His compositional style was often erratic, like his personality, with unconventional chord progressions, time changes and instrumentation, while his lyrics were far more abstract and suggestive than McCartney's. Lennon's lyrics were introspective and opinionated, writing primarily from the egocentric point of view of the 'I'. Lennon's music is, from this point of view, very choleric, reflecting the individuality of his personality. Though Lennon's style was mostly abrasive and opinionated, with a more rock 'n' roll edge than McCartney's, he could write a ballad as well as McCartney, though it tended to be less optimistic than McCartney's, and often with a strong sense of personal experience and pain. His vocal delivery matched his personal view, and there is usually an urgency in it, singing as if his life depended on it, and often with a sense that control is slipping away from him. McCartney, however, sang with a certain professionalism – clear, controlled and easy, even when he was rocking out.

Harrison's songs, too, reflect his personality, and in some ways were a kind of middle ground to the typical styles of Lennon and McCartney: neither fast and raucous like Lennon or slow ballads like McCartney, but instead often mid-tempo and slightly turgid. His first songwriting attempt (apart from his early co-write with McCartney – 'In Spite of All the Danger'), 'Don't Bother Me', was fast, but not overly so, while the lyric, as with other songs like 'Think for Your Self' and 'Within You Without You', suggested the typical Harrison personality of disdain, disinterest – expressing a desire to be alone and with himself. This is very much the personality type of those who are interested in the pursuit of mystical and spiritual experiences, reflecting Harrison's melancholic, quiet, analytical, idealistic and at times introverted nature, along with his later interest in eastern spirituality and the pursuit of spiritual knowledge in general. Harrison's musical style veered possibly closer to Lennon for its unusual approach, though it didn't have the same easiness that Lennon's often had, a sense which came from joyful experimentation and adventure with a delight in finding the unusual and unexpected. Harrison's style seems a little more forced, more as if he is trying to fashion something of himself, forcing his will on the music, rather like he would do when studying the guitar as a boy, working hard to master it, rather than the natural easiness that McCartney would display.

While Harrison's music has a melancholic drone to it, Lennon's painted the picture of an adventurer exploring new musical ideas and lyrical images. Lennon gives the impression of an individual leading his own way through the journey of life, a fiery and choleric egoism. McCartney's approach, on the other hand, was safe, pleasing and natural, and never too concerned as to whether he ventured over new ground. Though McCartney had a tendency to play it safe, he would often bring new ideas to the Beatles, and enthuse over new innovative styles of music, art and film – something in his personality that obviously connected him with Lennon – but McCartney always did this in his easy-going sanguine manner. Lennon, contrastingly, would take the ideas and recklessly throw himself at them, absorb them and then move on to something new and different.

Ringo, meantime, with his relaxed and phlegmatic nature, was happy just to be around. In his unassuming manner, he simply provided the three others with a backbeat to their creations, positive words and a companionship that would try and keep the others all anchored in the mayhem of being Beatles.

With these four distinct temperaments, the Beatles represented a complete human being, in which all the elements are equally mixed, standing for the various aspects of humanity's personality types.

The Fifth Beatle

Although there were obviously only four Beatles that were perceived to be by the public, there was in essence a 'fifth' Beatle working in the background. In some ways, this 'fifth' Beatle was the mystical result of their four energies working together. In some senses this was their artistic output and social influence, as well as the inseparable connection they made with the public, which would be influenced by, and in turn influence, the Beatles, in a kind of symbiotic relationship between them and their fans.

The four Beatles together brought what esoteric or mystic teachings consider the quintessence of 'the thing' or the 'fifth element'. It is the very purpose for the four other aspects existing together. In this sense, the four individualities of the Beatles would exist in order to bring about its truer meaning. In some respects, this fifth element is often seen as a change of consciousness, or *metanoia*, which is connected to the Holy Spirit.[161]

In a more practical sense, the 'fifth' Beatle was a physical personality that worked with the Beatles in order to bring out and co-ordinate the four extraordinary personalities and talents of the group. Who this 'fifth' Beatle actually was is rather mysterious, curious and even an esoteric idea. There were a number of individuals that received the title, including the American DJ, Murray the K, who promoted the Beatles endlessly in America, as well as the group's roadie and tour manager, Neil Aspinall, who ensured the Beatles were everywhere they were supposed to be. Pete Best, the drummer that almost became a global superstar, is also at times referred to as the 'fifth Beatle', often a symbol of the everyman, whose misfortune was not to be a global-superstar-Beatle, but who nearly was. The Beatles were ordinary, working-class lads, and this meant anybody could achieve success like they had – and Best was a clear example of what that meant.

However, there are three individuals who most represent this mysterious and elusive 'fifth' entity, namely Brian Epstein, the group's manager, George Martin, their producer, and Stuart Sutcliffe, their one-time band mate and friend; a gifted artist, who died tragically young.

Some would refer to the Beatles' manager, Brian Epstein, as being the 'fifth' Beatle, because of his managerial skills and his innate and rather astute ability to bring to public awareness the talents and skills of the Beatles as an entity. The fact that the group collapsed shortly after Brian's death, and when under the control of Alan Klein's management, showed just 'how effective the quiet Liverpool businessman had been in keeping four disparate characters on the same page'.[162] The Rolling Stones' manager and one-time assistant to Epstein, Andrew 'Loog' Oldham, said that, 'Brian made it all possible. He told them who they could be and helped them become it. The Beatles changed our lives. Brian Epstein changed theirs',[163] while McCartney admitted that, 'if anyone was the "fifth" Beatle, it was Brian'[164] (though he would also claim this about Martin, after Martin passed away in 2016).[165]

Many saw the 'fifth' Beatle in the personality of the group's producer, George Martin, the man who would harness their musical talents and direct them in such a way as to give their inspirations form and shape, polish up their sound and even enhance it with musical, as well as production and arranging, abilities. 'Working intensely with Martin,' wrote music journalist Timothy Malcolm, 'they would produce a collection of songs unparalleled in the pop canon. Martin, in many ways, was the key ... it was Martin who guided the work, brought us the idea that anything really is possible in music, and no barriers need to stand'.[166] Epstein and Martin were in a sense two sides of the same coin, both dedicated to the group, as well as very skilled and adept in the very distinct and clear-cut positions they held within the Beatles' camp. Stu Sutcliffe, however, served a different role as the 'fifth' Beatle.

Stu Sutcliffe was to have a spiritual and artistic influence on the group, one that directly influenced their look and image in the early days in Liverpool and Hamburg, as well as a close spiritual connection to John Lennon. One friend said that, 'Stuart stayed with the Beatles as a spectre throughout the Beatles career — the artistic look of the group was through Sutcliffe, his hair and collarless jacket. Sutcliffe gave the Beatles a new image — a post- World War Two artistic sensibility — an energy for something new.'[167] The group's *With the Beatles'* album cover was 'vaguely haunted by Stuart's gentle soul', while his spirit clearly overshadows their *Sgt. Pepper's* cover, suggesting that he was still alive in their memories and still considered an artistic influence on them.

After Stuart's untimely death, Lennon had himself photographed in Stuart's studio attic by Stuart's wife, the German artist Astrid Kirchherr. The photo somehow suggests Lennon stepping into Stuart's space and spirit. The connection between John and Stuart, as the *Pepper's* cover indicates, would remain, and Stuart's artistic search for truth would continue to fuel Lennon's artistic and musical creations throughout his life.[168]

The Esoteric Side of the Beatles

By all accounts, an alternative outcome to the Beatles' overwhelming success seems to have been an impossibility. It seems the Beatles, and the individual personalities like Lennon, McCartney, Harrison, Starr, Epstein, Martin, and even the minor characters of the Beatles' story, like Mal Evans, and Neil Aspinall, were destined to play a decisive role in the cultural developments of the second half of the twentieth century and beyond. Many commentators at the time, such as promoter Sid Bernstein, believed that the phenomenon of Beatlemania was self-propelling – with an inevitable cultural influence which was inherently connected – and a result of the cosmic forces (or what is more commonly termed the zeitgeist) that were forming and manifesting themselves in the post-war period and in the era of the Sixties.[169]

While Elvis was another cultural phenomenon, his significance, even if his commercial appeal continued, rapidly diminished, to be replaced – musically, culturally and artistically, as well as politically and socially – by more advanced forces like the Beatles, Bob Dylan and to a lesser extent British Invasion bands like the Rolling Stones, and the West Coast sound of the Beach Boys and the Byrds.

The Beatles were, in other words, a significantly necessary force that opened up and propelled the new impulses of culture and society that were bubbling under the surface. In this sense, the Beatles (and to a lesser extent the other groups) were a part of some kind of providential plan, in which all human beings and societies are intrinsically connected. McCartney would sum it up well when he described the Beatles in a *Rolling Stone* interview in the following manner: 'Life is an energy field,' he suggested, 'a bunch of molecules. And these particular molecules formed to make these four guys [The Beatles] ... I have to think that was something metaphysical. Something alchemic. Something that must be thought of as magic.'[170]

In essence, McCartney is pointing at something deeply esoteric – a cosmic force, a kind of divine plan, which brought the Beatles about and set them on their mission. Lennon would also suggest something mystical and prophetic about their forming and destiny, even if expressed through his usual surreal humour, when he wrote: 'I had a vision when I was twelve of a man on a flaming pie, who said you are Beatles with an a, and we are.'[171] For many, the Beatles were not just the result of four working-class guys coming together, nor were they the result of a series of social conditions, but were in essence the result of something much deeper, something that was a spiritual destiny. Beatles' historian Mark Lewisohn comments on the unprecedented contractual agreements made between Lennon and McCartney and their music publisher and record company, while they had only just released 'Love Me Do' and had nothing much else to show for their songwriting potential. Many of his comments seem to indicate the uncanny and mystical nature of the group's development, as if it was all somehow predestined.[172]

One writer, Jon Pompia, sees them as being divinely inspired and certainly much more than simply popular music makers. 'While talent, personalities, chemistry, musicianship, hard work, drive and drugs played their part,' says Pompia, the Beatles were, and even saw themselves, "as instruments of a higher power".' [173]

In an interview in 1968, John Lennon and Paul McCartney were asked: 'What do you think is the one single thing that has most contributed to your phenomenal, unprecedented success these past years? John answered 'God', to which Paul would reply, 'I'll go along with that.'[174] Following their move towards eastern philosophy and ideas of karma and reincarnation, the Beatles would often attribute their success to their own karmic relations. Pattie Harrison, George's first wife, would suggest as much: 'I know it was part of a pattern... it all follows a path, just like our path. John, Paul and George converged, then a little later Ringo. We were part of that action, which led to the next reaction. We were all just little cogs in an action that everyone is part of.'[175]

Others would view the Beatles as being somehow mysteriously connected to the deep psychological aspects of the human psyche, or at least their music seemed to find its inspiration from a direct connection to a realm of creativity that was connected on a level of collective consciousness – an idea that often surrounded the creation of Beatles' songs like 'Yesterday', and 'Yellow Submarine', while Lennon's 'Across the Universe' would directly express a spiritual connection to the collective unconsciousness. Pompia goes on to suggest that, 'The Beatles became worldwide conquerors in the fact that the songs the quartet "channelled" were always a part of a human's DNA. And once these musical creations fell to earth through the Beatles, everyone — from children to geriatrics — immediately took to them like a long-lost friend.'[176]

In this sense, the Beatles were seen as some kind of Jungian expression of the collective unconsciousness of the post-war period as expressed in popular culture, particularly through popular music. For reasons unknown, at least in this life, the Beatles were selected by destiny, if you will, to bring to a planet sorely in need of hope and happiness, the greatest and most enduring collection of songs of all time. 'I've never figured it out, and I don't think anyone has ever been able to,' said Matt Hurwitz, Beatles' historian. Even their publicist Derek Taylor said: 'It's something I've never been able to put a finger on. They just had an inexplicable charisma.' [177]

'Luck', McCartney said – in reference to the birth of certain songs, as well as to the Beatles' juggernaut itself – was often more of a factor than talent. This concept is reinforced by Lewisohn, who suggests that without breaks, coincidences and a lot of luck, none of us would have ever heard of the Beatles. But it was not 'luck' in the conventional sense, but more to do with a destiny that was laid out for the four individuals, as well as some deeper connection for humankind in the post-war years, which would resonate throughout the century and into the next one. This theory – as well as comments issued by both Lennon and McCartney throughout their career – would indeed indicate that a 'hidden hand' was at work to ensure that the world would not only know the Beatles, but would be forever changed by them. 'Believing that is what made us what we were,' Lennon once said, 'it was just a matter of time before everybody caught on.'[178]

One commentator echoed Lennon's words saying: 'The Beatles themselves were like other men, but the music and lyrics channelled through them contained magic and messages from beyond the mind.' Lennon would continue with his notions of cosmic influence on the group and his writing: 'When real music comes to me – the music of the spheres, the music that surpasses understanding – that has nothing to do with me, cause I'm just the channel. The only joy for me is for it to be given to me, and to transcribe it like a medium... those moments are what I live for.'[179] Pompia makes an interesting comment, saying: 'I believe they did not know the spiritual content of their songs until after they were written; that they came out of the air, as they say. They came from the collective unconscious or Holy Spirit, if you prefer, not their own minds.'[180]

The Beatles and the Cycle of 33

It's interesting that Allison Taich, in her essay 'Beatlemania', describes the Beatle phenomenon as a 'Second Coming' (see Chapter 3), attaching a religious, if not also a spiritual, significance to the Beatles and Beatlemania. If we make a slight leap of the imagination and consider the esoteric notion put forward by Rudolf Steiner but taken up by others, i.e. that the Second Coming had already presented itself in the year 1933, in which the Christ Being had returned 'in the cloud', or in the etheric realm, if speaking in esoteric terms,[181] and that this experience, similar in essence to Saint Paul's Damascus experience of the Christ, is to be had by more and more people who move away from materialism and embrace a deeper, more fully conscious spiritual view of life on earth, it may not be such an outlandish comparison that Taich makes when she says that rock was in its 'Second Coming' when the Beatles came to America.

In his book, *The Spiritual Event of the Twentieth Century, An Imagination: The Occult Significance of the 12 Years, 1933-45 in the Light of Spiritual Science,* Jesaiah Ben-Aharon suggests that this event, described above, was obscured by the atrocities of the Second World War, Nazi Germany, and the exploding of the atomic bomb.[182] Steiner, incidentally, states that the Christ event is not a physical one, in which this universal consciousness reappears in the flesh as such, as this task was already complete when the Christ was made physically manifest in the physical body of Jesus of Nazareth two thousand years ago. But if this is the case, and if we see the obscuring of such an event by the Nazis and the Second World War, then we must consider it being an event that still needs to be grasped in some way by humanity, most probably through imagination and intuition. Such, possibly, was one of the tasks of the Beatles and their contribution to waking up the new generation.

The above may also be considered in its opposite form as yet another mass hysteria, equal in many ways to that of Nazi Germany, in which the people are distracted from their real purpose of grasping this event within themselves, instead of looking outwards into the material world. This is an important consideration but really too big to deal with here. It is simply mentioned to point out how some express the Beatles' significance in religious and spiritual terms, as well as the possible justification of linking such a phenomenon to a wider cosmic view of cultural events which don't just have their origins and purpose encased in the socio-political arenas in which we, in this period of human evolution, are so entrenched. What is also significant about Taich's comparison is that the 'Second Coming' also suggests a rebirth or re-awaking, and that this is particularly significant in terms of the new beginnings that came about following the Second World War.

Interestingly, it would be 33 years – a cycle connected to Christ – after this event (Christ's appearance on the etheric plane in 1933), in 1966 that the collective consciousness underwent another major shift. Two books written solely on the subject — *1966* by Jon Savage and Steve Turner's *Beatles '66* – emphasize the significance of this year. 'Nineteen Sixty Six,' wrote Turner, 'was without question the pivotal year in the life of the Beatles as performers and recording artists.' He goes on to say that they, 'wrote songs that explored their psyches and the nature of society, and were frequently considered a threat to the established order by governments around the world'.[183] At the same time, the album, with its 33 and a third revolutions per second, became a major musical event corresponding with this date (1966), with *Pet Sounds*, *Revolver* and *Blonde on Blonde* being the most noteworthy examples. Even the title of the album *Revolver* was, curiously enough, a reference to the new-found significance of the album as a popular medium and as an emerging art form.

Chapter 5

Christ, You Know It Ain't Easy:
Bigger Than Jesus

The Controversy

In March 1966, John Lennon gave an interview in his mock-Tudor home in Weybridge, London, to the respected journalist Maureen Cleave, who had become close to the Beatles early on in their career.

Cleave's piece, 'How Does a Beatle Live? John Lennon Lives Like This', tried to give her readers some insight into the, almost regal, life of a Beatle. The Beatles, Cleave pointed out, were now so famous and so essential to British life and culture that to reject them or topple them from their exalted position would not only be an attack on youth culture and the future of Britain but would bring the values of the British system tumbling down. The Beatles no longer needed to play to anyone else's rules, no longer needed to take a position – they needed to do nothing, as their position, like the royal family, would be forever secure at the top of the pyramid. 'The Beatles fame,' she wrote, 'is beyond question, it has nothing to do with whether they are rude or polite, married or unmarried, 25 or 45; whether they appear on *Top of the Pops* or do not appear on *Top of the Pops*... They are famous in the way the Queen is famous... With her they share the security of a stable life at the top.'[184]

This is interesting in that it cast the Beatles as beyond reach, as something almost god-like; a position that could lead an individual, such as Lennon, dangerously close to becoming a megalomaniac. At the same time, Cleave points out quite accurately how this position has been put upon them by the public: 'they all tick over in the public esteem', the institutions around them, that mainly feed on them, as well as the cultural necessity to have such figures in England, as it secures the Empire its place in the modern world. It gives the

Empire relevance and significance once again, following its loss of position after the War.[185] It challenged the Americans in the cultural sphere and claimed that, although America was the strongest militarily, they were still superior culturally and artistically, for they had Shakespeare, Milton, Newton, Byron, Dickens, even Charlie Chaplin – and now they had produced the Beatles. What had America done in comparison?

Despite Lennon's wealth and fame, Cleave found a man, 'deeply dissatisfied by the trappings of domesticity and social status'. 'I'm just stopping [here] like a bus stop. I'll get my real house when I know what I want', Lennon said, as he gave her a tour of his mansion, littered with expensive 'toys'. 'You see,' he confessed to Cleave 'there's something else I'm going to do – only I don't know what it is. All I know is this isn't it for me.'[186]

Lennon and the rest of the Beatles had spent the beginning of the year enjoying a much-needed respite from four years' extensive touring, recording, media attention and Beatlemania. Lennon spent much of this free time in a period of intense self-reflection, expanding his mind with a regimen of psychedelic drugs, newspapers and books. He read, Cleave observed, 'extensively about religion', including Timothy Leary's take on *The Tibetan Book of the Dead*, *The Psychedelic Experience* and Hugh J. Schonfield's *The Passover Plot*, a controversial book that put forward the notion that Jesus Christ was a mortal man who faked his miracles and his death and resurrection. 'With Schonfield's book on his mind, and his tongue loosened by friendship,' noted *Rolling Stone* journalist Jordan Runtagh, 'the man who would later challenge the world to imagine no religions, spoke to his journalist friend with notable candor.'[187]

'Christianity will go,' Lennon remarked, 'it will vanish and shrink. I needn't argue about that; I'm right and I will be proved right. We're more popular than Jesus now. I don't know which will go first, rock 'n' roll or Christianity. Jesus was all right but his disciples were thick and ordinary. It's them twisting it that ruins it for me.'[188]

In Britain, the comment went unnoticed, but in America, when the article was published in the teen fanzine *Datebook*, just before the Beatles' 1966 American tour, all hell broke loose. Despite the general perception that the publication was nothing more than teenybopper fluff, *Datebook* was actually a boundary-pushing magazine for its day, covering serious social and political topics side-by-side with the usual showbiz fare. The magazine's editor, Arthur Unger, a gay man in an unwelcoming culture, who saw first-hand how minority groups could be oppressed and ridiculed, directed his vision of the magazine towards one of social justice. 'The magazine,' he explained in later years, 'was a serious attempt to help kids', and it published articles from critiques of patriarchal society to the abolishing of segregation in the south, and even gave its support for the registering of black voters there. It was, in effect, quite a radical teen magazine for the mid-Sixties.

Unger's work attracted positive attention from the Beatles and *Datebook* was occasionally given exclusive quotes and minor scoops. Unger accompanied the band on their future American trips, and a friendly relationship developed between them. For his coverage of their 1965 tour, Unger touched on Ringo Starr's pro-integration stance in the American South. 'Segregation is a lot of rubbish', he quoted Starr as saying. 'As far as we're concerned, people are people, no different from each other. We'd never play South Africa if it means a segregated audience. What a lot of rubbish.'

As they had with Cleave, the Beatles appreciated being portrayed as more than just loveable mop-tops, and continued to send Unger material. So, after Cleave's article was published in the *Evening Standard*, Beatles' press officer Tony Barrow sent it to Unger with a note: 'I think the style and content is very much in line with the sort of thing *Datebook* likes to use.'[189]

Barrow was right. The magazine's September issue, which also featured an article supporting interracial dating, seemed tailor-made to rankle bigoted southern values. Unger used two of Cleave's quotes on the cover spread to attack the twin pillars of racism and religion.

The first remark, 'It's a lousy country where anyone black is a dirty n****r' was a McCartney quote, but it was Lennon's 'I don't know which will go first – rock & roll or Christianity', remark that sent sections of America into uproar. Rumours about Lennon's quote spread quickly throughout anti-Beatle factions, mostly from the so-called Bible Belt, who took the quote out of context, declaring: 'John says Beatles are bigger than Jesus.'[190]

The quote attracted the attention of Tommy Charles, a DJ for Birmingham, Alabama's WAQY ('Wacky Radio') station and one of the first so-called 'shock jocks', that focused attention on the more sensational news stories of the day. Lennon's inflammatory remark was certainly the kind of news item the station relished, though the fact that the outspoken Beatle was actually complaining about the sorry state of spiritual affairs seemed of little consequence to him. With his side-kick Doug Layton, Charles launched an impromptu 'Ban the Beatles' campaign, refusing to play any of the band's music on the network in retaliation for Lennon's 'blasphemous' remarks.

Though the stunt was likely motivated by publicity rather than piety, Charles did his best to position himself as moral arbiter, taking a stand against godless foreign longhairs who sought to corrupt the American youth, admonishing the Beatles to 'grow-up'. This comment caused Harrison to retort that Charles himself should grow up as he had only banned the Beatles' records as a publicity stunt.[191] 'Because of their tremendous popularity throughout the world, especially with the younger set, [the Beatles] have been able to say what they wanted to without any regard for judgment, maturity, or the meaning of it, and no one has challenged them to any degree,' Charles crowed. The religious leader and writer David Noebel wrote a series of anti-Beatle articles stating, 'the major value of the Beatles to the left in general... has been their usefulness in destroying youth's faith in God...'. He mentioned Lennon's *A Spaniard in the Works* (1965) and Lennon's satire of 'Father, Sock and Micky Most.'[192]

Lennon remarked that:

> When it came out in England it was a bit of a blab-mouthed saying anyway… A few people wrote into the papers, and a few wrote back saying, 'So what, he said that. Who is he anyway', or they said, 'So, he can have his own opinion'. And then it just vanished. It was very small. But you know, when it gets over here and then it's put into a kid's magazine, and just parts of it or whatever was put in, it just loses its meaning or its context immediately… and everybody starts making their own versions of it.[193]

Lennon would be asked time and time again throughout the tour to clarify what he had said. 'My views,' he would explain, 'are only from what I've read or observed of Christianity… It just seems to me to be shrinking. I'm not knocking it or saying it's bad. I'm just saying it seems to be shrinking and losing contact.'[194]

Several dozen radio stations across the country followed the WAQY's lead and banned the Beatles' music. Some DJs went so far as to smash their records live on the air, and one even broadcast an anti-Beatle editorial each hour. While the English were able to laugh off Lennon's quote, literal-minded fundamentalist Christians in the southern United States were appalled to hear the Lord and Saviour equated to a pop group.

The destruction soon escalated to a series of mass burnings, uncomfortably reminiscent of the Third Reich, as stations publicly torched their entire stock of Beatles' music, while the Ku Klux Klan nailed several Beatles' albums to a cross and set it aflame at a 'Beatle Bonfire'. The outcry reached all the way to the Pope, who denounced Lennon's words in a statement to the Vatican newspaper, *L'Osservatore Romano*: 'Some subjects must not be dealt with profanely, even in the world of Beatniks.'[195] The governments of South Africa (where apartheid was still enforced) and Spain (ruled by General Franco's dictatorial regime) also issued official condemnations.

Lennon, ironically, was not making a particularly revolutionary point, and although his comparison with Jesus was a little too daring, no one could deny that the Church was certainly losing its popularity. Religious advocates in Britain, particularly, had been making similar arguments in the *Daily Mail* and the *Church Times*. Rather than respected and revered, the Church was a favourite subject for Sixties' satirists like Peter Cook, Alan Bennett and Peter Sellers. 'The clergy,' as Philip Norman pointed out, 'aware they had been reduced to joke fodder, were desperate to correct their image problem.'[196] The term 'Christianity' in Britain had become synonymous with the Church of England, an organization felt by many to be toothless and laughably out of touch.

'They themselves had been complaining about lack of congregations,' McCartney said.

> We used to get a number of Catholic priests showing up at our gigs, and we'd do a lot of debating backstage. We'd say, 'You should have gospel singing – that'll pull them in. You should be more lively, instead of singing hackneyed old hymns. Everyone's heard them and they're not getting off on them anymore.' So, we felt quite strongly that the Church should get its act together. We were actually very pro-church; it wasn't any sort of demonic, anti-religion point-of-view that John was trying to express.[197]

Others attacked the position of the fundamentalists. 'The truth of John's statement,' said the rector of Holy Trinity Episcopal Church, 'cannot be denied', while a Methodist pastor agreed with John's assessment that, 'Jesus was alright but his disciples are thick and ordinary. It's them twisting it that ruins it for me' – while a Memphis youth, attending Louisiana State University, wrote to the City Fathers asking, 'Is your religion so weak that four rock 'n' roll players can shake it?'[198]

The quote from Lennon trod a thin line of realizing the absurdity of their situation, while simultaneously not taking too seriously the position and titles put on them from those institutions that viewed them more as symbols rather than as real people. However, it also suggests that Lennon, though possibly, absent-minded in his remarks, feels, as Tommy Charles had rightly pointed out, that he can say whatever he pleases without his position being challenged to any real extent. This makes him different from the monarchy, and others who are beyond the normal placements in society. For often they are (at least officially) opinion-less; often they are without a personality, a stance and a point-of-view. They are not allowed to have one as it would colour the significance of their symbolic role, and thus diminish its power. In some ways, the Beatles were not supposed to have a point-of-view, a position that Lennon and Harrison often objected to, while at the same time they represented the very notion of individuality and personal opinion, often persuading and influencing the opinions of their own generation.

What exactly did Lennon mean when he made the statement they were 'Bigger Than Jesus'? As already mentioned, it seemed that Lennon and the other Beatles, being beyond reproach, could say and do as they pleased without criticism. When they were, famously, found in an illicit situation with the Rolling Stones, they were conveniently led out the back door – the spotlight was kept away from them in this instance. The media that followed them around presented only their better side – ignoring to report their more unsavoury behaviour, since, primarily, they wanted to be kept within the circle. The Beatles had a reputation for being cheeky, scruffy and insolent, but essentially moral, civilized and goodly representatives of both the British Empire, as well as modern youth culture. The Beatles' manager and his company, as well as other members of the Beatles' crew, like Derek Taylor and Mal Evans, were all hired to make sure nothing negative surrounded the Beatles, and people were often persuaded, most likely through pay-offs, to keep their mouths shut. Epstein built a strong army of protection around his charges, and thus they must have felt somewhat untouchable. Under such circumstances, Lennon felt he could say what he liked and no one would challenge him on it. In his defence, he was in conversation with a friend, someone with whom he felt he could speak candidly.

Essentially, Lennon was both brash and naive in giving his opinion on such matters as religion. It was simply his opinion about both the Beatles and Christianity, and though he may have been entirely qualified to talk about the Beatles, as he claimed he was doing, he wasn't really qualified to talk authoritatively about Christianity, even though he was genuinely interested in the subject (which would, incidentally, become a greater focus of his art and life in the later part of the Beatles and certainly throughout his post-Beatles period). But certainly, Lennon could only speak about Christianity and its purpose in people's lives from what he felt from his somewhat secluded and detached life as a Beatle, cut off from the rest of the world in Weybridge, Surrey.

Lennon should never really have been taken seriously when he put forward this opinion, saying things off the cuff, as was his manner, and seemingly that's how many British people who really cared about the remark felt. Others thought that he was entitled to his opinion, regardless of how ill-informed he might have been, while a few felt a little put out by his frivolous attitude to such a subject matter,[199] not so much by what he said but the casual and thoughtless way he said it. In fact, the British public probably responded exactly how they should have, not really making much fuss about some slightly naive pop star shooting from the hip.

However, such an attitude towards Lennon's remark was, in some ways, ironically, exactly what Lennon was referring to – that no one really cared about their religion, about Jesus or about what anyone said about it, or whether it was even worth defending, and because of that lukewarm attitude, Christianity was most likely going to become less and less significant in people's lives. This whole episode was a perfect example of that fact; so, inadvertently Lennon proved himself right, even though he didn't really mean to prove much at all. The statement, however, did prove one thing, that Lennon was, certainly at the time, preoccupied with thoughts of religion and was deeply searching in his soul.

While the Beatles, honourably, made no attempt to place the blame on Cleave by claiming Lennon was misquoted or had made the statements off the record, she did her best to put some perspective on the situation by saying he was simply observing that the state of Christianity was so weak that the Beatles were, to many people, better known.[200] *Datebook*'s open-minded editor also came to his defence, saying that Lennon, 'had a perfect right to make his statements – just as others have a perfect right to disagree with him. Our teenagers show a lot more maturity than many adults give them credit for and they are quite capable of reading what John has to say, weighing the points he has to make and then deciding for themselves where they stand.'[201]

The Apology

The one person who refused to comment or even apologize, however, was Lennon himself: 'I'd forgotten all about it. It was that unimportant – it had been and gone.'[202] Unable to persuade the somewhat confrontational Lennon to apologize, Epstein had no choice but to do so himself. Calling a Press conference on 6 August at New York's Americana Hotel, he read out a prepared statement that had been begrudgingly approved by Lennon.

'The quote which John Lennon made to a London columnist more than three months ago has been quoted and misrepresented entirely out of context', the statement began. 'What he said, and meant, was that he was astonished that in the last 50 years, the Church of England, and therefore Christ, had suffered a decline in interest. He did not mean to boast about the Beatles' fame. He meant to point out that the Beatles' effect appeared to be, to him, a more immediate one upon a certain cohort of the younger generation.'[203] Epstein brought the conference to an end with a reminder that any promoters were free to cancel their bookings in light of the controversy. Predictably, the almighty dollar won out and nobody did.

The Beatles departed London for their American tour on 11 August as planned, but as the situation remained volatile, it became clear that a statement would have to be made by Lennon himself. 'John had to apologise,' explained Starr,[204] 'not because of what he'd said, but to save our lives because there were a lot of very heavy threats – not only to him but to the whole band.' All the Beatles were concerned for their lives on this tour and, according to Peter Brown, the Beatles' personal assistant, Paul had 'a horror of being shot on stage'. 'We should be wearing targets,' he said.[205] Faced with the realization that both the tour and his life hung in the balance, Lennon finally cracked. 'He actually put his head in his hands and sobbed,' Barrow maintains. 'He was saying, "I'll do anything... whatever you say. How am I to face the others if this whole tour is called off just because of something I've said?"'

Already exhausted and disillusioned with being a Beatle, Lennon just wanted to put an end to the whole episode.

> I wasn't saying what they're saying I was saying. I'm sorry I said it – really. I never meant it to be a lousy anti-religious thing. I apologise if that will make you happy. I still don't know quite what I've done. I've tried to tell you what I did do, but if you want me to apologise, if that will make you happy, then – OK, I'm sorry.[206]

In a separate press conference, Lennon stated, 'I'm not anti-Christ or anti-religion or anti-God. I'm not saying we're better or greater, or comparing us with Jesus Christ as a person, or God as a thing or whatever it is. I just said what I said and was wrong, or was taken wrong, and now it's all this.'[207] He continued his explanation. 'If I'd have said television is more popular than Jesus, I might have got away with it... we meant more to kids than Jesus did, or religion at that time. I wasn't knocking it or putting it down, I was just saying it as a fact and it's true more for England than here.'[208]

The sight of a contrite Beatle did much to extinguish the damning hellfire raging across the country. WAQY DJs Charles and Layton cancelled their massive 'Beatle Bonfire' scheduled for 19

August, although officially they cited permit problems. A public burning, organized by a local radio station in Longview, Texas, on 13 August, did however take place, but the following day the station's transmission tower was struck by lightning, destroying broadcasting equipment and rendering the news director unconscious. Divine intervention or not, the incident surely amused Lennon to no end.

Despite the eventual success of the tour, the Beatles, already averse to being cooped up in hotel rooms and the continuous screaming and madness that followed them every time they pulled into a new town, decided it would be their last tour. 'I didn't want to tour again, especially after having been accused of crucifying Jesus when all I'd made was a flippant remark, and having to stand with the Klan outside and firecrackers going on inside. I couldn't take any more.'[209] Apart from their iconic 42-minute performance of 30 January 1968, on the roof of their Apple Offices at Savile Row Studios, the Beatles never performed live again.

Lennon the Believer

The reaction to the remark was an attack on Lennon, the Beatles and pop culture that some didn't like because it was beyond their control. Whatever the exact reason, it certainly wasn't to defend Christianity. The attack and the viciousness of it was, simply, characteristically un-Christian. The Press had built up the Beatles and now it was time to topple them – because it was more interesting, because it was more newsworthy, and because it showed that they, the Press, were still all powerful, particularly with regard to a brash group of young men from England.

'Newspapers had vested interest in keeping Beatlemania alive but they also wanted to be first on the scene when it began to experience its death throes… the unspoken rule was that those who benefitted from huge acclaim, financial reward, and natural talent should eventually suffer for their success.'[210] While in Britain, particularly at the time, value was placed in traditionalism, in things that had a lasting quality, the Beatles were now an institution. In America, the consumer culture placed greater value in the fad and not in that which had longevity, and for this reason the Beatles were, possibly, also attacked.

Lennon's estranged wife, Cynthia Lennon, would characterize the whole episode very well in her book *A Twist of Lennon*, as 'a mass orgy of self-righteous indignation', while during his December 1966 *Look* magazine interview, with some hindsight, John clarified the remark best saying: 'I said we were more popular than Jesus, which is a fact. I believe Jesus was right, Buddha was right, and all of those people like that are right. They're all saying the same thing, and I believe it. I believe what Jesus actually said — the basic things he laid down about love and goodness — and not what people say he said.'[211]

It is interesting that two things had happened in Lennon's life up to his conversation with Cleave, the first being that he was seemingly going through some kind of mental and emotional breakdown — he had written the song 'Help!' only one year previously, obviously completely lost in the world of Beatledom. During an interview with *Playboy* in 1980, Lennon recounted: 'The whole Beatles thing was just beyond comprehension. I was subconsciously crying out for help.' In fact, Lennon was feeling uncomfortable and depressed by Beatlemania long before he had even written 'Help!' Bob Stanley, for example, sees evidence of his disillusionment as early as 1964, remarking on the closing song from the *A Hard Day's Night* album, 'I'll Be Back', which, he suggests:

> Closes on a downbeat note [that] shows their fear of displacement and sense of loss as their lives were becoming irrevocably changed… throughout, its nasal harmonies are very English, steeped like a teabag in Merseyside melancholia. I'll be back is confused, resigned, mature, a goodbye to the initial heady rush of Beatle-mania. The lyric is self-defeating, resigned to its loneliness while the chords shift uncertainly.[212]

If the world was Lennon's oyster, why was he so miserable? This attitude must have made Lennon question where peace and salvation could really be found. He was surrounded with wealth and material nonsense, as Cleave would astutely point out, which gave him little happiness or sense of purpose. If it wasn't to be in money and fame, which he had always assumed, where then? If anything, he had become more and more divorced from the world, almost incarcerated by his own success. To lash out at superficiality of modern life was an obvious reaction, both at our attitude towards what were important things, like Christianity, as well as the superficiality of the institutions that are supposed to represent and encourage such thoughts and ways of life. Rock, John thought, was filling a void in people's lives once filled by religion — and he saw first-hand how young people were drawn to popular culture rather than conventional religions. The film *A Hard Day's Night* was more of a sensation in 1964 then the biblical *The Greatest Story Ever Told* a year later. Lennon had seen how myths could build up around ordinary people like the Beatles, misleading others, and felt that Christianity had become corrupted in a similar sense.[213] Christianity, Lennon felt, had declined in the modern world and no one, he told Cleave, was interested in saving it.

It most likely infuriated and scared Lennon that there was no direction for him or anyone, and the whole thing, including Christianity, was all a sell-out, a ruse and a pointless exercise that really just hoodwinked people. Lennon chose not to blame Christ for this. This was something that both his personality, as well as his intuition, wouldn't allow. Instead, he blamed those who were supposedly representatives of the Christ impulse, from the early disciples right through to the modern Church. Lennon felt let down by them, just as much as he had been let down by his father, his mother, school, and his beloved rock 'n' roll, which until most recently was his personal saviour.

Lennon's own intuition – as was the intuition of the younger generation – was to reject the lies, hypocrisies and double standards of the older generation and the institutions that they stood for, from World War Two to the Vietnam War, to the double standards that he experienced with the Beatles, even in his own soul. The Beatles, he would say, were 'bastards'.[214] Lennon would later realize that institutions and symbols couldn't lead us anywhere; salvation was to be found inside – 'I just believe in me', he would later sing. However, it is a scary and insecure road that leads one to this awareness, and Lennon was seemingly going through that stage, his 'dark night of the soul', as it were. He was becoming exhausted and disillusioned with the Beatles, particularly the live performances and what had now become the intolerable and superficial interviews and public appearances, as well as being public property. By 1965, the group, exhausted from touring, withdrew into the studio to record their first truly studio-focused album, *Rubber Soul*.

During this period Lennon gave some indication as to his real spiritual and religious leanings that would certainly help to dismiss any idea that, in his remark to Cleave, Lennon was mocking God or Jesus. Lennon seemed to have identified himself with the Apostle John, and John's Gospel certainly appealed to him, if only because he and the apostle shared the same name. In some sense Lennon saw himself in his role as a Beatle as a demi-god with a 'spiritual' mission. 'In the Beginning, I misunderstood. Now I've got it and the Word is good...', he would write, indicating that he was in effect writing his own 'Gospel of John Lennon', but also a confession that he had misunderstood what the message of Christianity was really all about.

But why would Lennon be at all interested in writing about something like this in a rock 'n' roll band? Because Lennon, with his expanding awareness of life through being a Beatle, and his voracious appetite for books and knowledge, was led to something beyond the scope of basic rock 'n' roll. Lennon had picked up on the first glimmer of this notion, which he was now ready to popularize culturally. In essence, the song ('The Word' on *Rubber Soul*) is the 'Gospel of John Lennon' and his 'In the Beginning...' was his delving into a deeper, esoteric understanding of life. Esotericism was something that clearly always fascinated Lennon, particularly through his love for books, like *Alice in Wonderland*. It was a subject matter that became particularly evident in songs like 'Tomorrow Never Knows' and 'Strawberry Fields Forever'. Lennon would intuitively exclaim what the next two years would come to embrace in a major way. It was the 'Word Love' that would release him and everyone else from the pain of earthly life – 'say the word love and you'll be free', as he would sing on *Rubber Soul*.

Lennon uses three esoteric terms in this song, all taken from John's Gospel: 'Love' 'Freedom' and 'the Word', all of which are in essence the spirit of Christ. So, was Lennon dismissing Christ or God? Certainly, in a deeper sense, he wasn't since he had just written one of his first rock 'n' roll songs based on the teachings of John's Gospel, though using the text as an artistic crutch – an experiment, possibly, to equal Dylan – but also to express the first inklings of his own basic philosophy, as well as the culture's grasping of the basic principles of 'Love', which would become a major movement the following year (and of which Lennon's song was one of the first major impulses). Much of his later music would deal almost exclusively with the subject, culminating in the hippy anthem, and the song that probably best captured the ethos and atmosphere of the late 1960s, 'All You Need Is Love'. This song, McCartney admitted, 'has affected a lot of people… It is what people need still'.[215]

Lennon was right, though his manner of expressing it to Cleave was clumsy and thoughtless, not realizing that many found comfort in religious institutions, as well as needing them. Though the British didn't bother too much with the remark (and rightly so in one sense), maybe they should have really thought about whether he was right, whether in fact no one really cared anymore about their spiritual destination.

In America, the quote was taken out of context and the media hype over it was simply another showbiz circus stunt, not really a religious debate, which the Beatles found themselves caught up in, while the Christian notion of forgiveness, the very essence of Christ's teachings, seemed to have passed those people by. Lennon had to concede his power to the media by apologizing and letting them know that they still had control; but ultimately they would not harm the Beatles because they made a lot of money for many people, and this was 'real' power. However, the threat that something ugly could happen to Lennon made him realize just how much he was caught up in a circus. Ultimately, Lennon was glad that he had this experience, bringing him to realize how absurd everything was, and how much his life was no longer his. At such a point, he realized he had to get out. Looking back, Lennon would comment on how significant this episode was, freeing him from the madness of the Beatles. 'I always remember to thank Jesus for the end of my touring days – if I hadn't have upset everyone I might still be up there with all the other performing fleas.'[216]

Two months before the 'Bigger than Jesus' remark, Lennon began to speak out against the Vietnam War. He said that the 'Butcher' cover for the *Yesterday and Today* album, which featured the four Beatles with the bodies of dismembered dolls and slabs of raw meat, was as relevant as Vietnam. Once it had been suppressed, Lennon cast the cover in that light, and aligned himself with anti-war students. When asked in America what he thought of the war, he said: 'We think about it every day. We don't like it. We don't agree with it. We think it's wrong.' British historian Eric Hobsbawn commented, 'most British people at the time would have said they thought the war in Vietnam was wrong, but very few would have said, "we think about it every day". That's remarkable.' [217]

Lennon expected that his anti-war remarks would be trumpeted by the media, but they virtually ignored them and decided to focus on the Jesus remark instead. Lennon would make sure his anti-war and political statements would not be ignored by the Press in the future, and '"the more popular than Jesus" controversy pushed John to take his first steps away from the Beatles and toward the anti-war activism that would become central to his life and work.'[218] The author Paul DuNoyer, who has written extensively on the Beatles, remarked: 'He was chastened by the reaction he got to his Jesus remarks and it probably made him think more carefully about religion... These comments would have been a great boost for churches if they had come out at the time.'

'For a long time, we always had specific little aims', Lennon told Beatles' biographer Hunter Davies:

> We never really looked far ahead. It was all a series of goals, to get a record made, to get a number one, to do another one, to do a film and so on. We just sort of glimpsed it all in stages. We never thought about any big things. Now I can. I'm not interested in little stages now. It's a waste of time for me... I suppose now what I'm interested in is a Nirvana, the Buddhist heaven... when I made the Jesus remarks, lots of people sent me books about Jesus. I read a lot of them and found out things. I've found out for example that the Church of England isn't very religious. There's too much politics. You can't be both. You can't be powerful and pure. Perhaps I'll find out that the gurus are like that as well, full of politics... but at the moment I want to find myself. [219]

It is clear from his interview with Hunter Davies that Beatledom had in fact isolated him even more from the 'real' world (as it seemed also with the other Beatles), and he spent more and more time looking inward, lost in his own reveries but disconnected from reality. His traditional background of Church of England 'Christianity' didn't provide him with any answers; in fact, it seems to have driven his quest for self-knowledge and spirituality towards Buddhism and eastern philosophies. Lennon, however, wouldn't rest here, but would later reconnect more with the spiritual values of Christianity. He would, in fact, announce to the other Beatles that he was himself Jesus returned,[220] not to mention equating himself to the crucified saviour in his song 'The Ballad of John and Yoko' – though this seems more a result of his heroin addiction than anything else.

Lennon's own detachment from reality at times would most likely cause him to have certain delusions, particularly when using drugs. From this point-of-view, again it seems easy for Lennon to in fact compare himself to the idea of Jesus, as had been presented to him through the conventional channels of western, particularly English, culture. Nevertheless, Lennon, though always a contradiction, seems to have transcended the conventional ideas of material Christianity, as well as the other relics of other religions, as he dismisses them outright in the song, 'God'. He rejects all figures of outward authority. 'I don't believe in Jesus...', he announces, but yet Lennon would continue to follow the essential teaching of the Gospel of John – in which the Evangelist presses us to 'Know the Truth and the Truth shall set you free' and in which Jesus announces himself as the 'Truth, the Way and the Life' – by searching for the 'Truth', as in the song 'Give Me Some Truth'. It seems that Lennon continually returned to Jesus and Christianity, feeling that there was something in it of immense importance but clearly rejecting the empty view of it as presented to him in conventional, often political terms. It is from this point of view that Lennon declares the Beatles as 'Bigger than Jesus'.

In a deeper, esoteric regard, however, Lennon seems to sense something of a much deeper and more sacred notion, which both his life and music pointed to and which he often sought for in other esoteric sources, like the *Bhagavad Gita* and Timothy Leary's *The Psychedelic Experience*, but which he understood to be in the Christian religion (although he may never have quite realized this in his lifetime, at least not in full consciousness). This is quite clear in the notions of both universal love and brotherhood, at the same time infused with intellectual and emotional development, which his songs like 'The Word', 'All You Need Is Love', 'The Ballad of John and Yoko', 'Across the Universe', 'Love', 'God', 'Imagine', and 'No. 9 Dream' clearly suggest.

Interestingly, Lennon's one-time musical collaborator and friend, Tony Sheridan, felt that Lennon was so in awe of Jesus that he was nearly envious of him. 'I think he was jealous of Jesus for many years, if you know what I mean. He was envious of there ever having been a Jesus, because Jesus is what he would have liked to have been, but a guitar playing Jesus...' – a political figure, but one with a heart and one with a message approaching a Jesus figure. 'He got as close as you can get to being Jesus,' remarked Sheridan, 'without actually being him.'[221]

In a BBC Radio 4 interview, not broadcast until twenty-eight years after his death, Lennon claims he hoped to encourage people to focus on the Christian faith. Despite his familiar image as a hippy icon who invited us to imagine a world without religion, Lennon says he was, 'one of Christ's biggest fans... And if I can turn the focus on the Beatles on to Christ's message, then that's what we're here to do'.[222] That Lennon was able to embody his own ideals was another question, but his thinking surely was bringing him to the conclusion that 'Love is the answer', and, in both a defiant way as well as out of petulance, he blamed 'Christian' institutions for not doing what they were supposed to do, i.e. to imbue the world with love.

It's clear from these remarks that Lennon was not in any way anti-religious or anti-God, as the American media tried to portray him. In fact, Lennon was and would continue to search for meaning, not just to his own life but to life in general. It would be apparent that every effort he made until his death would be an attempt to give his life some meaning, particularly since the material success of the Beatles had not at all been satisfying. Life as a Beatle had caused even more of a sense of meaninglessness. If the loss of his parents as a child, candidly expressed in his *Plastic Ono Band* album, and the loss of his close friends in early adulthood, had set him off on a journey of self-exploration – which he hoped he might discover through the world, particularly in the world of celebrity and the religion of rock 'n' roll – it seemed that it didn't fulfil anything. Like all the other Beatles, particularly George Harrison, John Lennon seemed to look for meaning in a supersensible reality.

Proof the Beatles are Bigger than Jesus!

Forty-three years after John Lennon compared the Beatles to Jesus, statistics emerge suggesting that he might have actually been correct. Steve Turner points out that in England, from 1964 to 2011, the number of people belonging to a religion and attending services dropped from 74 per cent to 13.1 per cent, while [223] Google's search traffic for the terms 'Jesus' and 'Beatles', over 30 days in September 2009, shows that the Beatles were, at least for this period, actually more popular than Jesus.

Chapter 6

I'd Love to Turn You On:
LSD and the Mystic Tradition

The Mystic Sixties

By the mid-Sixties, western society had gone through some major changes – politically, socially, as well as culturally, technologically and economically. The capitalist ideologies of western, particularly American, governments had accelerated after the war and had produced a culture of mass consumerism, which supported the white patriarchal constructs that were inherently connected to capitalism. While undoubtedly many prospered from this economically, encouraging a more prosperous middle class, it also created marginal groups. Feminist and Civil Rights groups, as well as a vast number of 'misfits' who had not found a place in the modern post-war society, and whose influence had encouraged much of the youth culture of the time, found little to celebrate in the immediate post-war social and political atmosphere.

Rock 'n' roll had originated from black communities through blues and gospel music (a music which spoke deeply about their economic and political hardships as well as their spiritual escape from such hardships). This music and these ideas would spread into white youth culture via rock 'n' roll and, ironically, through the consumer society which began to promote and encourage rock 'n' roll, once its economic potential was realized. The new generation was also more sceptical and questioning of their governments, and with cultural anti-heroes like Elvis, Brando and the 'beat poets', many young people decided to live life on their own terms and not be forced into a 'false consciousness' of consumerism.

Rock music had accompanied the American youth on its journey to the forefront of the nation's consciousness, but with songs like the Rolling Stones' 'Satisfaction', the journey took quite a radical turn. Historian Todd Gitlin suggests that the song's message, 'is the ordinary order of things is either broken or corrupt. The message in a sense is, cut loose.' It was through the music of the time that youth culture gained a sense of cohesion, as people began to 'wake up',[224] and by the mid-Sixties many people were in search of alternative lifestyles, rejecting the pyramid structures of capitalism. Many refused to live a life of quiet desperation, which seemed to them to be the only real result of the suburban middle-class consumer society that had developed after the war. They began to reject the values of their parent's generation, who were encouraged to conform and who were doing 'a poor job of running the country'.[225]

As a result of this mass 'waking up', new communities, built on higher principles than profit, began to evolve. In America, places like San Francisco were seen as 'new holy cities', supporting ideas of love and community. 'Suddenly, an environment,' remembered actor Peter Coyote, 'where your personal history did not matter. You would get up each day not knowing what the day would bring. There was random combinations and a sense of adventure to the time.'[226]

Drugs brought a new vision, as singer Jackson Browne observed: 'In the Sixties people took drugs to get out of the constraints of society and to see what life was all about.' Drugs became food for the soul, new ways of expressing 'ourselves', said the actor and leading counterculture figure Dennis Hopper.[227] The media promoted the drug culture along with the idea of 'mind expansion', with radio stations playing 'drug' songs by the Byrds' 'Eight Miles High', Jefferson Airplane's 'White Rabbit', and of course, the Beatles' 'Day Tripper', 'Tomorrow Never Knows', and 'With a Little Help From My Friends', which fuelled the 'mind expansion' aspects of the counterculture.

The unprecedented expansion of the youth and music industries encouraged a new, generational politics which was broadly libertarian (sex, drugs) and oppositional (on a wide variety of political issues). Thus the chasing of political power was most obviously concentrated in America, but coincided also with the social liberalization then occurring in the UK, where in 1967/8 the laws on divorce, abortion and homosexuality were relaxed. This was the period of pop's greatest outreach.[228]

In one of the more surreal media events of the decade, Rolling Stones' singer, Mick Jagger, was flown by helicopter to a televised summit meeting with four embodiments of the Establishment, including the British Home Secretary, Lord Stow Hill, and the Bishop of Woolwich, following a trial in which he received a conditional discharge for the possession of drugs. The scandal highlighted an essential fact that the more confident youth became, the more the adults were resistant to youth's perceived (and actual) excesses. Though this transformation was primarily led by the Beatles, it wasn't as if they had simply marched a generation of hippys and hipsters into a whole new realm of being, thinking and experiencing the world, but instead began to encapsulate the ideologies of the new youth through their music, giving it mainstream cultural significance. 'The Sixties was a ship discovering a new land and the Beatles were in the crow's nest,' Lennon was to remark, and 'for a brief moment there seemed to be no limits... pop became messianic, the harbinger of a new society.'[229]

The artistic and cultural transformation which took place in the mid-Sixties was taking place on a wider though more diluted manner before the Beatles unselfconsciously propelled it into mainstream culture. Hand-in-hand with these new ideas was a shift towards a significantly different philosophical and spiritual approach to life, particularly one of a more mystical variety. From being the obscure focus of a few individuals on the margins of society, in the 1960s magic, mysticism and unorthodox forms of spirituality had suddenly taken centre stage... Everyone, from anonymous hippys on the street to the most famous people in the world, took a trip through the looking glass, their entrance tickets coming, more times than not, in the form of meditations, tantric yoga, witchcraft, or one of the other weird manifestations of the irrational that saturated the popular consciousness.[230]

The occult works of Éliphas Lévi, Friedrich Nietzsche, Madame Petrovna Blavatsky (particularly her books *The Secret Doctrine* and *Isis Unveiled*) and stories of ancient lands, such as Atlantis, Lemuria and Hyperborea, all became popularized through Jacques Bergier's and Louis Pauwels' 1960s' sci-fi adventure book, *The Morning of the Magicians*, which had 'both banks of the Seine talking about alchemy, extra-terrestrials, lost civilizations, esotericism, secret societies, higher states of consciousness'.[231]

Other writers and thinkers, such as Hermann Hesse, Jack Kerouac and his Zen-inspired writings, which stimulated the notion of 'here, now' – a favourite phrase of Ringo Starr's and one readily adapted by the other Beatles, along with the mystical writings of Aldous Huxley – would also have a great impact in shaping the philosophies of the 1960s. Lennon was greatly affected by Huxley's writing and referred to him as the 'new guv'nor',[232] who had experimented with altered states through LSD. He was convinced that our individual consciousness was only a small part of a vast psychic sea, what he called 'Mind at Large', believing that society was in need of a new belief in spiritual values.

While writers like William Burroughs, with his 'cut up' technique, Robert E. Howards' *Conan* stories, which suggested the ancient worlds of Atlantis and Hyperborea, and H.P. Lovecraft's *Cthulhu Mythos* and the epic sci-fi novel *Dune* (1965), also had a great impact on the culture, probably the most influential of writers on 1960s' culture was J.R.R. Tolkien. Tolkien's *Lord of the Rings* (1954) was a modernized retelling of the Atlantis myth, which became a major success in America when published there in June 1965. New Wave musician and esoteric writer Gary Lachman points out that:

> With war raging overseas, and a youthful, King Arthur-like president only fairly recently shot down, American students were hungry for a hero and a purpose, some idealism to give their life

meaning... if in Lovecraft American students had found a pur-
veyor of other worlds that spoke to their subconscious, existential fears, in Tolkien they found an author who gave them a vision
of light, a good to battle the forces of evil.[233]

By 1968, approximately 50 million people had read the book.
It was 'more than a campus fad; it's like a drug dream', said the
manager of the college bookstore at Berkeley California, 'once you
had read it you had something in common with others who had
read it'.[234]

This new generation, including the Beatles, were earnestly looking for something spiritually and philosophically more satisfying
(the Beatles where aware of mystics by early '66, as McCartney's
reference to Blavatsky, in an interview with Radio Caroline DJ Tom
Lodge, suggests).[235] The Beatles, a result of the post-war outlook
and the misfit rock 'n' roller, were also the product of consumerism,
which sold a new and upbeat lifestyle to naive teenagers. It was
this consumerization of the 'Beatles', or Seltaeb (the Beatles spelt
backwards, which was their trade name for consumer products and
merchandizing) that pushed the Beatles, particularly Harrison and
Lennon, away from the hypocrisy of being Beatles and in search
of something more satisfying to their souls. Coinciding with this
move towards spiritual advancement was the introduction into the
culture of mind-altering and introspective drugs like marijuana and
LSD.

Lennon picked up a copy of acid guru Timothy Leary's *The Psychedelic Experience* (1964) – the first words being, 'Whenever in
doubt, turn off your mind, relax and float downstream', which
Lennon would essentially turn into a psychedelic mantra in his
song 'Tomorrow Never Knows'. Lennon would subscribe strongly
to Leary's exhortations, and for the next few years would live in
a virtual LSD reverie. Some, like writer and progressive thinker
Anais Nin, felt higher consciousness should not be reached so
easily without repercussions. But soon LSD would pervade popular culture, with even Hollywood actor Cary Grant becoming a

vocal proponent of the drug, claiming that through it he had been literally 'born again', and spoke of the era as a 'dawning of a new enlightenment'. [236]

Paul Saltzman, a typical teenager of the Sixties, and author of *The Beatles in India* (2006), summed up the era's new outlook:

> Like many of my generation, smoking marijuana was a pivotal experience in my conscious awakening. It was an invaluable door opener. I was twenty-one, and before trying marijuana I was a bright, talented, frenetic, under-achiever with low self-esteem and barely any conscious awareness of either who I was, or what I needed and wanted below the surface level of myself. The introspective, increased awareness aspect of 'getting high' allowed me to look within – to begin to see who I was, and who I wanted to be. It was also lots of fun. Then, having read Aldous Huxley's *The Doors of Perception*, I explored further using the soft psychotropic drugs: LSD, mescaline and psilocybin.[237]

LSD: The Path to Enlightenment?

LSD had first been isolated in 1938 by chemist and mystic Albert Hoffmann, while apparently trying to find a cure for migraine headaches. The story goes that he had ingested a minute amount of the substance and was both startled and profoundly impressed with his discovery. Five years later, following an intuition, he resynthesized it, and soon it was being sent around the world to researchers and psychiatrists as a very powerful psychoactive substance which, as described by R.E.L Masters and Jean Houston in *Varieties of Psychedelic Experience* (1966), was a 'concern with philosophical, cosmological and religious questions and, in general, apprehension of a world that has slipped the chains of normal categorical ordering, leading to an intensified interest in self and world...'[238] This drug, along with the more mood-enhancing marijuana, came at a very critical time and was one of the main reasons why the mid-Sixties moved into an era of psychedelia, hand-in-hand with the new interest in inner exploration and a regenerated pseudo-spiritual aspect that oriented the culture for about three years (1966–1969).

People of the 1960s, more than any other decade except for the 1920s, were deeply interested in things of a non-material nature. In the 1920s, the interest was due to the devastation of the First World War, the terrible existential crisis that left a whole generation, worldwide, in shock. The deep wound left in the aftermath of that war brought many people in contact with the beyond.

The 1960s was, in a sense, experiencing the same thing, following the aftermath of a World War, which like its predecessor not only saw the deaths of millions but which was once again caused by the inability of Britain and Germany to reconcile their differences. However, what emerged from this war was something potentially more disturbing, i.e. the emergence of two super powers, USA and Russia, who stood in a stalemate, facing off each other with the looming threat of nuclear attack. The 1960s was as a result a generation that was living constantly under the threat of nuclear devastation.

So, this generation needed to distract itself from the realities of this possible future as well as trying to prepare itself for it. The whole hippy movement was, in essence, an attempt to return to a 'magical way of living… with The Beatles at its centre…'[239]

Esoteric ideas, symbols and images soon began to pervade the culture. The Beatles began to associate themselves with the esoteric Dutch art group the Fool, who drew inspiration from Anthroposophy, Tarot and other mystical traditions. The Beatles thus became a kind of medium to bring new ideas and tastes to public awareness.[240]

The Fool were originally hired to design the artwork for the Beatles' major psychedelic work *Sgt. Pepper's Lonely Hearts Club Band* album, and although they didn't design the cover in the end, they did end up designing clothes for the Beatles – often with a mystical style – and painted the front of their Apple Boutique, on the corner of Baker Street, in psychedelic and mystical symbols and images. The council, however, complained and the building had to be repainted in white.

The Beatles would also display signs and symbols of an esoteric nature through their albums and in other works. A yin-yang symbol, for example, hung above them during their *Our World* live, international, satellite television production – the first of its kind. The programme, the brainchild of a BBC executive Aubrey Singer, based on the idea of Arthur C. Clarke's satellites in geostationary orbit, was an attempt to create a 'one world' consciousness. An estimated audience of between 400 to 700 million people tuned in. Other groups, like the Rolling Stones and the Doors, whose name was taken from Huxley's *Doors of Perception* (1954) – a title which was itself derived from the clairvoyant poet William Blake, who spoke of the need to cleanse man's perceptive ability in order to see within him an infinite potential ('When the doors of perception are cleansed, man sees what he truly is – infinite', wrote Blake) – also began to adopt this symbolic language, which seemed to go hand-in-hand with the LSD culture. The writer Tom Wolfe captured something of Blake's statement when he attempted to describe the LSD experience of cosmic consciousness on paper: 'His eye pressed against the sighting lens and gradually the whole whirlpool coming into his one eye, unity, I, vessel, receiving all. Atman and Brahman, letting it all flow in until – satori – the perfect state is reached and he realises he is God.'[241]

LSD had been seen for many, particularly in its early stages, and particularly within the scientific community, as a spiritual counterbalance to the destructive forces of war, and as a future spiritual antidote to the atom bomb. LSD was seen as a philosophical tool of advanced technology. Even the scientific community, usually more associated with a more materialistic worldview, saw Hoffman as a mystical figure (Alberich, the 'King of the Light'), whom angels had inspired during a very dark time in Europe.[242]

In 1958, Hoffman isolated the agent psilocybin from the fungus Psilocybin Mexicana, which came from the Mexican Mazatec Shaman Maria Sabina, through the help of ethnomycologist and banker Robert Gordon Wasson. As a result of Hoffman's work, the possibility of accessing shamanic religious and psychedelic experiences of the world's indigenous people was opened to the western world. Since Hoffman had been viewed as a mystical figure, LSD was introduced into the culture with a mystical aura surrounding it. This in turn led to the hope that a spiritual awaking was commencing, allowing the individual the ability to see or experience the world as it really was, unadulterated, unconstrained and unconditional. Essentially, an acid trip would allow the 'tripper' to experience the shaman's view of the world.

The sense of something magical found in the works of Huxley and his 'Mind at Large', or Tolkien and his fellowship – a utopia of connected individuals – led the culture to believe that LSD could open one's mind to the 'reality' that all individuals are inwardly connected and that the world should be more concerned with the task of creating a loving, life-affirming and peace-oriented community, that is not overrun by the competitive, slave-orientated, capitalist, patriarchal culture, that was mostly bent on war and destruction. A community of individuals with an underlying philosophy based, as Huxley felt, on a new belief in spiritual values, realized by the new generation, was the only possible way forward. LSD was seen as the key to this new realization and it was directly through his experiences with LSD that John Lennon would proclaim the philosophy of the decade in his song 'All You Need Is Love' – a philosophy which chimed perfectly with the psychedelic period of the latter half of the Sixties.

The connection between love and mind (or psyche) was an ancient one going back at least as far as the Greek myth of Psyche and Eros – a story about the search for love. It was a story which played a 'sacred' role in the ancient Mysteries and which the Greek philosopher Plato used (because of its mix of darkness, psychic search, revelation and transformation through desire) to illustrate his theory of how love brings about revelation in one's being.[243]

In his dialogue *The Symposium*, Plato describes love, 'as a dynamic, a flow of energy that operates throughout all levels of human awareness, uniting and transcending, or fragmenting and descending as it flows',[244] and identifies many different types of love including parental, sibling, love of self, Eros or erotic love, romantic love, love of life, love for humanity, and love of God. Plato suggests that it is through love that one connects with one's 'Immortality-union with the eternal'[245] and that through love one begins to recognize the divine within ourselves and others. All of these various concepts of love would become, in one way or another, subject matters for Beatles' songs. Songs, for example, like 'She's Leaving Home', 'Two of Us', 'I Me Mine', 'I Saw Her Standing There', 'Girl', 'In My Life', 'Give Peace a Chance', 'Within You Without You', 'Something', and 'God', all expressed a certain aspect of Love.

Love, for Plato, encompasses the potential to unite with the eternal, for in searching for and recognizing the Divine within the beloved, one also discovers the Divine within one's self, recognizing that in all its forms, divinity is One. Love elevates consciousness; it is a process not an end in itself, in which humans can touch the Divine. In this state of perception, we can enter into a mystical experience, a union of the human spirit with God.[246] It is through their many dealings with this subject, in its various guises, that the Beatles brought a greater awareness of these concepts into popular culture, thus encouraging a culture that would strive towards communities founded in love.

Jacob M. Held, in his curiously-titled essay 'All You Need Is Love: Hegel, Love and Community', considers that by the mid-Sixties the Beatles had outgrown their attraction towards the lower aspects of love, namely erotic love (from the Greek Eros – which often brings about self-interest and hence is antagonistic towards society) towards a more mature attitude on love based principally on Plato's idea of *Phila* or love for the other, based not on self-interest but on mutual respect. 'Through their mutual understanding of love,' Held explains, 'the Beatles are expressing the notion that our well-being is predicated on the development of healthy relationships with others. We are communal beings and can only get by with a little help from our friends. We are essentially other-regarding.' The Beatles are, he continues, 'working with the notion of love as mutually respectful interdependence'.[247] This idea would be central to the Beatles' Apple corporation, at least in its initial inception, as well as their attempt to start a commune on a Greek island, which they had planned to purchase in the latter half of the decade.

Modern society – the society which the Beatles and the counter-culture of the Sixties attempted to eradicate, as Held notes – tended to produce destructive ideals of greed, self-interest and materialism, with a master-slave dialectic at its foundation, and of which Held sees the Beatles' character Eleanor Rigby as a typical casualty, along, presumably, with all the other 'lonely people' of the rather Dickensian world that modern life was still creating. With 'All You Need Is Love', the Beatles grasped, though probably more intuitively than intellectually, the notion of the German idealist and mystical philosopher Georg Wilhelm Friedrich Hegel, whose essential philosophical outlook followed on from the hermeneutic tradition of Saint John's Gospel through to the mystical writings of Meister Eckhart and Jacob Bohme (who believed that mutual recognition is the ideal form of relatedness; an equal, respectful interdependence). The master-slave dialectic, on the other hand, is an account of failed recognition, namely inappropriate interpersonal relations that subvert self-realization.[248]

Held, in fact, sees the mutually self-regarding interpersonal relationships between the Beatles themselves as being a perfect example of this very notion, and why they were ultimately so successful.[249] The breakdown of this mutual respect into self-interest in the latter half of the group's existence, is ultimately what caused their breakup. Lennon's 'All You Need Is Love', calls for what Hegel also called for: a community which can provide 'a context in which we can realize ourselves'. 'Love', as the Beatles continually sang about, 'demands of us that we relate to others in a way befitting our nature as other-regarding. All human relations are, ultimately, to be regulated by the ideal form of relatedness, namely, mutually respectful interdependence.'[250]

According to Rudolf Steiner, it is the task of human beings to 'transubstantiate the wisdom and very substance of the Earth into love'.[251] 'What human beings will really give to the Earth,' Steiner says, 'is love, a love that will evolve from the most sensuous to the most spiritualised form. This is the mission of Earth evolution',[252] and in many ways it was the task of the Sixties to bring greater awareness to Love – through interpersonal relationships, as well as through the notion of Love as an all-pervading, if not *the* all-pervading force, in the universe, that binds all things and all peoples together, and that all things can be achieved through (i.e., 'Love is all you need').

As a result, LSD was seen as a pathway to a new utopia, a new religion, which the Beatles more or less introduced into the culture through their music, their cultural significance and their own belief in something more than the capitalist trap that they themselves had become entangled in. It was within such an environment that other artists were opened up to new realms of possibilities in their works, for example Jimi Hendrix's Sky Church – he called his music 'electric church' because he believed music was his religion[253] – and Dylan's spiritual searching, which led to him being 'born again' in the Vineyard Christian Fellowship and a 'gospel' tour in 1980.[254] Even Francis Crick's vision of the double helix structure of DNA and the new 'virtual' worlds envisioned by Steve Jobs, all owed something of their origin to LSD.

Cultural icon Ken Kesey and his gang of Merry Pranksters experiences with the drug revealed a collective consciousness among the group who, 'felt they were acquiring strange powers, and developing a group mind' – a possible example of Huxley's 'Mind at Large' – while simultaneously experiencing 'superhuman' powers like telepathy, psychokinesis and precognition. Kesey and his Merry Pranksters, writes Gary Lachman, 'began to believe that "nothing in the universe can resist the cumulative ardour of a sufficiently large number of enlightened minds working together in organised groups."'[255] This was certainly something that chimed with the 'one mind' consciousness of the Beatles themselves.

When the Beatles started in 1962, they were essentially drawing from the physical and sexual energy that rock 'n' roll, particularly Presley, had produced. The Beatles' earlier performances in Hamburg and Liverpool were mainly fuelled by Preludin (women's slimming pills), an amphetamine, which would give the group the energy they needed to tackle their gruelling touring schedules, but within a few years – mainly as a result of their meeting with Bob Dylan on their first American visit – the band were introduced to more introverted drugs, which certainly influenced them in perceiving their art in a more individual and self-centred manner. Held suggests as much when he states that, 'in their early songs, Love is often expressed as simple and juvenile', and Robert Arp, in his essay 'All My Loving: Paul McCartney's Philosophy of Love', says that the Beatles' early understanding of Love connected more to erotic love – 'the irrational part of the soul that is shared with animals' and which must be kept in check, but which later developed into a more Platonic view of Love, 'where one desires and pursues the nature of Beauty and other universal concepts'.[256]

Marijuana had a much more thoughtful and introspective effect on the group. It is for this reason that Lennon's major works on the Beatles' *Help!* album, the first major album they recorded after their meeting with Dylan and their introduction to marijuana, were introverted and self-focused. Consider 'Help!' as well as the turgid 'Ticket to Ride', and the introspective 'You've Got to Hide Your Love Away'. Even McCartney's famous 'Yesterday' drew on a sense of loss often brought about by inner self-reflection, again the result of the more introspective side-effects of marijuana. By the time the Beatles had given up touring and left the crazy days of Beatlemania behind, they were drawing excessively on their drug experiences, and by the time of *Revolver*, the Beatles had transformed themselves – artistically, musically and philosophically – even though it took until their *Sgt. Pepper's Lonely Hearts Club* album for to transform themselves on a physical level. *Revolver*, however, was a total breaking away from the Beatles as they had been in 1962, even beginning with its '1-2-3-4' count-in, echoing the opening of their first album *Please Please Me*, but with a double speed to counteract the original opening. The famous 'cough' which starts the album was also significant in presenting to the public the feeling of 'real-time' authenticity, giving the impression that the whole recording was a self-contained authentic event – although, like the recording of nearly all records, it was very much controlled.

What is different from these two albums is the shift from more physical interests, i.e. interests connected with the outside world – with 'the other' – and perceptions of the world that surrounds them. For *Revolver*, the perspective had moved inwards, towards philosophical exploration: 'turn off your mind', 'my head is filled with things to say', 'there was another kind of mind there'. In fact, they would, some considered, become so disassociated from the actual world that they opted to take up a kind of psychedelic residence with only themselves and their friends in a yellow submarine (the song 'Yellow Submarine' was recorded for *Revolver* and was released as a double A-sided single the same year).

Essentially, life was to be explored in the psychedelic world of the mind and the imagination. These musings were mostly the result of the Beatles' introduction to LSD. They simultaneously began to discover other cultures and philosophies, as well as lifestyles that were more in accord with the inner mind-expanding experiences of LSD. While *Revolver* was the first major psychedelic work, their previous album *Rubber Soul* had aspects of psychedelia within it. Songs like 'The Word' and 'Think for Yourself' gave a clear indication of this new direction, emerging side-by-side with a new philosophical approach, while the song 'Help!' had expressed how Lennon's first acid trip, taken without his knowledge, had 'changed his mind' and 'opened up the door', presumably one of Huxley's 'doors of perception'. By the time of the *Pepper's* album, the whole culture had caught up with the new religion of LSD and psychedelia. *Pepper's* had the effect of exploding a whole new, surreal perception of the world, beginning with the acid-induced view of childhood in the songs 'Strawberry Fields Forever' and 'Penny Lane'.

Immediately following the completion of *Sgt. Pepper's*, in the wee hours of 21 April 1967, the Beatles decamped from Abbey Road Studios to the singer Mama Cass' apartment in Chelsea, where they flung open the windows and blasted an acetate of the album, at top volume, into the London morning. In the surrounding buildings, windows slowly rose in reply, and neighbours leaned out to listen to the Beatles' newest songs. It's a delightful image, a metaphor for the flood of joy and wonderment that the four Liverpudlians loosed on the world and on England in particular – the windows, the minds, that were nudged open by the Beatles' sonically questing, love-affirming, sad, funny, irrepressibly tuneful music.

Jody Rosen, in her essay 'Everything You Know About Sgt. Pepper's Is Wrong', writes:

> Sgt. Pepper's is the definitive Beatles record not necessarily because it contains their best music, but because it captures them at their zeitgeist-commandeering peak: It is the Beatles album of, and about, history's Beatles Moment. It's a record about England in the midst of whirling change, a humorous, sympathetic chronicle of an old culture convulsed by the shock of the new – by new music and new mores, by rising hemlines and lengthening hair and crumbling caste systems. In short, it's a record about the transformations that the Beatles themselves, more than anyone else, were galvanising.[257]

Pepper's opened the world of the mind, of dreams and the imagination into everyday British and American life. Many saw 'Pepperland' as an actual place, essentially beyond time and space, but accessible to those wishing and willing to expand their consciousness. Some even thought that clues on the *Sgt. Pepper's* album pointed to a phone number that allowed one to contact 'Pepperland'. The phone number, according to Philip Norman, turned out to belong to a journalist for *The Guardian*.

Experiences of profound meaning could be discovered without even stepping outside; the self and the immediate environment could provide infinite different experiences, which would become vividly presented with LSD. The imagination was held as holy in the mid-Sixties, and Harrison would sum it all up with his transcendental song 'The Inner Light'. At the time of writing the song, however, Harrison was beginning to realize that enlightenment couldn't be achieved through forced psychedelic experiences, and instead looked for alternatives. However, it was a jumping-off point for deeper self-exploration. 'LSD was the self-knowledge that pointed the way in the first place,' explained Lennon.[258] Lennon is referring to LSD being a starting point for true self-knowledge, self-awakening, spiritual journeying. Lennon told Hunter Davies that he had to some extent always been searching, but LSD seemed to point to some kind of Nirvana: 'Perhaps I was looking, without realising it, and would have found it anyway. It would just have taken longer.'[259]

The Second World War had provided the desire to search beyond the material, while the literature and philosophies of the past had offered ample impressions of what such a world beyond the threshold could be like. The inner curiosity, the flowering imagination of the world's new poets, mostly in the shape of the pop musicians and songwriters like Lennon and McCartney, Harrison, Dylan and Brian Wilson, who were ready to express these ideas/feelings in their music, was much more digestible for the populace than *The Bhagavad-Gita* or Saint John's Gospel. Nevertheless, the outward conditions and the inner sensibilities were entirely ripe for the culture to venture into this new direction of the spiritual, non-material nature of man, the world and of life itself, focusing primarily on the concept that all things are spirit and that reality is to be found in the mind. Thus the mantra 'it's all in the mind' became a slogan of the 1960s, with the understanding that all things are connected through the mind and in the mind. There was no separation in the world of mind, as there was in the material world, and so, if there was no separation, if all was one, then everybody was intrinsically connected to everyone else.

'I am you as you are me as you are he and we are all together', began the opening line of Lennon's 1967 psychedelic epic, 'I am the Walrus' (a song that paid tribute to the nonsense work of Lewis Carroll and Edward Lear). It was Lennon's attempt to understand his own culture and to try to express its very essence in purely philosophical and non-material terms. He found it an impossible task and crashed into nonsensical imagery, a product of his childhood and childlike imagination. Interestingly, however, Lennon summed up his generation's mental and spiritual outlook perfectly with the colourful 'nonsensical' images he painted.

Beatle Nonsense

The use of nonsense in the Beatles' music is not entirely unrelated to magic and mysticism, and in fact 'non-sense' words, like *voces magicae*, are a key feature in magic, in order to tap into the subconscious mind, bypassing rational linear thought. They also create a sacred space delineated by the sounds, which 'enables the magician to communicate with elements belonging to this space and enable these elements to be active in this ritual space'.[260] Writing the text backwards, as a possible way of disguising a spell, might appear as non-sense, but it is also 'the reverse of normal behaviour', and 'abnormal behaviour belongs to the reverse world',[261] not unlike the world through the looking glass in Lewis Carroll's *Alice Through the Looking Glass* (1871).

Non-sense is a potent tool for stimulating altered states of consciousness, as magicians throughout the ages have known. The non-word 'abracadabra', for example, is thought to derive from the gnostic word Abraxas, which means 'I will create as I speak'

– though others believe that the word is derived from the Hebrew words for 'father, son and holy spirit' (*ab, ben and ruach hakodesh*). The word *hocus-pocus* is another non-word, while the word *gibberish* may derive from the eighteenth-century alchemist Geber, while the medieval word for magic spells, *goetia*, means to howl – which, incidentally, Beat-poet Allen Ginsberg worked into his classic poem 'Howl'. 'Howling' would be a form of abstract expressionism that Lennon would involve himself in as a result of his meeting and collaboration with his abstract-expressionist artist wife, Yoko Ono.

'Howling,' Lennon would explain in an interview, 'is just pure sound', and was for him, like much of his surrealist lyrics, an attempt to move away from the materialistic consciousness of so-called 'normal' society. Lennon would demonstrate, much to the amusement of the audience, the notion of 'howling' during his performance with Ono and the Dirty Mac band, on the Rolling Stones' *Rock and Roll Circus*. Another version of it – mostly as a result of his therapeutic sessions with the psychologist Arthur Janov and his Primal Scream Therapy, which Lennon had undergone in the late Sixties and early Seventies – is given expression in the opening track, 'Mother', to his deeply self-expressive ex-Beatles' album *John Lennon and the Plastic Ono Band*.

In fact, as Jere O'Neill Surber points out in his essay 'I'd Love to Turn You On', the Beatles, by 1965 onwards, were beginning to 'explore states of consciousness other than the rational, normative one of lucid awareness',[262] that had dominated society since the Renaissance and particularly since the French philosopher René Descartes' famous dictum of 'I think, therefore I am' – which presented logical, rational ego-conscious thinking as the basis for all reality. In one sense this was inevitable, since the human race, from a certain esoteric perspective, had entered into the era of the 'consciousness soul'.[263] This refers to a period in the evolution of human consciousness in which the individual begins to experience the world for the first time as an independent, thinking being, that can begin to act in the world as a responsible co-creator. Such a phase in human evolution is important in order to enable each person to develop themselves as an independent entity, with their own moral compass. Hence, through that, they become free agents – free from the forces of nature as well as the dictates of social and communal behaviour.

The negative aspect of such a phase is that the individual becomes spiritually or inwardly detached from the other, thus leading to a tendency towards egotistic selfishness, which in many ways creates the basis for a consumer-focused, capitalist ideology, which the Sixties' counterculture attempted to work against. Although the Beatles had begun to explore different states of consciousness – in songs like 'I'm Only Sleeping' (dream consciousness), 'Tomorrow Never Knows' (with its 'surrendering to the void' state of no-consciousness or all consciousness, akin to the Hindu notion of Brahman or the ultimate reality), 'Here There and Everywhere' (as a kind of cosmic consciousness), or 'Nowhere Man' (with its celebration of having no personal, ego-centric consciousness: 'he doesn't have a point-of-view' – it was in songs like 'I Am the Walrus', 'Dig a Pony' and 'Across the Universe' that the 'non-sense' language of Lennon directly challenged the notion of 'lucid awareness' as the normative consciousness.

Though Lennon had denounced any significant meanings to his nonsense lyrics, in fact stating they were deliberately non-rational to stop people from trying to read too much into them,[264] the philosopher Alexander R. Eodice, in his essay 'And of Course Henry the Horse Dances the Waltz', suggests that Lennon uses his lyrics not to make assertions or report facts about the world, but to attempt to display features of his own consciousness and inner mental states. He seemingly demonstrates, suggests Eodice, that while certain uses of language may not literally say anything, they may, in fact, show the limits and the value of nonsense from a purely linguistic perspective.[265]

Eodice also points out that the contradictory nature of some of Lennon's lyrics – particularly 'listen to the colour of your dreams', which leads Lennon into 'solipsistic fantasies' – creates a synesthetic view of the world (i.e., a view in which our senses relay different information to us than they normally would) and would certainly echo the mystical English poet S.T. Coleridge's poetic statement, 'a light in sound, a sound-like power in light'. [266]

The British occultist Aleister Crowley, who famously appears on *Pepper's* album cover, uses non-words or barbarous words, like 'arogogoruabrao' and 'athorebalo' as well as backwards writing, while the avant-garde writer William Burroughs also tried to extinguish all rational thought with his 'cut-up' technique, something which the Beatles had applied to their musical soundscapes by cutting up tape loops of sound and inserting them into the recordings. The avant-garde composers Luciano Berio (who had drawn much inspiration from the modernism of James Joyce) and John Cage, as well as electronics composer Karl Heinz Stockhausen, who also appears on the *Pepper's* cover, used a similar style of nonsense and randomness in their musical works.

The celebrated modernist writer James Joyce had transcended the everyday word with a whole new language of his own to capture the inner essence of human thought with *Ulysses* and *Finnegan's Wake*, while Lennon and McCartney's childhood heroes, the esoteric writers Lewis Carroll and even Edward Lear, had used nonsense language to capture the inner qualities of things, as well as creating magical and mystical lands and experiences. The nonsense style of the backwards writing in Crowley, as well as Carroll and Lear, allowed the Beatles to create some of their most profound work, particularly of the psychedelic period, like 'Nowhere Man', 'Yellow Submarine', 'Penny Lane', 'Strawberry Fields Forever', 'A Day in the Life', 'I Am the Walrus', and even Harrison's underrated 'It's Only a Northern Song' and 'It's All Too Much'.

For Lennon, non-sense and surrealism was something that made him feel sane in a world in which he felt he didn't belong.[267] The others, too, seemed to find something of profound worth in these strange and mystical ideologies, and although Harrison was drawn more towards the teachings of the Indian yogis, both he and Lennon saw the LSD culture as a means to delve into the true nature of reality – at least for the time in which they experimented with the drug. McCartney, not as adventurous but keen to keep his edge in the creative world of the ever-changing pop culture of the day, and afraid he might be thought of as 'Mr. Bland',[268] could not fall behind – thus he kept a professional interest in all that went on and a close eye on the literary and artistic trends of the day, mainly through his avant-garde connections with art collector Robert Frazer and Indica book gallery owner Barry Miles, who was on the Beatles' payroll as someone to keep the band informed of new and interesting publications.

It was Miles that introduced Harrison to eastern mysticism, through the book *Autobiography of a Yogi*, and introduced Lennon to Leary's psychedelic guidebook *The Psychedelic Experience*. Lennon had tried a year earlier to put his understanding of his psychedelic experiences in purely philosophical terms with 'Tomorrow Never Knows', in which he borrowed parts of the text from Leary's *The Psychedelic Experience* and tried to capture the sense of it in a purely tonal sense, with his eastern/avant-garde inspired soundtrack.

The cartoon film *Yellow Submarine* would attempt, too, to capture the essence of the late 1960s' spiritual awakening by blending the mundane with the childhood imaginations of another world, a world in which we also existed – a mirror world akin to the surreal world of Lewis Carroll's *Alice in Wonderland* (1865) and the comedy of Spike Milligan and the Goons, which the Beatles loved as teenagers. This spiritual awakening encouraged by LSD coincided with the astrological belief that the culture had come into connection with a new age, the Age of Aquarius.

LSD and the Age of Aquarius

Older cultures had considered psychoactive plants as 'teachers' that enhance healing, thinking and perception, believing that nature speaks to humans through these plants, often mediated by the shaman. Many contemporary cultures, however, have outlawed them as they have a shadow side and should not be approached casually – but this, then, is to curtail the individual's sovereignty over their own minds. With the emergence of LSD into the popular culture of the 1960s, people began to think outside society's 'normal' paradigms – but nothing is worse for authority than a society that can think for itself! While the authorities began to suppress LSD and LSD research, others resisted the suppression and argued for the discovery for oneself of a sacred reality. Timothy Leary, a professor from Harvard, was one of them.

Leary first took magic mushrooms in Mexico. It was a life-changing experience for him in which, 'he laughed at his own everyday pomposity, the narrow arrogance of scholars, the impudence of the rational, the smug naivety of words in contrast to the raw rich ever-changing panoramas that "flooded my brain".'[269] LSD, accompanied with meditation, felt Leary (like Hoffman) could lead the individual to an experience equivalent to something akin to the Eleusian Mystery schools. This was a 'school' where initiates experienced insights into a supersensible reality. Plato is considered one such individual, who experienced the spiritual nature of substance, i.e. the 'world of ideas', which became a major aspect of his philosophical teachings.

Leary, who called himself 'the most dangerous man in the world', as a reference to Aleister Crowley's pronouncement of himself as 'the wickedest man in the world', had in fact modelled himself on Crowley's public image. Crowley, like Leary, was familiar with the mind-enhancing effects of certain drugs, having written a number of books on the subject, including *Diary of a Drug Fiend* (1922) and *The Psychology of Hashish: An Essay on Mysticism* (1907) and was, as writer Gary Lachman suggests, the 'best example of the conjunction of pop culture and occult ideas in the mystic decade'. Lachman further considers that 'early on Leary twigged to the potential of LSD and other psychedelics as rally points for the emerging youth

culture'.[270] Leary promoted a culture that would abandon all traditional ways of thinking and living and targeted the open-mindedness – although some might call it naivety – of the expanding
youth population, with his famous slogan: 'Turn on, Tune in, Drop
out.' Leary, along with others of a similar ilk, like Robert Gordon
Wasson, Terence McKenna and Robert Anton Wilson, was intent
on transforming consciousness. Leary had attempted, as Lachman
points out, 'to start a new ecstatic religion based on the sacrament
LSD... a beyond good and evil ethic that characterised the time...
getting free of repressions and doing your own thing.'[271]

Leary was like 'a wild adolescent' whose mission was to popularize the drug, and as a result, by the mid-Sixties, LSD was a house-
hold word. Leary's 'Turn on, Tune in, Drop out' slogan became synonymous with the counterculture, and was blamed for the unrest
caused by the Civil Rights movement, the women's movement, the
ecology movement, and the rising tide of protest against the war in
Vietnam. Although LSD had undoubtedly opened the doors of perception to some degree, there was a terrible danger of being over-
whelmed by the unfamiliar landscape of one's psyche and the possibility of 'depersonalisation and ego dissolution'[272] without having
undergone quite rigorous training. Since only few took care in that
respect, there were many regrettable casualties. As well as the psychological risks connected to the drug, another problem with LSD
and mind expansion was that it tended to promote the idea that
mankind was on the cusp of some spectacular event – an entering
into a new, and usually considered 'higher', state of consciousness.

Since the discovery of electricity, the human race has been speed-
ing up, moving towards what many in the Sixties considered a possible 'New Age', an 'ascension' of sorts, and since World War Two
an apocalyptic thought has accompanied this acceleration, invading
modern life, exacerbated by the creation of the atomic bomb and
more recently by fears created by the changing climate. The result
of this has been to create a moral panic in western culture. It was in
such an apocalyptic environment that a suitable soil was developed

in which ideas of a New Age to come took root, and with the 'mind expansion' of drugs, mystical philosophies and science fiction, the colourful music of groups like the Beatles and the exploding youth culture, came the notion that the 1960s had entered the 'Age of Aquarius'.

This idea would later lend itself to the ascension ideas of the next generation and the new century, particularly linked with events like the '2012' phenomenon and the coming end-of-civilization-as-we-know-it, as well as the 'singularity' theories of trans-humanists, as found in the ideas of Ray Kurzweil.[273] Kurzweil presents what in esoteric terms might be referred to as an Ahrimanic/Satanic view of human evolution, in which the spiritualizing forces of Christ are rejected or opposed, heralding instead an age of spiritual machines, resulting in the end of biological humanity.

Rudolf Steiner described a future condition of humanity, the Sixth Cultural Epoch, which is referred to as the Church of Philadelphia in the biblical 'Book of Revelations'. It is to be an age of brotherly and sisterly love, 'when a new consciousness will arise giving birth to the Spirit Self within human beings'.[274] This, however, is only possible 'if and only if the transformation of soul forces occurs during our current cultural age, the Fifth Cultural Epoch'.[275] Thus, according to Steiner, building upon the spiritual achievements of the Fifth Cultural Epoch (i.e., our own time), 'humanity will have the potential to form communities arising out of individual freedom, around gnosis of Sophia, embodying a moral consciousness exceeding that of our current age'.[276] All notions of 'the other' as opponents, or as insignificant beings, must dissolve and give way to the realization that we are all spiritually connected. Such a notion is directly expressed in, for example, George Harrison's 'Within You Without You'. Karen L. Rivers, in her book *Love and the Evolution of Consciousness*, says that, 'for those individuals who develop this level of moral acuteness, love will be the reflexive response to all situations, for every person's condition will live within you as your own'.

Many people, however, had begun to predict when this new Epoch – the Aquarian Age – would begin, including the Russian mystic Madame Blavatsky. The Sixties' anthem 'Age of Aquarius', by the group the 5th Dimension, suggested that it had already arrived. Over the years some people have desired to prematurely force events to produce desired outcomes in history. The Puritans of the seventeenth century are a classic example of this manipulation of historical events, as they attempted to bring forward the New Jerusalem, Ezekiel's prophetic vision of a city centred around the rebuilt Holy Temple of Jerusalem. As a result of their impatience, the Puritans attempted to advance the process of time – to control cosmic events, so to speak – and to prematurely bring about, in their view, the Second Coming – and this they did by attempting to make it possible for Jews to return to Jerusalem.[277]

More recently others, such as Terence McKenna, deeply influenced by Leary and his own psychedelic experiences, came up with a mathematical model to accelerate history, which he called 'the Eschaton Wave' or 'Timewave'. Writing in 1975, he predicted that 22 December 2012 would be the pinnacle of the timewave construct, in which humanity, as we know it today, would collapse. McKenna, through experiments with psychedelic substances and the *I Ching*, had a revelation where a voice spoke to him saying that soon the human race would collapse and would transcend the Earth sphere, moving on to Jupiter. This was, in effect, what Rudolf Steiner refers to as a 'Luciferic impulse', essentially a premature attempt to bring in a new age and a new consciousness.

According to the historian and anthroposophist Terry Boardman, in his lecture 'Understanding 666: Age of Aquarius or Age of Anti-Christ',[278] the Age of Aquarius begins in 2375 AD, but its effects in human history are delayed by 1199/1200 years, meaning its effects will not be felt until the year 2375 + 1199 (3574). So, in effect we are now still only feeling the effects of the Age of Pisces, which began on the earthly plane in the fourteenth century and which will continue until approximately AD 3500.[279] According to Boardman,

Rudolf Steiner's interpretation of Saint John's Book of Revelation gives a strong indication of this fact. From Steiner's esoteric view, mankind moves through ages and epochs that operate on a system of seven. In other words, the evolution of the human race is subject to move through seven 'Great Epochs', each of which contain seven smaller epochs or civilizations. Each of these civilizations lasts approximately 2,100 years.

The number 666 occurs before the last of our ages. It is at this stage that human consciousness evolves the seven elements of the human being – physical, etheric, astral, ego (lower ego, the personality, and higher ego or the individuality). The ego is a stage of transformation where the individual transforms the lower aspects of the human being – which are connected to Sorath, a retarding and disruptive spiritual force in the universe, connected to the 'number of the Beast', 666 – into higher aspects of human evolution known as Atman, Manus and Buddhi. It is at this point that the first transformation takes place, with the individual transforming their lower nature, and this will be at the very end of our Seven Ages.

To enter this before our ego has properly developed would be premature and possibly disastrous for humanity. The '666' entity wishes to keep man in his lower state or to bring about the transformation too early – a particular aspect of the being Lucifer and a possible reason why the Age of Aquarius was prematurely promoted in some people's consciousness, who sought to influence culture (and hence the huge interest within some aspects of popular culture in the notion of 'Lucifer' himself). It is interesting that this New Age concept was expressed by the Sixties' film-maker Kenneth Anger in his art house film *Lucifer Rising* (1972) and *The Invocation of my Demon Brother* (1969), which he hoped would star Mick Jagger (though the Altamont concert put an end to Jagger's dabbling in the occult and forces that where simply way beyond his control).

The Beatles had undoubtedly influenced a generation in mind-expanding experiences, alternative religions and religious practices. They encouraged a philosophy based on a universally conscious experience, born out of the psychedelic feeling that all is one and everyone is connected. They encouraged their generation (and those that followed) to believe in the possibility of a new era founded on the indominable power of Love, as opposed to separation and war. With the influence of the Beatles, a generation embraced the notion that the world had entered a new consciousness, or New Age – the 'Age of Aquarius' and brotherly love.

Whether it had or not – or whether individuals like Leary and McKenna were keen to believe such and incorporate this view into their belief of 'mind expansion' and LSD experimentation, unaware of the dangers of unleashing this on a naive public – many popular figures were moving in this direction, giving the concept of a New Age more credibility. Brian Wilson and his experiments with psychedelia, for example, had produced a mind-expanding and musically adventurous expression of a psychedelic experience in the song 'Good Vibrations', while the anti-war stance of folk artists like Bob Dylan gave the new generation a political background based on 'Love not War'. The disastrous Vietnam War helped promote the notion of peace and love, of 'flower power' and a new religion of secular humanism – all inspired by a chemical substance, rather than a true spiritual epiphany, that was extremely personal and unstable. This approach, unfortunately, only created an illusory sense of a transcendental existence, one which could seem as terrifying as it could be overwhelmingly filled with bliss, depending on the state of mind of the individual.

Others interested in a culture that threw open the 'doors of perception' and 'broke on through' to a world beyond the material realm of political control, like the Doors' singer Jim Morrison, were in many ways attempting to bring humanity back to a tribal paganism – as, in effect, did most of the concepts and beliefs connected with LSD, promoting an old shamanistic clairvoyance that was immediate and not dependent on the inner development of the individual. In fact, this new religion was one that offered immediate enlightenment for anyone who simply took the drug, a little like *Alice in Wonderland*. Leary would support the idea of rejecting the suppressive capitalist culture, and the best one could do was to 'drop out' of such a society, the first step to experiencing psychedelic enlightenment.

Leary would use the popular status of the Beatles to push forward this new religion (Leary had Lennon compose 'Come Together', using the *I Ching* as a foundation, as his political campaign song) and did so with such a tremendous force that it would be almost immediate. In fact, Leary's promise was to offer an instant enlightenment, which still echoed the philosophy of the capitalist system in which things were immediate – have what you want *now* instead of tomorrow. In some senses, this was a contrasting notion to the 'here now' philosophy of the Sixties, and Lennon's first solo release, 'Instant Karma', would also echo a similar notion, even when it came to the dishing-out of cosmic justice.

In Lennon's view, a product of Sixties' consumer-driven 'now' culture, even karma, had to be immediate. Leary and the immature approach to LSD as a mind-expanding substance and a means of self-discovery, was abused by the more popular notion of immediacy. Spiritual enlightenment was something that was not to be waited for, developed and attained over time, but instead higher consciousness was to be experienced immediately, or as Jim Morrison would sing 'we want the world and we want it now'.

Unfortunately, things did not turn out so, and in fact the eastern mysticism that accompanied the ideas of psychedelia, in which the ego is abandoned, unfortunately left many people in a state of mental deterioration. Morrison himself would mentally breakdown, finding the pressure of pop stardom, as well as the weight of 'breaking through', too much to cope with, and was found dead a few years later. Jimi Hendrix also became a casualty of the drug, as did Brian Jones of the Rolling Stones – and most significantly Brian Wilson, who found himself at the mercy of drugs and psychiatrists for over ten years and in a state of psychotic distress for many more.

Lennon, and Harrison too, would realize the pitfalls of the drug. 'John,' wrote Steve Turner, 'began consuming LSD so recklessly that it affected his self-worth and sense of identity. 'I got a message on acid that you should destroy your ego', he told *Rolling Stone* in 1970. 'And I did.'[280] He would later abandon that avenue to enlightenment in favour of more natural ways – ultimately through meditation, which would later replace the drug culturally.

Lennon would effectively abandon all traditional ways of self-discovery, finally embracing the approach of psychologist Arthur Janov and his Primal Scream therapy. Ultimately, he would abandon all forms of offered enlightenment and realize that no figure or symbol could replace the individual's own inner truth. Unfortunately, Lennon particularly was so mixed up that it was difficult for him to find a real connection with his inner self. His childhood, in which his mother and father had abandoned him, his disillusionment with fame and wealth, and the promise of what the Beatles could offer him, were all empty. Elvis, rock 'n' roll, Dylan and Kennedy – all cultural icons – could not replace the truth of the inner self, and neither could religious figures like Buddha, Jesus or Krishna, or karma, yoga or the *Bhagavad-Gita* do so either. Lennon, ultimately, would realize that only his own higher self could show the way to enlightenment, but his inner radar was so disconnected that he would struggle with any way of finding his inner voice. Ultimately, it was a kind of abstract notion of Love that Lennon would continue to put his faith in.

Steiner suggests that the Sixth Epoch will also see 'the development of religious beliefs out of a free life of thought, independent of collective beliefs. The influence of institutional religious dictates will diminish as individual inner spiritual experiences increase, becoming the guiding inspiration for people in the Sixth Epoch.'[281]

This can be clearly seen in Lennon's attitude towards conventional religious and cultural leaders. The Beatles' rejection of conventional religious practice, which they saw as hypocritical,[282] was given expression in Lennon's comments about conventional Christianity declining, as well as in their sincere search for spiritual advancement and knowledge.

Steiner explains:

> If a sufficient number of people choose to prepare the soil of the future, to integrate transformative soul consciousness with spiritual striving, a radical, endemic shift in consciousness could take place, seeding the potential for a new wisdom culture, a culture of unity, a culture of brotherhood and sisterhood, arising out of selfless love for all peoples, and the kingdoms of nature.[283]

Again, this idea is well expressed not only in the Beatles' music and, particularly, in Lennon's solo work such as 'Imagine', but also in their commitment to creating Apple records to encourage and foster talent, their dedication to humanitarian causes through peace campaigns and charity concerts, as well as a commitment to vegetarianism, meditation and other spiritual practices.

The ideals of the LSD generation eventually hit a brick wall, particularly with individuals like Charles Manson losing a grip on reality, and as the decade ended, the dream of a utopia began to disintegrate. The world plummeted into more chaos, financial collapse and revolution, and the shift from spiritual enlightenment was replaced by more political concerns. By the end of the era, the Rolling Stones' Altamont concert had ended with the death of a young black man, Meredith Hunter, thus making people wonder what rock 'n' roll, LSD and flower-power could actually achieve. The reality of a young man's death made people realize that they were only dreaming; dreaming of what they hoped was possible, what they felt they wanted, and what gave them an identity in the face of a system which they railed against. In fact, by the time the Sixties had finished and the Beatles had disbanded, the generation found themselves leaderless and directionless. The Beatles themselves, the avatars and leaders of a hopeful generation, were even wondering about their own futures.

By the mid-Seventies, the realities of what the next generation faced was effectively expressed in the social-realistic movement of punk, which ultimately saw a world in which the protagonists played an insignificant role and in which their own destinies were ultimately outside of their own control. Instead of a 'brotherhood of man', which Lennon had idealistically imagined, a world free of hunger and greed, a world where people lived in harmony, the next generation saw only a world in which there was no hope, no possibility and essentially 'no future'. Idealism had turned to nihilism and once again the materialism of capitalism and social politics wiped away the dreams and hopes of the Aquarian Age. LSD and rock 'n' roll failed to inherit the earth and the world was back to the same march towards an inevitable conflict that had plagued the early post-war years, ultimately a disastrous conflict between Russia and America. By the beginning of the 1980s, the prospect a nuclear war was once again looming.

If, however, the drugs had not offered enlightenment, they had at least offered a glimpse of what was possible, of what might be on the other side. 'With drugs you do have a glimpse of a few things, they heighten your experience. But if you take a drug and hope that it will bring the subtlety out of this grosser level – well, it will never work,' said Harrison.[284] There was an overwhelming feeling that God did exist: 'It changed me and there was no way back,' Harrison claimed[285] – a sentiment that would be echoed by one of LSD's most prominent advocates, John Lennon, who would begin to realize that truth was not to be found in a chemical, but yet it did seem to point the way to something beyond the mundane. 'There was no going further. What it does is mainly finding out about yourself, your ego. With acid, it is all about yourself. The thing is that your true self is at a deeper level.'[286]

Despite this premature acceleration of the New Age, an age of brotherly love, there was a genuine interest in Love and Peace in the Sixties. While it was certainly not an actual shifting of consciousness into a new era, it was, or at least could be seen as, some kind of spiritual awakening, even if only in seed form. The esoteric philosophies and experimentation with drugs, music and language encouraged people to explore their own selves, explore the mind and also explore alternative ways of being and living.

The psychedelic experience made it possible for people to become more aware of themselves and, through their own self-awareness, they could become more aware of others and the notions of communities built on and out of Love. While the Sixties never really achieved its desire to create a society of brotherly (and sisterly love) – something that, as Steiner points out, is for the next cultural epoch – the thing it did, as Lennon astutely observed, 'was to show us the possibility and responsibility that we all had. It wasn't the answer. It just gave us a glimpse of the possibility.'[287]

Chapter 7

Here's Another Clue for You All: Album Covers, Films and Videos

Signs and Symbols

Things of a mystical inclination began to become manifest in the culture of the mid-Sixties, expressed, naturally enough, through the artistic movements of the time. It was the Beatles who, more than most, drove much of these cultural and artistic ideas, using an abundance of mystical, religious and surreal symbols and images in their work.

To what extent, however, did the Beatles themselves understand the signs, symbols, and images they used in their films, photographs and most significantly on their album covers? Did they use them primarily for superficial and decorative purposes, or consciously use them to influence the culture? To what extent, also, did other artists, like Peter Blake, the art designer who worked on *Sgt. Pepper's*, or the photographer Robert Whitaker, for example, influence the work, and did they do so with the intent on subliminally influencing a generation of drug-induced teenagers? To what extent did the Beatles become a vehicle for others to express their mystical and religious (perhaps even occult) ideas through? Did they become conduits for unconscious or even supersensible impulses to exert themselves? And, how significant was the role of the public's imagination in giving unintended meanings to these signs, symbols and images, which were possibly used only superficially to create interesting album cover designs?

Although this chapter aims to shed some light on these questions, what is clear is that the power of signs and symbols are a potent force in the evolution, or devolution, of a society. The famed psychoanalyst Carl Jung believed that symbols were carriers of

psychic energy and that they supplied the psychological and orga-
nizational foundations for social life, while the mythologist Joseph
Campbell also believed that living mythological symbols awaken
and give guidance to humanity. While the Beatles' use of signs, symbols and images influenced the culture tremendously, did it do so
positively or negatively?

Early Records

It seems fairly certain, though there are some claims to the
contrary,[288] that at the time of making their first album, *Please Please
Me*, the Beatles had little understanding of the music industry and
were totally unaware of how influential and significant they would
become within it. At most, Lennon and McCartney were hopeful
of becoming professional songwriters, with a number of original
songs featuring on the album.

With songs like 'Misery', 'There's a Place' and 'Please Please Me',
Lennon, the main author of these songs, was probably more intent
on finding an expression for his personal pain, while McCartney
seemed to be more interested in exploring his musical talent and
potential for melody and musical mimicry. Beyond this, the group
were most likely only interested in making money and playing their
favourite rock 'n' roll songs, with the added bonus of attracting
female admirers. There is little if any evidence that at this point in
their careers the Beatles had any real sense of wanting to influence
society in any permanent way. Rock 'n' roll was for the Beatles just
'a good laugh', as Lennon would remark in a Press conference.

The cover for the *Please Please Me* album was rushed, and the
recordings of the songs were done primarily by their producer
George Martin, and enhanced by him with piano overdubs. The
Beatles themselves had only spent one or two evenings in the studio, recording what was essentially a live set, and so their involvement in the production was extremely limited. Their thoughts
were, most likely, occupied by the usual thoughts of young men

(i.e., having a good time and meeting girls), as well as being enraptured by the excitement of finally being a signed group with records in the charts. There was little interest in anything else, particularly the notion of filling their album covers and songs with subliminal messages. If the album contained any untoward symbolism, then it was either the result of the photographer, Angus McBean, or else it was coming from supersensible realms – but this seems unlikely.

The same may be said for their next album, *With the Beatles*, although there have been some claims that the shaded photo used on the front cover suggests something of an occult nature.[289] However, the evidence for this is poor and it is more likely that the Beatles only liked the aesthetic nature of the photos, which were the initial idea of Astrid Kirchherr, who had photographed the Beatles in a similar fashion during their time in Hamburg. This style, which Brian Epstein and the Beatles very much loved, was reproduced by the photographer Robert Freeman.

The Beatles, while looking for a cover for their new album, obviously thought Astrid's photographic style would work for a strong visual image. The *With the Beatles'* cover *was* a powerful image of daring defiance, with an almost messianic significance, as Grail Marcus relates in his book *The History of Rock and Roll in Ten Songs*: 'The four black-and-white faces on the cover,' he says, 'were impassive, looking straight back at whoever was looking at them... the feeling that came off the picture was unsettling.'[290]

It is not at all surprising that the Beatles made the album cover such a significant element of the artistic presentation, considering Lennon's art college background, Epstein's sense of theatricality (as well as his impeccable taste), and McCartney's innate artistic sensibility. Although it seems unlikely that there were any specific hidden meanings in the album cover, at least as far as the Beatles (or Epstein, for that matter) were aware, it is nevertheless interesting to note one researcher's remarks:

With The Beatles! (released on 22/11/63 in the US – same date as the JFK assassination) shows all four Beatles featured on the front with only one eye showing. Their facial left halves (our right) have a shadow cast upon their faces. This brings to mind the left-hand path vs. the right-hand path and the eye of Horus and of course that 'all seeing eye' figure that seems to be here, there, and everywhere... Astrid has been described as a practitioner of Black Magic according to Lennon biographer Albert Goldman. Astrid had a HUGE influence on the Beatles, making the most significant image change of the band throughout their history – giving the Beatles their signature 'mop top' haircut. Considering her influence on the boys at the time, they may have been infatuated with her mode of spirituality. It's interesting that directly after meeting Astrid and Klaus in Hamburg, the Beatles' good fortune and popularity began to skyrocket. Astrid would also introduce the band to preludin.[291]

Although this is certainly interesting, and may require more investigation, little evidence has been found that Astrid was a practitioner of black magic and, according to The Beatles' historian Mark Lewisohn, it was the singer Tony Sheridan who had introduced the Beatles to preludin (a pep drug used for weight loss, which the Beatles, and nearly every other performer in Hamburg, would take when on stage). Although Astrid and her art college friends influenced the band, as did the whole Hamburg experience, it was not necessarily a major influence on their formative years.

Astrid and her friends were, according to Lewisohn, very much disenchanted with Germany and German culture, due to the dark shadow the Nazis had left hanging over the country. As a result, they associated themselves with things non-German, and were particularly interested in French culture, taking their nickname, the Exis, from the existential school of philosophy, made popular worldwide by French existential thinkers, such as Jean Paul Sartre and Albert Camus. The intellectualism of French philosophy, its association with café culture and its emphasis on personal freedom, has a fashionable reputation, and as a result has always been attractive to student culture. While existentialism often rejects conventions and traditions, in order for the individual to find their own 'truth', it is often seen as anti-religious (although other existentialists such as Soren Kierkegaard and Martin Buber were deeply 'religious') and so could be a possible reason why Astrid's worldview may have been seen by Goldman as being somewhat irreligious or occult-like. But this is not at all certain.

A Hard Day's Night evolved out of the need to outdo the cover design of *With the Beatles*. This requirement was coupled with the novel idea of the cover having a cinematic theme – an idea which married the album with the film, which itself created the effect that the songs were part of an overall soundtrack – possibly even a contemporary film musical. The idea that *A Hard Day's Night* was a musical of sorts catapulted Lennon and McCartney into the realm of serious composers, on the level with other musical partnerships like Gilbert and Sullivan and Rogers and Hammerstein, lending more credibility to the pop format. The film was a musical account of Beatlemania and the album cover, with its multiple images of the various band members, reflected that by offering fans different sides of their favourite Beatle.

Although this particular album cover managed to capture the essence of Beatlemania and incorporated a perfect mix of both commercial and artistic appeal, it is hard to see it as containing any major esoteric symbolism, apart from the semi-religious iconographic elements of Beatlemania that became attached to its image, which increased their cultural significance and already escalating commercial appeal. The album cover, as well as the film, presented to the public a definitive representation of the group, with distinctive, if two-dimensional, personality types of each of the group members, that has forever been etched in the public consciousness while simultaneously presenting the definitive blueprint of the pop band.

While many began to read things into the images on the Beatles' album covers and into their lyrics, causing Paul McCartney to comment that 'people take our music and read everything into that...',[292] some album covers and movies certainly do contain images that are very unusual and very potent, making the analysis of them quite legitimate. The religious leader David A. Noebel would suggest, in his 1965 pamphlet 'Communism, Hypnotism and The Beatles', that these symbols had a profound, and also detrimental, effect on the American youth — claiming that the Beatles were in essence a communist plot to destroy the intellectual abilities of the young. The Beatles' effect would make the youth unable to resist a communist neo-feudal type society, in which a small number of elite would control the vast majority, an idea still considered today by some; however, others like Leslie Woodhead, in his book and documentary film *How the Beatles Rocked the Kremlin*, as well as the one-time Russian Premier Mikhail Gorbachev, have suggested the contrary, i.e. that the Beatles were a symbol for freedom and authenticity, and were in fact instrumental in destabilising communism in the USSR.[293]

Whether at this point in their careers the Beatles used imagery for simply artistic purposes, or whether they had very deliberate intentions, doesn't seem to matter so much. What does matter is the fact that the images, symbols and other concepts employed – whether consciously or unconsciously – in their artwork, exerted an influence. It was for this reason that McCartney added, in his comment above, that 'it might mean all the other, we don't know, we're the last people to know about our songs'.[294]

The Beatles: Yesterday and Today, and Help!

Even though the images on *With the Beatles* and *A Hard Day's Night* were significant in presenting an 'idea' (not just a band, but also the beginnings of a mythology) to the world, it wasn't really until *Help!* and *The Beatles: Yesterday and Today*, an album released solely for the American market, that the Beatles' album covers employed more complex images, allowing for much more subjective and open interpretations.

The first of these albums, *Help!*, shows a definite set of symbols and images — the semaphores (a telegraphy system, using flags to send messages) for which few are readily able to decode, thus making the symbols much more open to interpretation. The most common reading of this 'text' is that it indicates the name of the album, which is also written in a stylized manner on the album cover itself. However, the semaphores do not read HELP!, and so straight away a space is created for all kinds of interpretations (what might be referred to as constellations, the subjective interpretation of signs – but more on this in Chapter 8), which may or may not be valid.

It is without doubt that the Beatles intended to create an artistic image to improve on their previous creations, and so the ideas naturally become more intricate and detailed. The fact that the group were highly successful meant that they were working with other artists who were equally creative, and who brought with them their own artistic visions and ideas, possibly using the Beatles – either consciously or unconsciously – as vehicles to present their own view of the world. Even if only a very small portion of the Beatles' collaborators exerted an influence on the final representation, it nevertheless colours the overall meaning.

Often these collaborators would bring ideas and suggestions to the Beatles – as was the case for *Help!* and many other covers, including *Sgt. Pepper's* – who would often happily go along with the suggestions, simply because they respected the artists and liked the idea, and also because they were so busy writing, recording and performing that they would leave the details of the album cover (or film) to the artist. McCartney admits the confidence they often put in those people around them, such as the photographer Robert Freeman, who photographed many of their early album covers. 'He,' said McCartney, 'was one of our favourite photographers during the Beatles' years who came up with some of our most iconic album covers. Besides being a great professional, he was imaginative and a true original thinker.'[295]

In the case of *Help!* the photographer, again Robert Freeman, suggested the semaphore cover to spell out the word Help. Freeman said the idea for the semaphores, however, got altered on the shoot, because the lettering didn't 'look good' and lacked a certain aesthetic quality for the cover. The group improvised with different gestures until they made up 'the best of graphic positioning of the arms'. Instead of 'HELP!' the signs spelt NUJV, while on the American cover the figure of Ringo is placed between Harrison and Lennon, to spell out NVUJ, which some claimed had a blasphemous intention (although it was more likely a record company decision to rearrange Ringo's position and not that of the Beatles). Any blasphemous suggestions, however, seem most unlikely, but if there is any truth to it, then it was the record company sending out the signal and not the band. From this point of view, there are some who feel that the cover was a blatant dismissal of Christian values, while others have interpreted the semaphores as ritualistic signs commonly used in Thelemic ritual magic,[296] as one researcher claims:

> If you look at the *HELP!* soundtrack cover, the boys are displaying the same type of imagery (i.e. that used in Thelemic magic). On the front cover of the *Help!* album, the Beatles are not spelling H-E-L-P in semaphore, they are actually holding positions of rituals used in The Hermetic Order of the Golden Dawn. George = in Osiris Slain, John = in Sign of Typhon/Apophis, Paul = in Isis Mourning, Ringo = in the Earth Sign, or the position of the Magician card of the tarot (as above, so below). I won't go into much more detail on this album cover here – but the point being is that throughout the Beatles' career, we see references to Crowley's Thelema and the Greater/Lesser Mysteries that cross over photographers and even over Managers.[297]

It is interesting, considering the above suggestion, that in the film *Help!* Ringo seems also to be depicted as the Hanged Man in Tarot, which correlates to the number 23, a number which seems to occur a lot in modern pop culture and in many media events. Strangely enough, the number later also appeared on the Beatles' *Yellow Submarine* album cover, on the jumper of the Butterfly Stomper.[298] Incidentally, the occultist and Tarot expert Manly P. Hall explains the meaning of the Hanged Man, which is interesting if one thinks of the Beatles as fulfilling a cultural mission. Esoterically, the Hanged Man is the human spirit, which is suspended from heaven by a single thread. Wisdom, not death, is the reward for this voluntary sacrifice, 'during which the human soul, suspended above the world of illusion, and meditating upon its unreality, is rewarded by the achievement of self-realisation',[299]

If it is true that these symbols are related to Crowley's Thelema and to the Tarot, the question arises as to what extent the Beatles had incorporated these ideas into their work themselves, or if they came into Beatle mythology as external factors, such as cultural influences, or something of a supersensible nature that expressed itself through the Beatles and into the culture – or through individuals closely connected to the group, such as the photographer Robert Freeman, etc.?

The film *Help!* itself deals with ideas that are multi-layered, with notions of secret societies, freemasons, cult groups, sacrificial and ritualistic magic, as well as a representation of non-western cultures as being, among other things, primitive, pagan, manic and foolish, paying little regard to the fact that Britain's empire had relied for its global dominance on the resources and wealth of these countries. As well as this, the film also pokes fun at many other things, such as the pomposity of certain elements of British society, the contradictions between the private Beatles and their public image: 'They haven't changed. They're still the same as they was before they was', observes one onlooker (wrongly). The invisible presence of the United States as the dominant power pervades much of the film (Paul's playing baseball, the creation by the US of a superior laser weapon, etc.) an obvious presentation, as Schneider observed, of the dominant power of the Anglo-American Establishment, which many considered to be endorsed and enhanced by the Beatles, cementing in the public mind – particularly that of the youth – relations between these two countries after the war.

The Beatles themselves would eventually be drawn more towards those eastern elements that the film had ridiculed and rejected – 'your filthy eastern ways', as Lennon mocks. Within the space of a year of the film's release, however, eastern philosophy and culture would take hold in the West, and notions of karma and reincarnation would soon begin to find their way into mainstream western thought; a concept which had been making its presence felt more and more since the nineteenth century, with works such as the German philosopher Gotthold Lessing's essay *The Education of the Human Race* (1883) and Emerson's Brahma-inspired poetry, societies such as the Theosophical Society and the Anthroposophical Society – and even in a Sixties' favourite, Nietzsche, who had expounded the notion of eternal recurrence.

The concept of reincarnation would become a major philosophical truth for the Beatles, particularly Lennon and Harrison, with their connection to Hinduism and Hare Krishna, and major themes in their songwriting. Both Beatles would continue to adopt ideas from Hinduism in their songs, with references to devas, karma, and so forth, re-establishing centuries' old ideas, held not only by eastern religions, but by Plato and early Church Fathers, such as Origen of Alexandria, but which had been eradicated by more recently developed materialistic religions and modern materialistic, scientific thoughts about the world.[300]

Another album, *Yesterday and Today* – a bastardization of *Help!*, *Rubber Soul* and *Revolver* – has a cover which would become probably the most controversial of their career. It was disturbing, not just for the depiction of mutilated babies (symbolized by dismembered plastic baby dolls) but also because of the raw slabs of meat placed on the Beatles, who were dressed in white butchers' coats. This was an image far removed from the band's cute and cuddly image not even a year earlier.

Was it a significant symbol that revealed some clue to more sinister motives behind the group? Was there some kind of hidden occult message in the picture that would justify the fears of Noebel and others, who felt the band were undermining the values of American society? Or was there another perfectly good explanation for such a move by the Beatles? Whatever the answer, the image certainly gave rise to a variety of interpretations and speculations. Although fans didn't seem to object to it, the album cover was not well received by radio stations, which forced the Beatles' record company, Capitol, to withdraw the album and change the cover.

The Beatles were not altogether squeaky clean; in fact they had a rather dark sense of humour at times, as suggested by many of their lyrics ('fish and finger pie', 'come together over me', 'baby you can drive my car'). The Beatles were happy to be subversive and felt frustrated that they were always made to tone things down. In this sense, they may have been content to present a side of themselves that was real, but which had been suppressed. At the same time, they were also happy to destroy what to them had become their annoyingly cute, mop-top image.

The idea for the cover was actually that of photographer Robert Whitaker, who had planned a whole series of images with a particular theme that had not been intended as a cover in the first place. It was Capitol, strangely enough, who had decided on that, despite the image's obviously non-commercial appeal. So, the big question is why Capitol (and not the Beatles) chose such an image in the first place?

Whatever Capitol's reason, the Beatles were keen to explore new concepts and avenues of artistic expression. Whitaker gelled with the Beatles, who trusted him and shared a similar artistic vision. For Whitaker, props were symbols, and he drew his inspiration from Greek drama and surreal art. For this particular project, Whitaker was influenced by the German artist Hans Bellmer, who was known to use disturbing images as an attack on Nazism, and his aim here was to demythologize the Beatles, a response to what he saw from the fans on their US tours.

Whitaker was shocked by the crazed fan-reaction to the Beatles, whom he felt were, 'not an illusion, not something to be worshiped, but people as real and substantial as a piece of wood', comparing it all to the biblical account of the Israelites' worshipping of a golden calf as the Ten Commandments were being written. Whitaker originally intended to give the photo, entitled 'A Somnambulant Adventure' (the idea came to him in a dream[301]) a gold-coloured background and illustrated silver-jewelled halos over the Beatles' heads. The butcher-album 'carve-up', as *Disc* magazine referred to it that summer, was the first time the Beatles were involved in a real controversy. In the eyes of the media, they had lost their innocence forever. Coincidentally, John Lennon's 'bigger than Jesus' comments started another controversy about a month later.

The album cover was also considered a response to the treatment of the Beatles' music in America, in which Whitaker, as well as the Beatles, felt that their American record label would often 'butcher' their original album concepts by altering the tracks (mixing and matching from different albums) and changing the running order. This, according to many sources,[302] does not appear to be the case, but what is interesting is that this was the narrative that many American fans had gone with, as Candy Leonard, author of *Beatleness* (2014), suggested in a radio interview,[303] realizing that the albums they were buying were not the ones the Beatles were actually making. From this point-of-view, this story could be seen as a fan response, rather than a Beatles response, to the treatment of Beatles' records.

The series of images created by Whitaker evoked ideas popular in the mid-Sixties, particularly in relation to the psychedelic impulses that were manifesting at the time, including references to trepanation – a process of accessing the 'third eye' by hammering a sharp instrument through the forehead (see Harrison pretending to hammer nails into Lennon's head, for example), which enabled the person to 'see people as they are, and not as they pretend to be', essentially by seeing people's auras.[304]

The Beatles never questioned Whitaker's idea but were happy to do anything that would distance them from their cute, loveable Beatles' image. Harrison was seemingly uncomfortable with the slabs of raw meat,[305] and later Lennon and McCartney would claim that the cover was their artistic comment on the Vietnam War,[306] while Philip Norman suggests the idea was in fact Lennon's as a definite comment on Vietnam,[307] but this seems unlikely. A further point on this comes from one Beatles blogger who is fascinated by Beatles' symbolism, suggesting that Robert Whitaker remarked that the complete vision went unrealized. The album was intended to be a gatefold, forming a triptych of images, the left side symbolizing the birth of the Beatles, the right symbolically representing the death of the Beatles, and the centre image – the infamous 'butcher cover' we have today – representing the apotheosis of the Beatles. 'Regardless,' says the blogger, 'even without the envisioned gatefold, the album in my opinion is still revealing deep symbolism.' He continues:

> The meat could symbolise the 13 pieces of Osiris – that Isis had to put back together after he was slain by Set according to the Egyptian mythological tale of Isis and Osiris. The doll parts could symbolise the falcon-headed God Horus, the god-child of Isis and Osiris. Crowley taught that the Abrahamic religions were 'Osirian' religions – rooted within the 'Aeon of Osiris' dominated by patriarchal values. He taught that this aeon would fade away and be replaced with something else. Crowley interpreted he was to help aid the ushering in the new age, or the 'Aeon of Horus', which was controlled by the child god, symbolised by Horus. The butcher cover says to me that the Beatles have 'killed' or 'butchered' the old ways – and are now helping to usher in the new age, the age of acting upon your own will, and self-realisation. The age of Horus.[308]

Finally, according to Whitaker the cover shoot was part of a much more elaborate work and intended as a surreal comment on celebrity and as a reaction against the usual Beatles' publicity shots, which the group had become bored doing and wanted to try something more interesting and arty.[309]

On their US *Beatles '65* album cover, which was another butcher attempt by their American record company of the *Beatles For Sale* album, another series of images were used, this time to indicate the four seasons. One of the photos, again taken by Bob Whitaker, had the group sitting under umbrellas whilst another featured a basket of witches' broomsticks. Whether intended or not, such images could certainly be read as having occult associations: the umbrellas signifying some kind of Mephistophelean contract, as the idea that fame and fortune will rain down upon the one who makes such a deal, while the witches' broomsticks are self-explanatory, i.e. that the group might be dabbling in magic (either black or white). Whether the Beatles were aware of these associations seems unlikely, however the use of umbrellas has a great many levels of meaning, one of which is the 'umbrella of protection', where allegiance is given over to an authority figure. Obedience is thus rewarded and rebellion is punished. According to one source:

> The concept of an umbrella of protection is illustrated in what the prophet Samuel said to Israel's King Saul when Saul disobeyed God's instructions: *'Rebellion is as the sin of witchcraft'* (I Samuel 15:23). Those who participate in witchcraft directly interact with destructive, satanic influences. Rebellion is similar, because through disobedience you remove yourself from God's full protection and are therefore far more susceptible to the attacks of Satan.[310]

Being 'under the umbrella', it would appear, has in cabbalistic lore a connection to Lilith and the taboo of sexuality.[311] Whether these symbols within the Beatles' images are imbued with these specific occult meanings or similar ones is not so easy to say, but it is quite likely that many similar images are elaborately employed in modern music and music videos for very specific purposes, and from this point-of-view it may be possible to interpret, on a psychic energetic level, the symbols and images on the Beatles' albums as a seed planted in the subconscious mind of modern culture that is coming to fuller expression in modern music, much of which is deeply filled with very dark and negative images.[312]

Was the image stating that the Beatles were under protection and were now untouchable, as long as they did what they were told? Though there are certainly those that might suggest so, and it is not impossible to think that this could have been subconsciously depicted, in that symbols are carriers of psychic energies. It is without doubt that the Beatles were heavily protected on every level, but whether or not they were also used to promote certain ideas and attitudes by those whose protection they were under, is another matter.

Rubber Soul and Beatles '65

The cover photograph for *Rubber Soul*, taken again by Robert Freeman, was by all accounts a complete accident. Paul McCartney recalled that, as Freeman presented to the group the pictures projected onto an album-sized piece of card, 'we had just chosen the photograph when the card that the picture was projected onto fell backwards a little, elongating the photograph...'[313] While the cover, with its psychedelic distorted look, was a happy accident, it chimed perfectly well with the surreal-ness of the mid-Sixties and the psychedelic influence that was entering the culture, and it seemed to marry well with the musical experimentation that was developing, particularly with this album.

Such accidents show just how tuned in the Beatles were with the times, as they were able and creative enough to incorporate these random occurrences into their work, allowing space for the universe or zeitgeist, as such, to contribute to the creative process and in turn to influence itself on the culture. What is also interesting about the cover is that the band's name, as with *Revolver*, didn't need to appear on the cover – the four faces of the Beatles had become so iconic that they were recognized without even being named.

The title of the album *Rubber Soul*, created by McCartney, played on the idea of a rubber sole on a shoe, as well as a metaphysical rubber soul, thus mixing the mundane with the sacred. In the case of the shoe metaphor, the title would suggest something inauthentic, while the metaphysical connotation of a 'rubber soul' brought another layer of the surrealism into the Beatles' work, as well as into the culture as a whole. McCartney's title was, of course, also a pun on black 'Soul' music – something that white musicians, it has often been thought, could only poorly imitate. Thus it was 'plastic' ('plastic soul' was another title McCartney had been toying with during the making of the record).[314]

The faces look distant and somewhat aloof, as if they are deliberately distancing themselves from their cute and loveable Fab Four image. Although it is not surprising that such intelligent and creative individuals would become exasperated with a one-dimensional representation of themselves, which is what the Fab Four image had done, and would want to present other sides of themselves and their musical creativity, the group look as if they have no interest at all in being Beatles or playing up for their public in any way at all. John Kruth, the author of *This Bird Has Flown: The Enduring Beauty of Rubber Soul*, points out that Harrison looks as if he would rather have been anywhere else than 'messing about with this pop star nonsense' and observes that there is 'something ghostly about the image, not just in their drawn, stretched out faces, but in the way the boys lean together, pale washed out, like tombstones. You can almost feel the chill in the air... their hair hanging in their eyes... creeps towards their shoulders like wild vines.'[315] Kruth's tombstone analogy is pertinent in that the album certainly signified the end of Beatlemania and the Fab Four image that the group had come to despise.

This association with magic on the American release of *Rubber Soul* is interesting for the fact that their next album was to be called *The Magic Circle* or *Abracadabra*. Eventually, however, it would be given the title of *Revolver*.

Sgt. Pepper's Lonely Hearts Club Band

Paul McCartney would originally employ the work of the Dutch art group the Fool to design the artwork for the *Sgt. Pepper's Lonely Hearts Club* album cover, but was discouraged by his friend, the art enthusiast Robert Frazer, better known as 'groovy' Bob, an extremely well connected and successful impresario in London at the time. 'Groovy' Bob would suggest that the Beatles use artist Peter Blake instead, and between the two of them (and Blake's American wife, the artist Jann Haworth, who had designed the costumes for Kenneth Angers' *Lucifer's Rising*), they designed the album cover.[316]

The initial idea behind the cover design seems to have come from McCartney, who had the inspiration to create alter egos for the Beatles, the purpose for which was to allow the group to escape from their mop-top image, which they and the public were beginning to tire of. 'As we're trying to get away from ourselves – to get away from touring and into a more surreal thing – how about if we become an alter-ego band, something like, say, Sgt. Pepper's Lonely Hearts?',[317] McCartney would explain to the other band members in an attempt to move away from the defunct Beatles' image, while still keeping the other disinterested members excited about another Beatle project.

For a variety of reasons, the *Pepper's* album cover has often been interpreted as a funeral scene, some claiming it is the funeral of Paul McCartney (see Chapter 8), while others read it as the 'death' of the old Beatles. Considering the Beatles wanted to distance themselves from their former selves, as suggested by McCartney above, this view is quite a legitimate one, which even the Press at the time read it as.

> The cover photo, then, shows the Beatles assuming this new identity and laying to rest their earlier image as the Fab Four. Though their expressions seem subdued, their eyes glint with a new awareness tinged with a little of the old mischief. As for the grave in the

foreground: it has THE BEATLES spelled out in flowers ... With characteristic self- mockery, the Beatles are proclaiming that they have snuffed out their old selves to make room for the new Beatles incarnate, and there is some truth to it.[318]

It's possible, given McCartney's delight in teasing and fooling with the public's perception of the Beatles, that he may have suggested including his supposed 'death' into the album (which will be investigated in Chapter 8).[319] But many of the so-called 'death clues' may also be connected to the death of the Beatles' close friend Tara Brown, who had died tragically around the time of the making of the album, while the spectre of Stuart Sutcliffe (a close friend and one time member of the Beatles, who died while in Hamburg with the group) finds its way onto the album's cover — giving it an even more deathly atmosphere.

However, it seems quite unlikely that the other Beatles had thought of inserting 'hidden' clues into the cover design, as they had expressed little interest – beyond suggesting some figures for the cover – in the whole project. Harrison was more consumed with his spiritual pursuits and eastern philosophy, Lennon had almost lost himself to LSD at the time, and Starr had simply left it up to the others to make any artistic decisions.

While there is undoubtedly an enormous amount of imagery in the cover design of the *Pepper's* album (which will be dealt with in Chapter 8), what is most significant is that the cover introduced a considerable number of esoteric thinkers, writers and spiritual gurus to the general public. From this point of view, the Beatles brought esoteric, occult and mystical thinking to the masses. It also mixed the notions of mysticism and spiritual thinking with popular culture, placing individuals like Aldous Huxley, Carl Jung, Edgar Allan Poe, the Hindu goddess Lakshmi and a host of Indian Swamis, alongside figures such as Shirley Temple, Diana Dors and Snow White, thus democratizing all levels of culture, suggesting that there was no hierarchical system of knowledge, and that per-sonal fulfilment could be found in all aspects of culture.

Paul in particular, through his new circle of friends, was trying to 'reconcile the standards of classical art, literature and music with those of popular culture'.[320] This was also akin to the artistic philosophy of Peter Blake, who was also intent on challenging 'the status quo's idea about what constituted art and broke down barriers between traditional fine art and the new cutting-edge field of Pop'.[321] By 1966, the Beatles had combined traditions as diverse as Hindustani and European classical, experimental electronic, and southern Soul, seeing all as an expression of art and not distinguishing between high art and popular art. This influence had spread to all artists, photographers, designers, and painters of the period,[322] including Peter Blake.[323]

Musically, the album merges the cultures of East and West, while also drawing influences from the mundane, such as Corn Flakes' adverts, TV shows, newspaper stories and childhood memories, along with everyday places and people, like Penny Lane, 'lovely' Rita, Billy Shears and Sgt. Pepper himself. The use of a kaleidoscope of instruments and styles mixed with the childhood perspective of many of the songs' images (with a nostalgia for the past), creates the feeling that time is distorted. 'Nothing of *Sgt. Pepper's*,' says musicologist and composer Howard Goodall, 'is quite what it seems.'[324] Another aspect of the album cover's imagery is that it mixed childhood heroes with present-day heroes and individuals that were seen as representing a futuristic outlook, like Huxley, H.G. Wells and James Joyce, again creating a kind of psychedelic distortion of time. The past, present and the future were merged together.

The notion that 'nothing is quite what it seems', or as Lennon would sing, 'nothing is real', deepens the album's mystery and allows for a much more open interpretation of the album's cover design, whose over-abundance of colourful images was enough to spark the imaginations of an already LSD-stimulated youthful population. From this perspective, many of the images were possibly interpreted in a very particular way by the album's fans. Jann

Haworth suggested as much, seeing it as 'the result of a brilliant collaboration and happenstance rather than rife with the deliberate hidden meanings widely offered throughout the past half century'. Haworth was puzzled by her own creation, asking: 'What the heck is going on in that cover? Who are the crowd? Are they "lonely hearts" or is it a fan club of the Lonely Hearts Club Band? Is one of them Sgt. Pepper? Where is Sgt. Pepper? Nothing actually fits when you really analyse it.'

The notion of distorting time and culture is again the theme of the two videos accompanying their double A-side single from this period, 'Strawberry Fields Forever' and 'Penny Lane', where old Edwardian army tunics and other period-piece properties, along with time manipulation and super-imposition of images and surreal lighting suggested an unidentifiable space, particularly in 'Strawberry Fields Forever'. Alongside all this were single eye images, prevalent in much of today's pop music iconography, creating a psychedelic atmosphere. The outdoor dinner space in 'Penny Lane', with servants resembling the Mad Hatter's Tea Party, also creates a sense of distortion and a kind of, to quote Crowley, 'dream reality', thus contributing to the idea that 'nothing' is indeed 'real' and that reality and fantasy are one and the same. The filming of the filming in the 'A Day in the Life' promotional film, and the sense that the watcher is being watched, are other examples of this distorted perception of 'how things are', or at least how they are perceived by modern western perception.

While much of this can be seen as a definite attempt to democratize art and eradicate the differentiations between types of art, others have considered that it was designed – along with the LSD culture that flourished vis-à-vis these artistic developments – to bring about confusion in thought, making all levels of cultural thought both acceptable and equally relevant, dumbing down the public's capacity to think rationally and making attempts to attain 'truth', both meaningless and futile. (This latter subject is dealt with further in Chapter 10.)

The recording of the *Pepper's* album was finished by April 1967, and it is possible that Blake and his co-designers, or even McCartney himself, included little signs as to the supposed 'death' of McCartney, a 'rumour' which was already circulating in London society by 1966 – possibly to spark the fans' imagination. It is difficult to say for sure if these 'hints' were intentional or not, or if there was an even more macabre reason behind many of the faces and images on the cover. There is some indication, according to the Sixties' singer Marianne Faithfull – who was at the centre of the London Sixties' scene – that an intellectual hub, created around Barry Miles and Bob Frazer, tried to create, or at least encourage, a counterculture in England at the start of the decade, an Ur-Myth based on a dream of Carl Jung's, in which Liverpool was the centre of the world – though they shifted the scene to London.[325]

David Livingstone, in his book *Transhumanism: The History of a Dangerous Idea*, points out that Miles' Indica bookstore and gallery was named after a term Aleister Crowley had used in his book *The Psychology of Hashish*. Crowley was particularly symbolic of a new attitude in post-war Britain which was greatly encouraged by this particular group of intellectuals, who had seen London as being the centre of a New Age and possibly saw themselves as New Age heralds. The group was linked to Michael Hollingshead, 'the man who turned the world onto LSD', and who was, interestingly, linked to the Institute of British-American Cultural Exchange.[326] This brings us to the controversial representation of the British occultist Aleister Crowley on the album's cover.

Crowley is a controversial figure and self-professed 'Satanist', but his idea of 'Do what thou wilt is the whole of the law' strongly resonated with the Sixties' ethos – although unfortunately has also been seen as a licence for an immoral, or at least amoral, lifestyle. Crowley intrigued the Sixties' generation, with time on their hands, money in their pockets, and an ability – unlike previous generations – to indulge in intellectual as well as social pursuits. Like the aristocratic Greeks, who could spend their days philosophizing, the middle-class British were comfortable enough to engage in reading Crowley, Leary and other mystics, whilst tripping on acid! To the new generation, who were granted these luxuries, Crowley was not a wicked man but one well ahead of his time, who anticipated the later generation's rejection of outmoded pieties of duty and restraint. What Crowley stood for, ultimately, was self-gratification: no mere aimless indulgences but the healthy and liberating pursuit of one's deepest will and desires against the soulless and shallow expectations of authority. Crowley's elaborate credo of Thelema (Will) gave young people's enjoyment of sex, drugs and rock 'n' roll a dimension beyond their immediate pleasures; from a Crowleyan perspective, such joys could be considered sacred.[327]

Miles and the Indica Gallery crowd, like Frazer, were more concerned with intellectualism than were the Beatles, and were happy to spread alternative, even subversive, thinking to the group, as well as to the general public through their bookstore. Some believe it was McCartney who had chosen Crowley for the cover, although Haworth claims it was Lennon, saying in an interview that Lennon had Hitler down as one of his choices, along with Crowley. He explained Lennon's unusual selections as being, 'probably the folly of youth, but it's a real whopper. John was provocative to a fault and to the point of almost being rather rude to people',[328] but whether Lennon, McCartney, or the other Beatles were really all that interested in Crowley, at least in any meaningful way, seems unlikely, since – considering their gruelling schedule – they simply would not have had the time to immerse themselves in his teachings. Thus Crowley only usually appears as a footnote in Beatles' biographies, mostly connected to the *Pepper's* cover. The Beatles were intrigued with Crowley and the occult in an experimental sense, as Harrison would suggest in his song 'Try Some Buy Some', where he indicates as much before finding a more sincere calling in religion. He sings there: 'After a time when I tried them, denied them, I opened my eyes and saw you.'

What is particularly interesting about the cover, however, is not who *is* on it but who *isn't*. Elvis, for example, probably the most influential figure in the Beatles' musical career, does not appear, although this is likely because they saw him as being *too* iconic. However, other figures, particularly African-American singers like Little Richard, did not appear either[329] – or, for that matter, the French actress and Fifties' sex symbol Brigitte Bardot, the fantasy of the teenage Lennon, McCartney, Harrison and Starr. In her stead, Blake used the English actress Diana Dors, thus keeping the cover primarily Anglo-American, with the exception of a few Indian personalities. Such a design would certainly enhance the impact on world culture of what the historian Carroll Quigley would refer to as 'the Anglo-American Establishment'.

Magical Mystery Tour

Magic seems to have intrigued the Beatles, who had originally planned to call the *Revolver* album *Abracadabra* or *The Magic Circle*.[330] The idea behind *Magical Mystery Tour* came from the psychedelic and esoteric collective that were the Merry Pranksters, led by author and semi-mystical acid guru of the 1960s, Ken Kesey. The Pranksters were a kind of Robin Hood and his Band of Merry Men, or what would later become more popularly known as 'hippys', who lived outside of the conventions of the time. They had traded their middle class consumer lifestyle for an alternative, free-spirited one, primarily inspired by the changes that were taking place in the mid-Sixties, as well as by the new drug LSD.

The Pranksters dedicated their existence to finding a more magical and illuminated form of living. They travelled in a bus around America, simply 'being'. Their experiments with LSD, which had become a part of their daily diet, had led the group to having a kind of deep collective conscious experience, as if their minds had 'merged into one'. They became a kind of prototype for the 'new society', which it was hoped would consist of individuals who would be inwardly and spiritually connected to one another – in other words, a society of one consciousness, with each member independent but connected.

The Beatles, in their own mysterious way, were both an inspiration for the Merry Pranksters, as well as being consciously inspired by them. The Pranksters were in some sense a self-conscious reflection of the Beatles, in other words, the Beatles had inspired such a group intuitively, whilst the Pranksters became a kind of conscious realization of such a group in society, which allowed the Beatles in turn to consciously look in at themselves. However, instead of creating a deeper collective consciousness among the Beatles, this process tended to separate their individualities more – something that would become evident by the time of what is popularly referred to as *The White Album*. Writer Bill Gibron observed that, if you place *Magical Mystery Tour* alongside their previous feature movies *Help!* and *A Hard Day's Night*, 'we get a telling triptych, a sequence of statements that argued against their continued marketing and marginalisation and for the furthering of their own individual artistic goals'.[331]

The *Magical Mystery Tour* was an attempt to emulate this notion and to create a kind of fantasy-odyssey film, which also fused the traditional English seaside day trip with a modern psychedelic consciousness (similar to how James Joyce represented Homer's theme of the Odyssey in modern literature). Again, the Beatles were bringing together something old and traditional with something new and innovative. Unfortunately, it didn't quite become the adventure film it was hoped to be. Despite these artistic problems with *Magical Mystery Tour*, the film shows an unusual side to the Beatles. At their artistic peak following *Pepper's*, the Beatles had begun to embrace a new vision of themselves and the world. *A Hard Day's Night* was traditionally British, with the Beatles very much a representation of this new 'Elizabethan Age', and *Help!* was somehow mocking of itself, though keeping entrenched in ideas of the British Empire and American consumerism while simultaneously mocking the unorthodox impulses coming from the East that were beginning to find their way into western culture, mainly through literature and philosophy. *Magical Mystery Tour*, however, is something of a complete turnaround – a rejection of what the old world had stood for whilst embracing eastern ideas, mysticism and the occult in a very overt sense.

The film is magical, mysterious and colourful from the outset, hinting at Indian mysticism. (Hostess Wendy Winters, played by Mandy Weet, has her pineal gland – or third eye chakra, an indicator of higher consciousness – decorated by an Indian bindi, the sacred symbol of the cosmos in its unmanifested state.) Lennon wears a feather in his cap, as if some kind of 'fool' figure with magical powers, and Harrison, too, sports an unusual costume suggesting, if not something mystical, at least unconventional. McCartney, at his artistic best at this stage, presents himself as the 'Fool on the Hill', the flower in his hat and the set piece of him 'above the world', a symbol of a transcended consciousness, like Shakespeare's fool characters or the symbol of the Fool from Tarot, which indicates knowledge and wisdom beyond the conventional and mundane. The hermetic magician and Christian mystic Valentin Tomberg describes the Fool as one who has 'memory of the future' but has forgotten the past and present; the Fool contemplates eternity and lives outside time. The medieval mystic Jacob Boehme says: 'You still say that you will be taken for a fool, which is true, for the Way that leads us to the love of God is folly to the world.' The Fool is the footloose Bohemian, the Exile, the Expatriate, the Cosmopolitan, the one who has abandoned the struggle for existence.[332]

The *Magical Mystery Tour* album cover and film contain many more images that carry, either consciously or subconsciously, certain ideas and suggestions (e.g. the Walrus sequence) but one of the most intriguing is the sign on the album's inside sleeve – next to John Lennon – that reads: 'THE BEST WAY TO GO IS BY M&D C...', thus spelling out the initials of Lennon's future assassin, Mark David Chapman (his murder would happen thirteen years later).

Although this may be just a coincidence, the sign does not appear in the film version of this scene, from which the still image is seemingly taken.

Such strange coincidences, or serendipitous occurrences, are ubiquitous throughout the Beatles' story, such as the figure of Fred the seaman in *Yellow Submarine*, who shares the name of Lennon's father (Alfred or Alfie Lennon), who was also a seaman. It was likewise the name of Lennon's personal assistant, Fred Seaman. Lennon's life also closely paralleled that of his mother, who became short-sighted at around the same age as John (six or seven years of age), became estranged from her parents, was rebellious and attention seeking, was sexually active throughout her life, was musical and played the banjo, became pregnant with John in her mid-twenties (roughly the same age John became a father), was married, divorced and estranged from her child at almost identical times in her life (as John was from his first wife and child), and died a tragic, untimely death at the age of forty-four – just four years older than John when he was assassinated.

Another unusual parallel is with the film *Rosemary's Baby* (1968) and Lennon's *Imagine* album. Lennon based the cover design of his record on the film's promotional poster, while the film itself is set in the Dakota building, the very building Lennon was shot outside of. A scene from the film also contains a white Beetle car covered in blood. Interestingly, the film's director, Roman Polanski, is also strangely connected to the Beatles through the murder of his wife, Sharon Tate, by the Manson family, who claimed the murder was inspired by songs from the Beatles' *White Album*.

Whether these connections have any real significance requires a lot more investigation, but what is significant is the power many of the images and symbols are given by the imagination of society as a whole. Peter Bebergal, in his study of the occult in rock 'n' roll, sensibly observes that what really gives these album covers occult significance is the power given to them, as with any graphic form, 'to function as an emblem'.[333] Bebergal quotes the graphic designer

Paula Scher about her experience with the *Sgt Pepper's* album: 'Everyone I knew,' she said, 'stared at the cover for hours on end, unlocking special, secret clues to its meaning… and we debated our obscure findings forever. Nothing before or since affected me as strongly.'[334]

Yellow Submarine

The *Yellow Submarine* album and movie certainly contains images and symbols that are full of esoteric meaning, although it is almost certain that these meanings, particularly in the movie, did not derive from the Beatles themselves, and in most incidences they didn't come from the creators of the movie either. Dr Robert R. Hieronimus, in his book *Inside the Yellow Submarine*, observed that 'most of the co-creators of this film insist they were too busy with their deadlines and the frenzied, script-less beginnings of their production to create the multi-layered allegories many of us fans read into it', yet he suggests that, 'the colours reflected the feelings of the people working on the film, and the flower power LSD culture too'.[335]

Released in November of 1968, the same month that *The White Album* came out, *Yellow Submarine* was produced with little involvement by the Beatles themselves. Although the premier of the film, at Piccadilly Square in November of 1968 (which caused a near-riot) is often seen as the last expression of Beatlemania, the genesis of *Yellow Submarine* was simply business. Beatles' manager Brian Epstein negotiated the movie deal in order to satisfy remaining contractual obligations, and the only contribution the group made was four songs (which were actually out-takes from unrelated recording sessions). The movie's message, though hardly original, is simple — the power of music and love to defeat melancholy and to tame our harsher impulses. It's a sentiment perfectly summed up in the anthemic 'All You Need Is Love'.[336] 'Although The Beatles in fact had little to do with the making of the film,' said George Martin, 'it is surprisingly in line with their own ideals.'[337]

Hieronimus is certain that the film does indeed contain symbols and images that found their way into the movie, mostly through the subconscious and collective consciousness of the period. He assigns to the film the idea that 'throughout history, great artists have described the experience of the creative force flowing through them, being scarcely conscious of what they were creating until it was done'. The boys' voyage,' wrote a *Time* magazine critic, 'is filled with stilted symbolism',[338] while another *Time* critic observed that the film's main creator Heinz Edelmann's 'outright inventions came from everywhere, including the unconscious'. Edelmann was a cutting-edge artist who more or less invented psychedelic art, and whose style in this film spawned a genre known as 'Yellow Submarine Art'. He even referred to this unconscious aspect himself, saying: 'I knew that part of my subconscious would go into these things, but I chose to disregard that.' John Coates, the film's line producer, said, 'we knew we wanted to say something about the Sixties and that whole scene. There was a certain consciousness of doing that.'

The song 'Yellow Submarine' was, according to McCartney, inspired in the twilight hours,[339] a time when the mind is between sleep and waking, between the conscious and subconscious, between this world and the next, when supersensible ideas stream into the conscious mind and spiritual influences find their way into the sense world. The British magazine *Punch* observed that the Lennon/McCartney songs used in the film seemed to have been conceived and brought forth in the pure, simple spirit of mystical innocence, like the paintings of Chagall. And like Chagall's works, the film tries to include everything in the world in order to make up its own cosmos. The animation style ranges from storybook simplicity to pop art and psychedelic shimmer.

The very title of the film can be seen to represent the act of creation, or creativity. Throughout history, yellow, explains Hieronimus:

> Has been used to symbolise the sun, fire, spirit or mental activity. It represents an active, outer-directed, centrifugal force, or

masculine energy, expansion. Submarine could be considered a symbol for matter or the body. It is necessarily linked to the symbol of water, which throughout history has been considered representational of lunar or feminine energy. It is a passive, intuitive, centripetal force. The submarine is also something that dwells within, hidden and internal rather than external and obvious. By combining the two words 'Yellow' and 'Submarine', one can see a pairing of opposites or a balance between spirit and body, sun and moon, or a uniting of male and female, which is an obvious symbol for the act of creation that produces a unity or oneness. In the film, the yellow submarine lands on top of a Mayan pyramid in 'Pepperland', it is the pyramid with a sun symbol on top of it. The pyramid is a mother symbol. The eye in the triangle of the pyramid, which means male and female are balanced. It must be balanced for life to be nurturing and flowering.

'We all live in a Yellow Submarine' has become, as Hieronimus points out, a symbolic phrase for environmentally-minded groups, and in the 1960s the song was used as an anthem against the Vietnam War by the American peace movement.

The Beatles' press officer, Derek Taylor, suggested that there was a zeitgeist they represented, which was extremely warmly disposed to the human race and to the mode of goodness. (The album's central song is 'All You Need Is Love'.) The overall message of the title song is that, 'We all live in a Yellow Submarine', and our friends are all aboard – a kind of eternal ark. A Yellow Submarine is a symbol for a vessel that will take us all to safety. Some, however, argued that the friends were simply those 'beautiful people', rock stars and celebrities that were out of touch with reality and lost themselves in a fantasy world, essentially shutting the doors on the common people, the fans, who put them there. They were not something to be looked up to and certainly were not the answer to society's problems.[340]

Hieronimus takes Derek Taylor's view, that *Yellow Submarine* provided a society desperately in need of healing with the right symbols and images that could allow this to take place on a subconscious level. Hieronimus explains that without meaningful myths and symbols which work on a deep subconscious level, 'a worldwide cultural malaise is developing, which leads to increasing anxiety and mental, emotional and spiritual disintegration'.

It's interesting that since the 1960s society has seemed to plummet further and further into a state of anxiety, and many of the re-invigorators of the Sixties, like the Beatles, and particularly Lennon, felt that they had subscribed to an over simplistic and unreal philosophy of 'love and peace' in which they inertly got 'stoned' – rejecting, as Bebergal put it, the 'starry-eyed naivete of their own "Love Is All You Need" absolutism'.[341]

'An ever growing "us and them",' observed Derek Taylor, in an England that 'still hadn't had it so good' – but all that changed and changed rapidly. Roger McGuinn, the Byrds' lead singer, would point out this fact in an interview saying, 'as it turned out there are more bombs than ever before'.[342] From such a point of view, not to mention the trend to see conspiracies in everything (justified in some senses in that there has turned out to be a hidden hand behind many of the century's historic events), many believe that the symbols contained in the Beatles' later works, and particularly in the *Yellow Submarine* movie and album cover, display signs and symbols which are not of the positive variety but ones which have led to increasing mental and spiritual 'disintegration'.

Whether the above is true or not, the Beatles appear on the original *Yellow Submarine* album cover making unusual hand signals – signals that many would associate with the occult. John gives the 'devil's horns' (corna) hand signals, one facing forward and a 'mirror image' facing backwards, a symbol of the spiritual realm and 'as above, so below', an indication of the Crowleyan 'Law of Reversal', which urges the practitioner to train himself 'to think backwards by external means'. Lennon's use of it here popularized the sign that has since been used by many bands. Paul is making a '666' hand sign, which is also a yoni (the female anatomy, or sex worship). On the cartoon version cover, the cartoon John makes the 'Devil's horns', while the deeply significant occult number 23[343] is also displayed.

It is difficult to know exactly what the Beatles are trying to indicate here, and often these signs have multiple meanings – while the meanings themselves also get confused in popular culture. It is unlikely that the Beatles are unaware that they are making particular gestures. But whether they are simply experimenting with signs and symbols or are purposely trying to make an impression on their fans is certainly deserving of more research. What is certain is that esoteric symbols, whether consciously or unconsciously, found their way into the *Yellow Submarine* film and both album covers.

The White Album, Abbey Road and Get Back

The *White Album*, the first on the band's Apple label – itself a symbol packed with deep esoteric meaning – is some indication of the Beatles breaking away from their stereotyped image – as well as evidence of each members' move away from group identity towards individuality. Nowhere in their career do the singular elements of each of the Beatles' songs seem more fractured – and the result of a group of individuals expressing their independent thoughts and feelings, moving away from a collective consciousness – as much as this album. A possible indication, if we take the Beatles as a microcosmic representation of 1960s' culture, that society itself was moving towards individualism and a breaking-down of the collective consciousness.

By 1968, there were revolutions across the globe, an assertion of independence. The Sixties per se had moved toward independence for minority groups, such as the civil rights' and feminist movements, which were themselves splintering as individual movements emerged within them.

The cover of the Beatles' *White Album*, a reaction to the elaborate design of *Pepper's*, was in itself symbolic. The Sixties had reached its peak during 1967, the 'Summer of Love' and the anthemic ideology of 'All You Need Is Love', and like all things that go through cycles of time, this period bore its fruit and saw its end. The *White Album* expressed the collapse of the Sixties' dream. It is a cynical and quite dark album which had lost optimism. It has stared the reality of change in the face. The new anthem was 'revolution', and the all-white cover, with even the name of the band in white, suggested a nihilism, a completion, a returning back to itself, while at the same time a blank canvas onto which a whole new consciousness could be projected. Some, like Charles Manson, supposedly, took the symbols to mean 'revolution' in the extreme. In general terms, the album reflected the direction in which the culture and society were moving. A new beginning was definitely nearing.

While the album cover was a dualistic symbol of the end and the beginning, other symbols were to be expressed in sound, particularly the sound collage of Lennon's 'Revolution No. 9', with other backwards messages featuring throughout. 'Revolution No. 9' was Lennon's supposed attempt at avant-garde expressionism, something his new association with Yoko Ono had brought. While some claimed to hear in the music Lennon presenting a subliminal message of his 'dead' friend Paul (see further in Chapter 8), others felt this was an expression of Lennon's occult leanings towards Aleister Crowley, representing the occult practice of backwards writings and recordings (which, in occult terms, provides an insight into the spiritual world).

There is no doubt that the Beatles were aware of such notions, but whether they practiced them to any extent is another matter. Other backwards recordings and non-sensical gibberish (see Chapter 6) occur throughout Beatles' songs, such as at the end of 'I'm So Tired', 'Strawberry Fields Forever', 'Rain', 'I'm Only Sleeping', and the end of the *Pepper's* album. It seems, like much to do with the Beatles, that these were the result of 'chance', happy accidents (like the feedback on 'I Feel Fine', or the cover photo of *Rubber Soul*) that chimed with the times and which were the by-product of modern technology. The notion of 'chance' may not necessarily mean something that happens without purpose, but in fact is the opening up of a space that allows 'something' else to enter in to the process. This 'something else' is often considered something super-natural, or possibly even divine. In the Gamelan music of Bali or Java, for example, this notion of 'chance' can be recognized, as with modern composers like John Cage, and even in the poetry of the German mystic Novalis.[344]

The technological aberrations within some Beatles' songs, which were employed later on purpose by other artists for artistic purposes, suggest the distorted nature that technology can bring into the sphere of nature — man's print in the manipulation of matter and energy (acoustic instruments don't generate feedback and backwardness; these occur in the realm of sub-nature and technology), but were embraced by artistic inventiveness.

These sonic 'glitches' would provide a new colour and mode of expression to the Beatles and many Sixties' pop artists, giving the music a freshness, a contemporariness, that was unique to the time and place, but which also suggested something dark and disturbing — in other words a distortion of nature and reality. The Beatles remained contemporary by intuitively incorporating these elements into their work, while also exploring other avenues of a political nature, as in the case of 'Revolution No. 9', which was not only Lennon's attempt to capture the idea of revolution in sound, but also his way of subverting the Beatles' myth.

It seems unlikely that the Beatles really knew what they were doing in relation to backwards magic. They probably dabbled with such ideas, as magic was certainly something that interested them, if only superficially. Interestingly, 'Revolution No. 9' took its initial form from the fade-out of another revolution song, 'Revolution No. 1', which also featured on the *White Album* (with added sound effects, voice-overs, and instrumental music from a variety of classic composers such as Sibelius and Vaughan Williams). In essence, the two songs were the beginning and the end of the same take,[345] paralleling the beginning and ending symbolism of the album's plain white cover.

While the *White Album* cover symbolized the end of Sixties' psychedelic dream and the possibilities for something new, the band's *Abbey Road* album certainly represents the death of something. Whether the Beatles consciously knew it or not, the album is representative of a funeral procession – it is too uncanny for it to be a coincidence, although synchronicity and serendipity, in their spiritual sense, were certainly major elements of the Beatles' phenomenon. The cover is very significant of the final end, not just of the band but of the decade, and clearly indicates that this is the end of the Beatles' and the Sixties' dream. The fact that the album finishes with the song 'The End' suggests that the band were definite about it being so.

The end, so to speak, had more or less come when the Beatles returned to the stairwell of EMI studios to re-shoot the original *Please Please Me* album cover shot, with the original photographer Angus McBean capturing the band almost seven years on (the original was taken in February 1963 and the re-staged version was taken in May 1969). 'We all felt very spooky: This is pretty final. This is full circle. We've started and ended', McCartney told journalist Paul Du Noyer.[346] Mysteriously, the group had intuitively recognized the end of a seven-year cycle in which things have, by necessity, to move on.

Rudolf Steiner had developed a theory of human development based on seven-year cycles, which he had also linked to astrological cycles, and which also feature in Steiner's approach to child education.[347] The Beatles, as ever, intuitively realized as much.

While the *White Album* is full of individual pieces, so too is *Abbey Road*, though these lack the cohesiveness that the *White Album* captured. Though the final medley on side two re-creates a sense of the camaraderie that the collective approach of the earlier work had, and its optimistic flair, it also suggests that the band were running out of ideas, with nothing substantial enough to stand on its own.

Hence, in essence it was for the best that they broke up. Some suggest the album cover was not intended to mean anything and was done on a whim, with the photographer, Iain McMillan, taking a few photos of the band walking across the road of their studio.[348] But if that is so, it is uncanny that it represents a funeral procession, with each member playing their part perfectly (Lennon in white, representing a priest; Ringo all in black, the mourner; Harrison in working man's denims, suggesting the grave digger; and McCartney, in an ordinary suit but strangely barefoot, representing the dead), while simultaneously capturing one of the most iconic images of the twentieth century. Some cosmic force working itself into the process could be an explanation, as it would certainly be for many other 'happy coincidences' in the group's career.

The end (or death) of the most loved pop group of the Sixties, if not of all time, with each individual Beatle beginning to move in their own individual directions – a process which was happening over the last few years of the group's career (possibly even before the *Pepper's* album) – is finally realized in their final album release, *Let It Be*, coming after the group had officially split up. Each member is pictured in an unelaborate, if even conventional setting, against a black background. They appear as separate individuals contained within their own separate box, no longer really part of a cohesive group.

Chapter 8

He Blew His Mind Out in a Car:
Paul Is Dead

The Rumour

'The seventh of January was very icy, with dangerous conditions on the M1 motorway linking London with the Midlands, and towards the end of the day, a rumour swept London that Paul McCartney had been killed in a car crash on the M1. But of course, there was absolutely no truth in it at all, as The Beatles' press officer found out when he telephoned Paul's St. Johns Wood home, and was answered by Paul himself...' Thus, goes the article entitled 'False Rumour' in the February 1967 issue of *Beatles Book Monthly*, the magazine of the official Beatles' Fan Club.[349]

McCartney's Mini Cooper did in fact crash, with some newspapers reporting his death as a result. However, McCartney wasn't in the car at the time, but seemingly at a party in Sussex. The man driving the car was one Mohammed Hadjij, an assistant to McCartney's art gallery friend, Robert Frazer, who, it is alleged, was transporting drugs up to the party.[350] The rumour of Paul's death, however, would gain a certain momentum over the next few months, and McCartney would himself allude to it during a Beatles' Press conference later that year.

The rumour, like many about the Beatles, soon faded but resurfaced about two years later, this time in Des Moines, Iowa, when on Wednesday 17 September 1969, the student newspaper at Drake University published an article by student Tim Harper entitled: 'Is Beatle Paul McCartney Dead?' The article came to the attention of art student John Summer, who was so intrigued by it that he compiled a dossier of evidence substantiating Paul's death and offered it to United Press International, who agreed to carry it.

Around the same time, DJ Russ Gibb at WKNR-FM introduced the 'Paul-is-Dead' rumour to the airwaves. His show had been heard by yet another student, this time at the University of Michigan at Ann Arbor, named Fred LaBour. LaBour was scheduled to write a review of the Beatles' new album *Abbey Road* for the next issue of the university's student newspaper. Inspired by Gibb's show, LaBour decided to do away with the standard review format and composed a piece of pure imagination. It began, 'Paul McCartney was killed in an automobile accident in November 1966 after leaving EMI recording studios tired, sad, and dejected?' The article claimed that Paul had died in a car crash three years earlier, the top of his head sheared off. The Beatles, conspiring to conceal his death, held a lookalike contest and hired the winner, a Scotsman named William Campbell (also known by the names Billy Campbell and Billy Shears), to replace him. The mysterious clues, claimed LaBour, were held to be part of a strange and disturbing plot orchestrated by John Lennon, who had it in mind to found a new religion, with himself as God and the 'reborn' McCartney as a Christ-like figure at his side. The article appeared in the university's student paper, *The Michigan Daily*, on 14 October 1969, sparking widespread interest in the rumour.

At first, mainstream news organizations were reluctant to report on the matter without more evidence, but when the Beatles, and particularly McCartney, chose to ignore requests from the Press for a statement – and thus, having no way to verify or dispel the rumour, they had no choice but to acquiesce to the public demand for information – they began to cover the story. It wasn't long before the rumour became an international sensation, with articles appearing in every leading newspaper. *Time* magazine even devoted a feature essay to the subject, and special 'Paul-is-Dead' magazines appeared on newsstands and were snapped up by the hundreds of thousands of readers. The song 'Saint Paul', by singer/songwriter and radio DJ Terry Night, was released and at least four different 'Paul-is-Dead' novelty songs were rushed into production, with titles like 'Brother

Paul' by Billy Shears, 'We're All Paul-Bearers' by Zacherias & The Tree People, 'The Ballad of Paul' by the Mystery Tour, and a number called 'So Long, Paul', recorded under the pseudonym Werbley Finster, who turned out to be none other than the Puerto Rican singing star, Jose Feliciano. In June 1970, even DC comics used the rumour for a background story for their *Batman* strip. Not surprisingly, sales of the Beatles' own records and licensed merchandise, especially their new *Abbey Road* album, went through the roof.

During the climax of the 'Paul-is-Dead' media frenzy, RKO produced a one hour television special called 'Paul McCartney: The Complete Story, Told for the First and Last Time'. This programme was videotaped on a set resembling a courtroom, in which various 'witnesses' involved with the rumour, including Gibb and LaBour, were formally questioned by an attorney, celebrity lawyer F. Lee Bailey, whose most infamous client was Albert DeSalvo, better known as the Boston Strangler. RKO's 'Paul-is- Dead' TV special was syndicated on the Thanksgiving weekend of 1969. After the broadcast, all videotapes of the programme appear to have vanished without a trace, but fortunately the soundtrack was preserved for posterity by an anonymous Beatle fan, who had taped it from his television set.

There is very little doubt that the whole article was fictitious. LaBour had even told Bailey during a pre-show meeting that he had made the whole thing up. Bailey responded: 'Well, we have an hour of television to do. You're going to have to go along with this.' On the programme, LaBour explained why he wrote the article: 'I didn't wanna just, um, write a review *(for Abbey Road)* about, you know, Paul does this song and George does this song… So, I decided to make it work symbolically, on a religious level.' LaBour's article presented for the first time what was to become the definitive legend of Paul McCartney's death.[351]

As the hysteria reached its peak in the last week of October, McCartney reluctantly granted *Life* magazine an exclusive interview, mainly so he could be left in peace. Paul appeared with his family on the cover, in one of the biggest-selling issues in the

magazine's history. The accompanying article presented a cynical analysis of the 'death clues', along with a statement from Paul
in which he summarily dismissed the clues and declared that the
whole matter was 'bloody stupid'.

According to Beatles' biographer Philip Norman, reports of McCartney's death were not new: 'Paul had already been the subject of a
good many, started by people trying to make money from newspapers or simply to discover where he lived,' wrote Norman.[352] What
was even more curious than the reports of Paul's death, though,
was that during the *Life* interview, McCartney announced that, 'The
Beatle thing is over. It has been exploded...', but strangely nobody
paid any attention to the statement, just as they had ignored Lennon's statement – during the 'Bigger than Jesus' controversy – about
the Vietnam War.

The Clues

Throughout October 1966 McCartney had little if any presence in
the media – as if, some felt, he had just suddenly disappeared. Even
though McCartney had given an adequate explanation of his scant
media presence, and also of how the rumour might have started –
stating, 'I haven't been in the press much lately... I would rather be a
little less famous these days'[353] – some people were not (and are still
not) satisfied with this explanation. McCartney's desire to be less in
the public eye might not appear that strange if one considers that
for the last four years there was non-stop coverage of the Beatles'
every move, and that the need to disappear from the public eye
and public pressure was a feeling generally felt by all the Beatles in
1966 – particularly after their unsettling incident in the Philippines,
in which the band were in fear of their lives.[354] Others, such as
researcher and anthroposophist Nicholas Kollerstrom, however,
have seen more sinister reasons behind the band's, and particularly
McCartney's, absence towards the end of that year, namely the
'death' of McCartney and his replacement by an 'imposter'.

Brian Moriarty, game designer and professor of Interactive Media and Game Design at Worcester Polytechnic Institute, in a very enjoyable and insightful talk on this very subject (given at a Game Developers' Conference in San Jose, CA in 1999, suggested that:

> You might think that this authoritative appearance by McCartney would be enough to make the 'Paul-is-Dead' issue dry up and blow away. It wasn't. The *Life* article was indeed enough to convince most people that Paul was still alive. But what about those death clues? Who put all those creepy artefacts on the album covers and in the songs? It is these questions that seem to provide the more mysterious elements to the rumour, thus indicating that although the rumours themselves were mostly fabricated, there seems to be some inexplicable truth to them. Why was that stuff in there? Even the Beatles' publicist Derek Taylor had to contact McCartney, so unsure was he of the rumour. Why did it re-emerge three years later and why did Tim Harper revitalise the rumour? Maybe it wasn't really in there at all. Maybe we were just deluding ourselves. Or maybe somebody was having a bit of fun, and making a bit of money, at our expense.[355]

The focus, as Moriarty continues to explain in his talk, suddenly shifted from concern over McCartney to a morbid fascination, not just with his supposed death but more with the clues and indicators, possibly planted by the Beatles themselves, regarding the possibility of his death. In other words, the whole affair became a game of clue-hunting and puzzle-solving, and not about Paul's death at all. In more recent times, following on from this rather innocent preoccupation of clue-hunting into more vicious attitudes towards conspiracies and nefarious activities, primarily fuelled by today's internet, the theories behind Paul's 'death' have become more and more preposterous, so that reason and common sense seem to be the real victims in this whole saga. This is a clear example of the 'cognitive dissonance' permeating the whole of our modern culture.

The clues regarding McCartney's death mostly appear on two Beatles' albums: *Abbey Road* and *Sgt. Pepper's*, and if LaBour's review had presented *Abbey Road* as a funeral procession – with John as the anthropomorphic God, followed by Ringo the undertaker, followed by Paul the resurrected Christ, barefoot with a cigarette in his right hand (the 'original' Paul was left-handed), followed by George, the grave-digger – then *Sgt. Pepper's Lonely Hearts Club Band* was his burial.

In fairness to LaBour, the *Abbey Road* cover *was* uncannily like a presentation of a funeral procession, and if it was to be so, then it's possible that *Pepper's* could be seen as Paul's burial, especially since the album cover was originally conceived as a kind of burial – not just of Paul, however, but of the Fab Four image the group wanted to distance themselves from. 'As we're trying to get away from our-selves – to get away from touring and into a more surreal thing – how about if we become an alter-ego band, something like, say, Sgt. Pepper's Lonely Hearts?',[356] McCartney would explain to the other band members, in an attempt to move away from the defunct Beat-les' image, while still keeping the other three disinterested members excited about another Beatle project. The cover photo, then, shows the Beatles assuming this new identity and laying to rest their ear-lier image as the Fab Four. The new psychedelic Beatles stand at the centre, while wax images (Lennon had once claimed they could have been just four wax works for all anybody cared about the music)[357] of the younger Beatles look mournfully on the grave site, symbolic of the fact that the Beatles were no longer the same band.

The album was full of the most colourful imagery, much of which would later be interpreted as clues that re-enforced the myth of Paul's 'death'. There are too many to consider here, but many of the more crucial ones concerning the myth have been disproved, like the 'Officially Pronounced Dead' badge that Paul was wearing on his sleeve, which turned out to be 'Ontario Provincial Police' (although some feel the badge was doctored to purposely fuel the rumour, the evidence of which is thin). There were also some musi-cal clues, like John singing 'I buried Paul' at the end of 'Strawberry

Fields Forever'. With the release of original recordings from the *Anthology* series, it emerges that Lennon was actually saying 'cranberry sauce', not untypical of Lennon and his surreal imagination.

Since the internet, however, a whole host of sites have emerged to uncover the mystery of the 'Paul-is-Dead' conspiracy, bringing forth even more supposed evidence that McCartney is in fact dead, including a statement by Emilio Lari, the photographer on the Beatles' film *Help!* In an interview, Lari claimed that McCartney had, in fact, been replaced in 1966. However, in a more recent interview, Lari recanted his statement, saying: 'I was convinced that it was like that, I mean that Paul was dead in an accident in 1966 and that he had been replaced by a double. Now, after months and months of consideration, I came to the conclusion that it is, without a shadow of a doubt, that the story is a hoax.'[358]

In his book *The Life and Death of Paul McCartney*, Nicholas Kollerstrom, known for his work on the London 7/7 bombings, presents his readers with numerous 'clues' to suggest that Paul McCartney did indeed die in a car crash and was replaced. 'The show,' he suggests, 'had to go on.'[359] His reasoning is that the Wilson government of 1966 was able to avoid devaluing the pound because of the Beatles' contribution to the revenue and exports, and that it was an actual 'government imperative' for the Beatles to provide a replacement.[360] Kollerstrom also suggests that anyone aware of the fraud was silenced by the Official Secrets Act, with pressure coming from 'high level masonic governmental involvement'.[361]

If the above was indeed the case, that the Wilson government had encouraged the defrauding of the general public by insisting the Beatles cover-up Paul's death in order to save the British financial system, then so be it, but unfortunately Kollerstrom's book is full of all kinds of inconsistencies and unsupported claims, which make any of his theories difficult to entertain. For example, he claims that the original Paul couldn't play the piano,[362] and certainly not the piano parts on 'Lady Madonna', yet in the same book he writes that Paul had composed 'Eleanor Rigby' on the piano,[363] and that he was waiting for a piano to be delivered to his house at Cavendish Avenue to finish a new song, most probably 'Penny Lane'. Paul is also seen playing piano in the films A Hard Day's Night and Help! and was certainly talented and dedicated enough to improve to the standard of playing on the 'Lady Madonna' track four years later.

Kollerstrom also tells us that Jim Fetzer, a former Professor of Logic who had researched the 'Paul-is-Dead' phenomenon, seems to validate his claims that the 'real' Paul was much smaller than the 'imposter'.[364] Fetzer must not have been much of a logician, since any basic search on the internet clearly shows that the 'two Pauls' are exactly the same height, relative to the other Beatles (John, Paul and George were about 5'11', Ringo was approx. 5'8',[365] and also to Paul's girlfriend of the time, Jane Asher). In an early Beatles' interview, Paul is asked his height, which he gives as 5'11.[366] Kollerstrom attempts to support the claim of the different sizes by showing two different photos of the 'real' Paul and Jane against another photo of Jane with the 'imposter'. However, Kollerstrom shows the photos only from the waist up, which means we are unable to properly determine the comparisons — is Jane in high heels in one photo and not in the other, for example? Again, a simple search on the internet would clear this point up.

Kollerstrom also points to Lennon's Imagine movie, where Harrison makes a reference to 'Beatle' Bill, which is supposedly a reference to the real name of the imposter William Campbell (or Billy Shears).[367] However, Harrison is actually referring to the producer Phil Spector – or 'Beatle' Phil (an in-joke among the band) – who is sitting across from Harrison as he makes the remark.

Kollerstrom, and others, have suggested that the 'true' McCartney was a baritone with a full round timbre to his voice; that he had difficulty hitting notes above E and F and, particularly, struggled with the higher notes G and G sharp – whereas the 'imposter' could soar into the heavens, effortlessly. There are claims that later McCartney songs don't employ the same baritone timbre that the 'real' McCartney did in songs like 'Yesterday' and, presumably, other ballads like 'And I

Love Her'. Both these statements are inaccurate and cause another problem for those trying to prove the 'Paul-is-Dead' argument. The 'real' Paul was 'a compulsive mimic and performer',[368] with a wider, if not necessarily deeper, range than Lennon, and would often perform Elvis and Little Richard, indicating his extensive range to his classmates while at school.[369] Paul had recorded many songs which reach at least a tone, if not two tones, above G sharp — for example, 'Long Tall Sally', which the Beatles covered very early on and recorded in 1964, and 'I'm Down' recorded in 1965.

It's not unknown for singers to improve their range or their vocal quality, and certainly McCartney did seem to make his vocal adapt more to the stadium-rock style that his post-Beatles' group Wings required. The idea that the 'two Pauls' have different vocal abilities is just not convincing. While a study was done on McCartney's vocals pre- and post-1966, the scientist involved was seemingly convinced that there was more than one Paul singing the songs (he claims there were three!), and thus the results are a little dubious – particularly since the experiment was left inconclusive, with the negative initial reaction supposedly forcing him to abandon the work. More recent studies on Paul's vocal, with modern voice analysing technology, have suggested quite convincingly that the same vocalist is singing on songs pre-1966 (the supposed year of the alleged death of Paul McCartney) and post-1966.[370]

There is also the suggestion that the 'real' Paul was not so well educated and could not have incorporated all the musical and artistic ideas he would later bring to the Beatles' work. This is not the case since Paul was absorbing all kinds of influences through his friendship with Jane Asher's brother, Peter, and his circle of friends, particularly the intellectual Barry Miles and the art dealer Robert Frazer. Paul spoke to DJ Alan Freeman, in an interview in February 1966, of all his new and varied influences, from playwriters to modern art and even Stockhausen.[371]

The question of McCartney's changing eye colour has also been a major point in the 'Paul-is-Dead' controversy. McCartney has brown/hazel eyes which sometimes appear green or blue. The most famous example of changing eye colour, and one which has caused much of the controversy, is the Beatles' performance of 'Hey Jude' on the *David Frost Show*. However, it would seem that hazel eyes can often appear green and sometimes blue, as the following paragraph, from Allaboutvision.com, explains:

> Hazel eyes are a bit of a mystery. For starters, people describe this magnificent eye colour in many different ways. Some say it looks like hazelnut, while others call it golden or brownish green. One of the reasons it's so hard to describe hazel-coloured eyes is that the hue itself seems to change, depending on what you wear and the type of lighting you are in.[372]

There is also some considerable concern over Paul's general facial appearance, many claiming that his face looks considerably different from a number of aspects. Possibly, McCartney might look different in different photos, but so did all the Beatles at times, in particular Lennon, who became almost unrecognizable towards the end of the Sixties from when the group started. Interestingly, the English playwright Joe Orton, who was commissioned by the Beatles to write a film-script for the band called *Up Against It* (1967), noticed on meeting McCartney to discuss the project with Brian Epstein, how, 'He [McCartney] was just the same as his photographs'.[373]

The negative DNA test of Bettina Hubers, a woman who has claimed to be the daughter of the 'real' McCartney, has led some to suggest that there was a replacement, but of course it could also be possible that Bettina is not actually the daughter of Paul McCartney, and therefore not proper evidence that a 'replacement' took place.

Other, supposedly forensic, evidence from a scientific team in Italy, consisting of Francesco Gavazzeni and Gabriella Carlesi, has supposedly proven that Paul McCartney was 'replaced' in 1966. The scientists conducted a biometrical analysis of Paul, pre- and post-1966, and discovered discrepancies in his facial features that could not be accounted for by error or plastic surgery. The original article was entitled 'Chiedi chi era quell (Beatle)' and was included in the August 2009 Italian edition of *Wired* magazine. Gavazzeni and Carlesi had, they say, originally set out to prove that there was no replacement and that the 'two' Pauls were the same people; however, they were surprised to discover the opposite to be true. Although this would appear to be conclusive, Gavazzeni and Carlesi have strangely appealed to other forensic scientists to carry out investigations to validate their findings, thus leaving their own investigation somewhat inconclusive.[374]

Kollerstrom feels that it was uncharacteristic for the 'real' Paul to have left his fiancée, Jane Asher, for Linda Eastman, but this is not so difficult to understand when Jane, a promising actress, was career focused and did not want to be at home minding children.[375] Linda did, and that's what Paul, a traditionalist at heart, wanted. Paul was a typical Gemini, the sign that most signifies change, novelty, trial and error, while often appearing to be several different people. These 'twin spirits' would, as Sandford suggests, 'be clearly recognisable in the Sixties when the barefoot hippie became a company director and, ultimately a multimillionaire tycoon.'[376]

Other, rather creepy and unusual, images are the model of an Aston-Martin, the type of car that some say Paul was driving at the time of his supposedly fatal accident, as well as a pair of blood-stained driving gloves, that appear on the cover of *Sgt Pepper's*. It is likely that the car and the blood-stained gloves are, however, a reference to the death of the Beatles' friend Tara Browne, who had been killed in a car crash earlier that year. In fact, it is very likely that the line, 'He blew his mind out in a car', in 'A Day in the Life' refers to Browne's death, not McCartney's, despite claims that this song is in fact the Beatles' official announcement of Paul's 'death'.

Other clues, however, have proven quite difficult to explain. As such, the tale about Paul's demise survives to this day in some quarters as something of an urban myth. But as the story unfolded at the time, the whole affair certainly helped raise the Beatles' 'mystical' appeal.[377] Some of these more inexplicable clues are the following:

In numerous situations, a hand hovers over Paul's head – not just on *Pepper's*, but on the *Yellow Submarine* album cover, as well as in many scenes in the *Magical Mystery Tour* film. This is quite bewildering, particularly since the placement of the hand never occurs over the heads of the other Beatles. Other more bizarre clues, which sometimes call for serious leaps of the imagination, include what is probably the most elaborate of all the so-called 'clues', i.e. the bass drum on the *Pepper's* cover. If a mirror is held across the middle of the words 'LONELY HEARTS', written across the centre of the bass drum (designed by one Joe Ephgrave, a fairground painter), the image 'IONEIX HE<>DIE' is seen. When arranged as, 'I ONE IX HE <> DIE', this suggests the date that Paul supposedly died (11-9, or November 9 1966 – or September 11, rather than November 9, if reading from an English perspective, which is, incidentally, a favoured date for occult groups and conspiracy theorists). While this reading of the image on the bass drum seems to be the product of an overactive imagination on the part of some Beatle fans, the designer's name Ephgrave (of whom little is known, which also seems somewhat odd) is a hybrid of 'epitaph' and 'grave'.

According to McCartney's biographer Christopher Sandford, the crash was on Wednesday 9 November 1966 – this day is consistent with other 'clues', like the lyric from 'She's Leaving Home': 'Wednesday morning at 5 o'clock', referring to the morning of the accident; and a lyric from 'I Am the Walrus', 'Stupid Bloody Tuesday', i.e. the evening McCartney supposedly stormed out of the studio to his doom. However, according to Sandford, McCartney was actually on holiday, travelling abroad with Jane Asher on 9 November 1966, so that date could not possibly be the one of the supposed crash. Again, according to Sandford (and many others), McCartney fell off a moped on 9 November (presumably while on holiday in Kenya) and cut his upper lip. He grew a moustache to cover up the cut. From the point-of-view of the bass drum 'clue', this means 11 September must have been the date of the crash, but that was a Sunday, which does not match up with the above lyrics (if they are to be taken as actual 'clues'). What is more significant about the 9 November date, however, is as Sandford points out, 'if McCartney didn't die on November 9th it was the beginning of the end... John met Yoko that night at an exhibition at the Indica gallery, while Epstein announced formally that the band were finished with touring.'[378]

In the promotional film for 'I Am the Walrus', Paul is again not wearing shoes, singling him out from the other three. His shoes are seen to one side, and it appears that they are stained with blood. In the film, Paul sits in front of a sign that reads, 'I Was' (possibly a reference to the 'voice' which dictated the *Book of the Law* to Crowley), while in the set piece for the song 'Your Mother Should Know', Paul is once again singled out by wearing a black carnation while the other Beatles wear red ones. The black carnation seemingly symbolizes death. On the *White Album*, a number of songs draw attention to the 'Paul-is-Dead' myth, the most famous being on the sound montage 'Revolution No. 9', which if played backwards is supposed to contain the line 'Turn me on, dead man'. Lennon would give more fuel to clue-hunters with the *White Album* track 'Glass Onion', when he sang the line: 'Here's another clue for you all / The Walrus was Paul.' Lennon, though, was entirely fed up with people looking for hidden meanings and signs in his music, which was being interpreted, as he said, 'like the Holy Scriptures'.

The most bizarre idea about Paul's supposed death comes from the book *The Memoirs of Billy Shears*, which claims to have been written by the personality that today is considered to be the true Paul McCartney, but which is actually written by the 'real' William Campbell. The level of detail contained in the book by 'encoder' Thomas E. Uharriet is incredibly extensive (e.g. 666 pages), and leaves the reader with the impression that we have not been listening to James Paul McCartney for fifty years, but to his replacement – who at the time of Paul's supposed death, on 11 September 1966, was a talented yet unknown studio musician. It is so elaborate that it claims that McCartney's words are interpreted by the individual

Thomas E. Uharriet, who claims that he was spiritually connected to McCartney. However, from the start the book states that it is fiction, yet for many 'Paul-is-Dead' conspirators it has a strong confessional element to it, although disguised as fiction. The book claims the following:

1. Shears and McCartney are spiritually connected (referred to as 'Paulism', based in Satanism) — Billy is Paul and Paul is Billy.
2. Plastic surgery was used to recreate Billy as Paul.
3. Billy was trained by Brian Epstein on Paul's mannerisms (Epstein had an interest in acting, though by all accounts he was not very good) and had to work hard to copy Paul's way of arching his eyebrows.
4. Billy had to learn to play left-handed, which he did by listening to *Revolver* continuously – also by channelling Paul – but played right-handed in the studio.

This last claim is easy to disprove, since images of McCartney in the studio, around 1967 and beyond, show Paul playing bass left-handed. It is highly unlikely that these were staged photos. Also, Paul plays the bass live on TV on 'All You Need Is Love', not to mention the *Let It Be* movie of the Beatles live in the studio – and he even manages to play live and sing (a very impressive feat for a few months' work). Also, a quick internet search easily reveals photos of McCartney in the studio playing guitar left-handed during the *Pepper's* session – so, in a matter of months he must have learned to play guitar left-handed as well!

As regards 'Billy Shears' being groomed by Epstein, this seems outlandish since there was very little time for him to learn Paul's mannerisms as well as to learn all the Beatle's songs and to play instruments left-handed – although it is almost impossible to disprove the spiritual 'channelling' of McCartney. However, the above shows just how detailed these ideas have become, and that connecting them on such a deep level indicates just how involved the whole affair is. But again, the internet age is full of theories and ideas that include the supernatural as well as science fiction.

It would be good to bear in mind, as with the LaBour article, that the Shears' book was presented as a piece of fiction and it is another good example of the cognitive dissonance that modern consciousness is working under, particularly with the delusionary tool of the internet, which is often part of what documentary film-maker Adam Curtis presents as 'perception management', in which individuals engage in controlling society's perception of reality.[379]

The book claims that people see what they want to see regarding the 'true' McCartney, even though he is physically different in shape and size (as we have seen, this is not true), as well as there being many lyrical clues as to his death. This last remark is also not true, as the only clue was Lennon's in 'Glass Onion', which was not a clue to anything at all, and was actually – by Lennon's own admission – due to his frustration at fans looking for deeper meanings in his words.

Another example of this confusion around the subject, and of conflicting evidence and accounts, is in the *Last Will and Testament of George Harrison*, which gives a very different but equally fictitious account of the Beatles' covering up of the 'death' of McCartney and his replacement by an imposter. All of this is very entertaining, but is totally in contrast to the Uharriet novel. Even those who support the theory that Paul has been replaced admit that there are widely differing accounts and deliberate confusion between those accounts. The 'plastic-macca' website, for example, criticizes *The Last Will and Testament of George Harrison*, stating that, 'the Harrison film is extremely misleading in general, though someone went to a great deal of effort to present it as a real film of testament'.[380] *The Last Will and Testament* seems to refer to the whole myth as a mind-control operation, thought up by the CIA and MI5 (see Chapter 10).

Yet a third account is the documentary *The Winged Beatle*, which again is very different in its tone and presentation of the facts to the two others. A lot of these claims can be dismissed. The dates of the crash, for example, are not even consistent. Kollerstrom even admits that no one can prove that the car crash actually happened.[381] It seems very odd that someone would devote a lot of time to develop theories based on a premise that cannot be proved...

But despite the fact that LaBour announced that he had made up the whole 'Paul-is-Dead' thing; that Paul himself quickly dismissed the rumours; that many of the so-called clues have been proven to be false; not to mention Lennon's denouncement of the whole affair (when he sarcastically sings, 'those freaks were right when they said you was dead', referring to McCartney's artistic death and his commercial greed in his song 'How Do You Sleep?') – there are still enough unexplained factors and anomalies on Beatles' albums, films and music as a whole to keep the legend alive.

Explanations of Paul's 'Death'

Over time, the Beatles became less and less interested in being Beatles and more interested in exploring their individual pursuits. Beatlemania was good for business, but, as Steve Turner points out, there was no time to 'reflect, explore or develop meaningful friendships beyond their small circle. Their identity was bound up in being the Beatles... This was a time for them to develop as individuals and bring this to their art.'[382] They were tired and uninterested in the mania that surrounded them,[383] and found themselves prisoners of their own adolescent dreams: 'We don't plan anything. We don't do anything. All we do is just keep on being ourselves,' said George Harrison.[384] So, consciously leaving clues behind as to the death of McCartney seems beyond comprehension. If McCartney had in fact died in that ill-fated car crash in 1966, after storming out on a heated recording session, then it would most likely have been the very excuse the band would have needed to free themselves from their over-burdening obligations of being Beatles.

The music industry, interested in making money, unable to have predicated the success of *Pepper's* the following year, and supposing that the Beatles had probably reached their potential, artistically and commercially, would most likely not have wanted to keep the idea of the Beatles going, replacing a deceased Paul with a look-a-like, but instead would have found it more lucrative to cash in on the ill-fated accident, selling the band's back catalogue and compilations (which is exactly what happened when the rumour resurfaced for the second time in 1969). This possibility is supported by Steve Turner's remarks that,

> By late 1965 the British press was anticipating, not without a smidgen of relish, that the Beatles might be nearing their end as the kings of Pop and so were scrutinising the group's output and image as well as the behaviour of fans, for the first signs of decline. Two to three years was the predicted lifespan of pop stars...[385]

However, considering McCartney was aware of the rumour before the *Pepper's* album was finished, is it possible that the Beatles, under the encouragement of McCartney, imagined something of these macabre incidents into the album cover. The inspiration to adopt a pseudonym for the band was ingenious, allowing the band to replace their familiar image with something entirely different. The *Pepper's* album and image chimed perfectly with the drug-induced period of the late Sixties, where the culture had aspired to something entirely surreal and imaginative. The Beatles' album covers were often as celebrated as much as their music, and with album covers like *With the Beatles, A Hard Day's Night, Help!* and particularly *Revolver*, which was a huge leap forward in the area of album cover design, *Pepper's* had to be something hugely impressive. Filling it with symbols and clues would certainly have added to the surrealism of the time.

Their final album, *Abbey Road*, was a very concerted effort to muster together all their strengths to recreate a farewell album, making a conscious effort to recapture the magic they had had

throughout their career. Possibly, they managed to succeed in capturing the magic for the last time but in reality *Abbey Road* shows,
more than any of their other albums, the difficulty the group had
in continuing being the Beatles. 'Relations,' according to one article
on this subject,

> had deteriorated to such an extent that the group abandoned their
> original title of *Everest*, together with a shoot in the Himalayas,
> and were photographed instead walking away from the studios
> and everything they had once shared. The photoshoot for their
> new *Abbey Road* album happened just yards from the eponymous
> recording studios and took ten minutes – only six frames were
> taken by the photographer, Iain Macmillan, who was perched on a
> stepladder.[386]

Although, according to Philip Norman, the *Abbey Road* album 'had
never been intended to mean anything whatsoever',[387] this does seem
unlikely, as it clearly represents a funeral procession, a complement
to the *Pepper's* cover, while at the same time an indication that the
Beatles were in fact splitting up. McCartney had mentioned their
intention in his *Life* interview, and of course the final song on the
album, 'The End', certainly indicates that the Beatles were calling it
a day and were most likely communicating so to their fans on this
album cover – just as the burial symbolism on *Pepper's* indicated the
end of Beatlemania.

The Beatles certainly worked symbols and signs into their artwork – Lennon even admitted doing so – and while of course it
is common in art to utilize signs and symbols, could the Beatles
have purposely fed the 'Paul-is-Dead' idea to the public in 1969 as
a publicity stunt? Both Capitol Records and the Beatles definitely
had a financial motive to devise such a scheme. The 'Paul-is-Dead'
rumour led to massive sales of all the Beatles' albums. People were
actually buying multiple copies of the albums in order to play
them backwards to listen for hidden messages. But Capitol denies
having started the rumour, and it does seem far-fetched to think
that record executives would have been imaginative enough to

dream up and pull off such a hoax, although it is undeniable that once the rumour took hold, Capitol didn't do much to discourage it.

More suspicion is usually focused on the Beatles themselves, because they had the creativity to initiate such a thing. There is also some suspicion of this possibility surrounding the re-release of the Terry Knight song 'Saint Paul' by their publishing company Maclen Music in May, five months before the rumour broke. Why would Maclen publish this one non-Lennon/McCartney work? All of Knight's other songs were published by Storybook Music. Perhaps it's because Lennon or McCartney suggested that Knight write it? Andru Reeve, the author of *Turn Me On, Dead Man: The Beatles and the Paul is Dead Hoax*, writes:

> The enigma of a virtually unknown musician's original song being published by The Beatles may be a greater mystery than the 'Paul-is-Dead' rumour itself. Would its inclusion in The Beatles' catalogue (and its recent and mysterious disappearance) have something to do with Terry Knight's visit to Apple in early 1969? Was the song instigated by none other than Paul McCartney himself?

In April 1969, Terry Knight, who was a very successful radio DJ in Detroit (the place where the rumours of Paul's death started), and was nicknamed 'the sixth Stone' (after more or less making the Rolling Stones famous in America through his continued radio support of them) released a song supposedly reigniting the rumour in Detroit. Knight had been invited to Apple by McCartney in August 1968, and although some claim Knight never met McCartney, other sources say that he met all four Beatles and was witness to their personal bickering during the *White Album* sessions. Knight it seems was disenamoured with both his perception of the Beatles as a harmonious unit as well as with Paul McCartney, who never signed the contract with him and Apple.

On returning to Detroit, Knight wrote and released the song 'Saint Paul', which some have interpreted as disclosing the death of

McCartney, which he apparently had been privy to during his short time at Apple. However, it seems it was more of a jibe at McCartney, for promising something which he did not deliver on. It also seemed to mock the other Beatles, at least the public's perception of them as a tightly-knit group of friends, which is not what Knight had witnessed. Knight contented himself to the use of many musical and lyrical references to the Beatles' music; in fact, on the original release of the song, Knight had virtually plagiarized whole sections of Beatles' material, particularly 'Hey Jude'. As a result, Knight received a cease-and-desist order from Maclen.

What seems to have aroused suspicion is that Maclen would later release the song, but in a different form, in May of 1969, just as the 'Paul-is-dead' rumour was gathering momentum and a month before the Detroit DJ, Russ Gibb, began spreading the rumour across the airwaves. If its release was only coincidental the rumour certainly helped with the sale of the groups' *Abbey Road* album, and is why many, like WAKR DJ Tony Jay, felt it was 'the most well-planned publicity stunt... *Abbey Road* was out four weeks but wasn't selling so well.'[388]

It seems unlikely that, at least from the point-of-view of the Knight song, that Maclen and the Beatles used this as a conscious publicity stunt, though certainly they were not willing to stop the rumours once the records were selling. However, the Knight song is not convincing evidence of any duplicity, but simply suggests that they didn't want Knight using Beatle material (although obliged in re-releasing the song, re-worked without the copyright infringements, and had worked out a deal with Knight in doing so). It's also possible that McCartney, having not honoured the contract with him and Apple, was happy to make some kind of amends, particularly since Apple was supposed to be a philanthropic venture, aimed at discovering and promoting new talent.

Since the growing popularity of the internet and social media sites, the Paul-is-Dead conspiracy has resurfaced to a greater extent.

While some of this interest has been promoted by amateur bloggers and film-makers, it seems that a number of them, including 'Iamaphoney' and 'The Winged Beatle', were produced by Stand By Films, a subsidiary company of the Beatles' Apple company, and managed by Neil Aspinall, who was a very close friend and personal assistant to the Beatles. When the Beatles set up their Apple company to make records and films, Aspinall was appointed managing director.[389] After Aspinall retired, Paul McCartney took over as managing director.[390]

So why did the Beatles' close friend and managing director of their Apple company allow a film to be made on the subject of Paul McCartney's alleged death – particularly since they tried to distance themselves from the rumours as 'bloody stupid' soon after the initial media coverage of the subject? Is it possible that debate on McCartney's death would have kept him in the public's consciousness, particularly since his music no longer has the impact it once had. That McCartney himself is behind these films, in order to keep him relevant in the public's mind, is a possibility. If we accept John Lennon's claim that McCartney is a 'master of publicity', then certainly it is not beyond the imagination that he may have encouraged the rumour to grow in recent times.

One researcher in this area makes the following point:

> Is McCartney now funding Iamaphoney? I cannot be certain, however, that none of Iamaphoney's YouTube material has been hit with a copyright infringement by Apple seems a little too good to be true and, that the purported reason for the delay in his RevelAtion film seems to be because of a 'cease and desist' order from EMI rather than Apple is also strange.[391]

Esoteric Dimensions to Paul's 'Death'

The *Pepper's* cover was so colourful and so chock-a-block with strange images. Coupled with the LSD culture of the time, that produced an over-active imagination, it is not surprising that such outlandish theories like the death of a Beatle were taken so seriously. The clue-hunting and suggested meanings hidden in the album covers certainly made it seem as if the Beatles' own culture was as mystical and colourful as the fantastical literature that was popular at the time – like *Lord of the Rings*, which was a companion piece to all acid trippers of the day. During that era, there were all sorts of theories about the actual existence of 'Pepperland' and clues as to where it was – and even a telephone number that you could call if you took all the numbers on the album together. The number, it turned out, was that of a British journalist, who remarked that,

> Most callers sound perfectly self-confident, not to say a little 'high', and quite unapologetic about ringing up on a transferred charges basis in the middle of the night... The only common link of the calls is the consistent use of Beatles song language ('Is it true Paul died Wednesday morning at five o'clock?')[392]

Characters such as Lucy in the Sky, Sargent Pepper and Billy Shears became realities for the confused LSD generation, who partly wanted these imaginations to be true.

The *Abbey Road* album appeared – though only two years later – in an atmosphere almost devoid of colour and imagination, at a time when the utopian vision promised by the counterculture had sadly been abandoned, and the cracks in the optimistic outlook of this generation were clearly beginning to show. In this sense, the death clues offered to the imagination, although distorted and nihilistic, could fill the void left by the cultural decline of the decade.

The fact that Beatles' fans, stimulated by the pseudo 'mysticism' of the psychedelic era, might have desperately wanted to have their fantasies realized, was re-enforced by Brian Moriarty, who concluded, in his presentation at a Game Developers' conference in 1999, that the 'Paul-is-Dead' idea was most likely the result of rumour, mischievous, insider joking, and most of all the over-active imagination of the people who became engaged in the idea.[393] Moriarty explains that, as game makers, it is this last element, the imagination, that is the most powerful. Even he, as a young boy, invested, together with his friends, weeks and weeks to clue hunting, unleashing the powerful forces of his own imagination to discover the 'truth' about McCartney.

He says that he never had so much fun hunting for clues with his friends about the rumour, and it was possibly this period in his life that began his interest in gaming. It was, he explains, searching for clues in relation to the 'Paul-is-Dead' rumour, that gave his life meaning at that particular time. It also gave more meaning to his friendships, providing him and his friends with something that only they knew about – a 'Paul-is-Dead' club. All this made the Beatles and their music even more significant to them, even if it was something that had nothing directly to do with the Beatles and more to do with the product of their own imaginations.

Moriarty calls this power of imagining, as applied to gaming, 'constellation', which he describes as a powerful design principle. Constellation is used here as a verb related to pattern recognition, based on the principle of applying order to chaos. When strange and novel ideas are projected into the environment, i.e. into the game, the mind tries to give meaning to these novelties, resulting in something that we expect to see or want to see, a form of self-recognition. The most powerful experiences, which evoke the greatest constellation, are the most novel ones. This is certainly one of the most plausible explanations, and it is almost certainly a huge part of the 'Paul-is-Dead' affair.

Another esoteric consideration is, if we think of the physical world as being the final manifestation of all events that come through the levels of spiritual existence, that things must exist in some other form (akin to Plato's 'world of forms') before they become a physical reality. In relation to the personality of Jesus, for example, as the writer C.S. Lewis explains in his book *Mere Christianity*, his life was the physical manifestation of other stories and mythologies – which it did not copy, but which were fulfilled completely on the physical plane. Those other mythologies, which described the story in non-material forms, were the same story, but understood in the form of the imagination. In other words, the myths preceding the story of Christ's incarnation were the experience of the Christ event on the spiritual or 'imaginative plane', before its final manifestation in the physical world.[394]

Another, though mundane, example can be observed in architecture, where the idea comes in the form of inspiration. It is then sketched out in some basic idea, a blue print, two-dimensional, and then finally into the three-dimensional arena of physical space.

All things must go through the same stages before they become a physical reality. This same notion applies to the Beatles in many of their aspects, such as their formation, Beatlemania, and their break-up. Their break-up was the result of many things, but what made it extremely problematic was the distance that seemed to form between McCartney and the other three, which was primarily the result of Paul's enthusiasm for remaining a Beatle whilst the other three had lost their enthusiasm for the project.[395]

This separation became deeply evident in their relationship with Alan Klein, whom Lennon, Harrison and Starr all welcomed as their new manager, but who McCartney vehemently rejected; also, in the fact that he was unmarried, while the other three were married, and that he lived away from the other three in London, while they lived in Weybridge and socialised more together.

McCartney seemed to be, more often than not, presented somehow differently to the other Beatles, most noticeably on album covers such as *Pepper's*, where he holds a wind instrument instead of the brass instruments the other three hold, while the back cover shows him with his back to the viewer, in contrast to the other three who face forward. The bare-footed McCartney on the *Abbey Road* cover is another example of his appearing different from the others, as is the black carnation instead of the red one in the video for 'Your Mother Should Know'. In the *Yellow Submarine* film, Paul's character is once again set apart, as his is the only character of the four Beatles not sporting a moustache.

Bizarrely, McCartney often 'plays dead' in a number of scenarios with the Beatles, including their mock production of Shakespeare's 'play within a play', *Pyramus and Thisbe*, (not to mention the strange report that he had been born 'dead', due to oxygen-deficiency in the brain).[396] Much of this suggests that McCartney was perhaps separating himself, maybe unconsciously, from the other three – something that became a complete separation when he recorded and released his first solo album, as a distinct project away from the band. From such a perspective, it's possible that McCartney's 'death' was more of a symbolic one, as he began to move himself away from the group, or as the Beatles' publicist Derek Taylor remarked, that deep down there was a 'death wish' that Paul harboured[397] (or again, possibly a subconscious memory of his being 'born dead').

The interesting point of the 28IF licence-plate number on the beetle car on the *Abbey Road* cover, is possibly connected to McCartney's departure from the group, symbolically. He was 27 when the images emerged in public. His 'death' or separation, or possibly his rebirth, resulted when he was 27, a notable age within the realms of pop stardom, where many rock stars had tragically died at this age[398] – an age often associated with certain spiritual laws in which the forces of the individual begin to deteriorate[399] (and if not renewed somehow, bring about the end of the person's creativity, or in many cases their self-destruction, if there is no other means of escape). Lennon also displays this by the time of *Pepper's*, because in 1967, at the age of 27, Lennon had withdrawn into himself, rejecting his position of the Beatles' leader and main songwriter and, subconsciously, handed this role over to McCartney. Lennon would later begin his relationship with Yoko Ono, in some ways a saving grace for him, and into a world of heroin and other unusual activities, with Ono replacing his one-time 'partner', McCartney. Harrison would also go through such an experience, as he was 27 when the Beatles split and he started his major solo career, allowing a rebirth as a major songwriter. Thus, possibly LaBour intuitively picked up on the symbolic 'death' of the group, as presented to the public through their final album *Abbey Road*.

Another thought is that the Beatles were fully aware that this was to be their last studio recording and was a farewell to their fans and the public at large. McCartney's 'The End', which finishes the album, is no accident and was consciously conceived to be the closing song, indicating the final Beatle song ever, and as such the end of the band, their music and the 1960s as a whole. If this was very conscious on behalf of the group, it is possible that their final funeral procession image, on the *Abbey Road* album, was also a conscious symbol and indication to its public that this was in fact the 'death' of the group and the end of the Beatles. If *Pepper's* had been consciously conceived as the death of the Fab Four, again, it is possible that *Abbey Road* was a conscious representation of the death of the Beatles as a band. It's also possible that McCartney's separation from the group – the two symbolic and artistic representations of the Beatles' 'deaths' – mixed with the overactive imagination of the public and the macabre initial rumour of McCartney's car accident, were all misread as McCartney's actual, physical 'death'.

One last consideration is the idea of preserving romantic notions of youth, talent and untimely death within the human psyche. Again, referring to Moriarty's constellations, it was the need to preserve the idea of the youthful romantic symbol of the 1960s (which Paul stood for) and in a sense immortalizing that, as Lennon's death would do two decades later. In relation to the 'Paul-is-Dead' rumour, McCartney supposedly died at 24 – an 'English Orpheus, the beautiful boy' – as Kollerstrom referred to him, or as 'so good, so true, so beautiful that he just had to be … the perfect sacrifice?'[400] Others described him in even more idealistic terms, as if he had no flaws whatsoever – a very one-sided and unrealistic view of a human being. One fan wrote that Paul will be remembered for his 'love', 'heart', 'kindness', 'gentleness', 'compassion', 'empathy', 'genius', 'talent', 'humbleness', 'sincerity', 'generosity', and so on.[401]

Other rock 'n' roll groups had their romantic 'dead god', as encapsulated in the 'I wanna die before I get old' theme. This is an aspect of the Dionysian cult – which became a major part of the rock 'n' roll mythos, through the deaths of iconic figures like Robert John-son, Buddy Holly, Richie Valens, Brian Jones, Jimi Hendrix and Jim Morrison – as Dionysus was an example of a dying god, with many images depicting him as a beardless, sensuous, naked or half-naked androgynous youth — a perfect description of the young McCart-ney. Since the Beatles were the perfect embodiment of the pop-rock culture, surely they too had to have their 'dying god'? By the end of the Sixties, this was captured in the imagination through the invented death of McCartney, but became a reality in 1980 when Lennon, sadly, became the real embodiment of the 'dying god', thus making the story of the Beatles, through all their various stages, the complete expression of the rock 'n' roll myth.

Chapter 9

Ja Guru Deva:
India and Spiritual Regeneration

Maharishi Mahesh Yogi and Transcendental Meditation

By the second half of 1967, the Beatles were searching for answers to some of life's bigger questions. This search would lead them to meditation, eastern philosophy and, eventually, to Rishikesh, India, where, on 16 February 1968, they began a period of study with the Maharishi Mahesh Yogi. The Beatles, growing up as teenagers in Liverpool, were vaguely familiar with the Maharishi through his occasional promotional tours in England. Paul McCartney remembered that:

> We'd seen Maharishi up North when we were kids. He was on the telly every few years, on Granada's *People and Places* programme, the local current-affairs show. We'd all say, 'Hey, did you see that crazy guy last night?' So we knew all about him: he was the giggly little guy going round the globe seven times to heal the world (and this was his third spin).[402]

They began to pay more serious attention to him after George Harrison, who had already become interested in Buddhism and Yoga,[403] had been introduced to the Maharishi's practice of Transcendental Meditation by his friend Ayana Angadi, an Indian intellectual, Trotskyite and critic of colonialism, who was living in England with his English wife Patricia Fell Clarke, both of whom founded the Asian Music Circle.[404] Angadi had been under surveillance by the British Government during the 1940s for his anti-imperial activism and the suspicion that he was a Cominform agent, intent on spreading socialism internationally.[405]

It seems unlikely that Angadi had tried to use the Beatles (through Harrison) to promote Communist ideologies, since Angadi didn't know who the Beatles were until they had contacted him regarding the sitar, which they were recording on Lennon's song 'Norwegian Wood'. Though Harrison became friends with Angadi and his family, and became more acquainted with Indian culture and religion through musicians such as Ravi Shankar, Harrison parted company with Angadi and the Asian Music Circle only about six months after their initial meeting. It seems that Harrison and Angadi did not depart on friendly terms.[406]

It was mainly due to the Beatles' reading of *An Autobiography of a Yogi* by Paramhansa Yogananda – who had started the Self-Realization Fellowship – which told stories of his encounters with yogis and holy men with magical powers, that eastern thought entered into their lives, and subsequently into 1960s' mainstream culture. Harrison, particularly, was impressed by eastern philosophy and culture, and he included many yogis, like Sri Yukteswar, Sri Mahavatara Babaji and Sri Lahiri Mahasaya, on the *Sgt. Pepper's* cover. This finally led him to take a greater interest in the Maharishi.

The Maharishi, who had moved to England in 1959, had begun teaching a very simple, easy-to-learn form of Hindu meditation. What seemed to appeal to westerners was the notion that inner peace could be accomplished without the traditional ways of eastern asceticism. In this sense, the Maharishi was very shrewd. In a radical departure from traditional Hindu teaching, he said there was no conflict between the materialistic ways of day-to-day living and the spiritual path as embodied in his form of meditation. Though spiritual knowledge and techniques are never, traditionally, sold, the Maharishi said – even more shrewdly – that westerners wouldn't value his teachings if they were free.

The Maharishi described his technique 'as a simple, scientific system that brings peace, happiness and success to all who use it'.[407] It was this simple philosophy that most impressed the Beatles. 'I was impressed because he was laughing all the time,' said

Ringo.[408] The feeling was mutual, as the Maharishi told a reporter after the lecture that he thought the Beatles were 'the ideal of energy and intelligence of their generation, and will really bring up the youth on a good level of understanding and intelligence'.[409] Maharishi had connected himself to the School of Economic Science,[410] based on the work of Peter Ouspensky, a Russian mathematician and key exponent of the esoteric doctrines of the spiritual teacher George Gurdjieff. But the Beatles soon became disillusioned with the guru's 'woolly sentiments of universal love' and their feeling that he seemed to have gone from 'innocent mystic to worldly wise business man' shortly after they got involved with him.

The Beatles had essentially been searching for something to counteract their irregular and often complicated Beatle lives, while simultaneously searching for something that couldn't be satisfied by the wealth and fame they had accumulated. The photographer Paul Saltzman recollects an encounter with George Harrison, as he reflected on the emptiness of Beatle life: 'like, we're the Beatles after all, aren't we? We have all the money you could ever dream of. We have all the fame you could ever wish for. But, it isn't love. It isn't health. It isn't peace inside. Is it?'[411] In fact, with their positions as the world's greatest cultural figures, they felt great pressure. They had tried drugs as a distraction and as a crutch, but it soon became ineffective. 'We'd been into drugs, the next step is, you've got to try and find a meaning then', McCartney would later explain.

For the Beatles, the Maharishi and meditation embodied the hope of finding meaning to life's mysteries; of finding 'an end to the confusion and pain that plagues life, often when lived unconsciously, no matter how rich or famous you are'. Before they left for India, Paul expressed to his friend, singer-songwriter Donovan, that they hoped the Maharishi would offer them some answers for both personal and global peace.[412] During an interview with David Frost, Lennon would explain his own, and his generation's desire to find something beyond what their materialistic culture could offer them. 'The youth of today,' he told Frost, 'are really looking for some answers – for proper answers the established Church can't give them, their parents can't give them, material things can't give them.'[413]

This sentiment was again echoed by Saltzman, who like many of his generation would – via the drug culture of the early Sixties – find himself on a journey of self-discovery a few years later. 'Although it was truly helpful', admitted Saltzman,

> within a couple of years I found 'getting high' actually brought me down. I was more tense 'stoned' than 'straight'. I was more perceptive 'straight' than 'stoned'. Hallelujah! For me, drugs were about getting into life, not avoiding life. Going deeper, not shallower. And while people still use soft drugs that way, and sometimes even get such benefits when it is not part of their intentions, unfortunately it's often a tool of escape from one's own inner self. It was at that point, when getting high was occasionally fun, and more often not, that the next step for me was to get away from the environment that had had so much influence in forming me, and I left for India. It seems that often we only need to consciously know the next healthy step in our unfolding. Lao-Tzu wrote: 'The journey of a thousand miles begins with one step.' And for many of us, including John, Paul, George and Ringo, that next step led to long-known wisdoms of the East. To meditation. To Rishikesh.[414]

Maybe Transcendental Meditation was exactly what they needed to carry on being Beatles once again, the chance to retreat into the calm, away from their hectic lives. 'I don't really enjoy being a Beatle any more, its trivial and unimportant. I'm fed up with all this *me, us, I,* stuff and the meaningless things we do... thinking about being a Beatle is going backwards — Hinduism, meditation, philosophy is what matters', confessed Harrison.[415]

The two who were most engrossed in Maharishi's teachings were John and George. They would meditate for hours. Ever keen to put his faith in others, John Lennon proved particularly eager to learn from Maharishi, hoping 'he might slip me the answer!' McCartney commented that this was 'very revealing about John. I suppose everyone is always looking for the Holy Grail. I think John thought he might find it. I think it shows an innocence really, a naivety.'[416]

Shortly after their first meetings with the Maharishi, though about four months before their famous trip to India, the Beatles willingly began to discuss in television interviews the virtues of their newfound belief in Transcendental Meditation. George Harrison would tell David Frost:

> The energy is latently there every day, anyways. So, meditation is just a natural process of contacting it. So, by doing it each day you give yourself a chance of contacting this energy and giving it to yourself a little more. Consequently, you're able to do whatever you normally do – just with a little bit more happiness, maybe… Your actions – whatever they are – are your actions. It's all about your attitude toward other people. If you treat them good, they'll do the same; if you hit them in the face, they'll probably do the same thing. And that's not much to do with religion. Action and reaction, that's the thing Christ was saying. Whatever you do, you get it back. Jesus was one of the divine incarnations. You know, some people like Jesus or Krishna because they were the divine the moment they were born. They chose to reincarnate, to come back in order to try to save a few more people. Whereas others manage to be born just ordinary and attain divinity in that particular incarnation.[417]

A Sudden Exit

The first of the party to leave Rishikesh, less than a fortnight after their arrival, were Ringo and his wife Maureen. Ringo would compare the whole experience as like being at a Butlin's holiday camp. Paul and his girlfriend, Jane Asher, left a few weeks later. Paul was keen to get back to business as usual and start preparations for the launch of the Beatles' Apple record label. 'Paul was more of a businessman than the others and a month of meditating was enough for him.'[418]

A couple of weeks before they were due to leave, one of the Beatles' party accused the Maharishi of behaving improperly with a young American girl, the actress Mia Farrow. 'Without allowing the Maharishi an opportunity to defend himself, John and George', wrote Cynthia Lennon, in her account of her Beatle ex-husband, 'decided we must all leave.' John later told Cynthia that 'he had begun to feel disenchanted with the Maharishi's rumoured sexual misbehaviour. He felt that, for a spiritual man, the Maharishi had too much interest in public recognition, celebrities and money.'[419] Lennon recalled the situation in an interview:

> So we went to see Maharishi, the whole gang of us the next day charged down to his hut, his very rich-looking bungalow in the mountains. And I said, 'We're leaving.' 'Why?' And I said, 'Well if you're so cosmic, you'll know why and he gave me a look like, 'I'll kill you, bastard.' He gave me such a look, and I knew then when he looked at me, because I'd called his bluff. And I was a bit rough to him.[420]

Upon their return, a reporter asked Lennon if the Maharishi was 'on the level'. Lennon quipped, 'I don't know what level he's on, but we had a nice holiday in India and came back rested.'[421] Later, Paul said: 'We made a mistake. We thought there was more to him than there was. He's human. We thought at first that he wasn't.'[422] Years later, John would completely renounce his connection with spiritual leaders like the Maharishi: 'There is no guru. You have to believe in yourself. You've got to get down to your own God in your own temple. It's all down to you, mate.'[423] Farrow would later say that she felt that the Maharishi's attentions hadn't been sexual.

To the Beatles, the Maharishi's rumoured sexuality, however, was really the final straw. They had earlier been concerned about two things: the Maharishi using them to promote himself, and what seemed to be his focus on money – unexpected by them in a spiritual teacher or holy man. Soon after they had been given their mantras, as Apple insider Peter Brown recounts in his book *The Love You Make*, the Maharishi began to use the Beatles, without their permission, to promote himself and his work. It wasn't until Paul and George flew to Sweden, with Peter Brown, and told the Maharishi to his face, that he finally backed off.

In addition, the Beatles were surprised and upset when they learned the Maharishi expected between ten and twenty-five percent of their annual income, deposited to a Swiss bank account in his name. Bill Harry, in his *Encyclopaedia of The Beatles*, concludes:

> Despite the fact that the Beatles' association with him had been brief, the Maharishi's cause had blossomed with the international publicity. The money poured in as the converts grew and the Maharishi immediately began to buy property. In England alone he bought Mentmore Towers in Buckinghamshire, Roydon Hall in Maidstone, Swythamley Park in the Peak District and a Georgian rectory in Suffolk. He set up his headquarters in Switzerland and at one time he was reported to have an income of six million pounds per month, with two million followers worldwide.[424]

Of the Beatles, only George Harrison kept a significant spiritual connection with India. He visited the country a number of times subsequently, consolidating his interest in Indian spirituality and music. And it was Harrison mainly (though Lennon as usual would show a novel interest) who got involved with the Hare Krishna movement.

A.C. Bhaktivedanta Swami Prabhupada, born Abhay Charan De in Calcutta in 1896, was the son of a cloth merchant but became interested with the ancient tradition of Vaishnava Hinduism, a sect founded in the sixteenth century by the monk Chantaiya Mahaprahbu, who believed that by chanting the name of Krishna and studying his life and works, one could become free of the wheel of re-birth. Swami Prabhupada was struck with a revelation in 1965 to bring Krishna consciousness to the 'most spiritually dark place on the planet', namely New York City, and luckily – at least for him – the notion of Krishna consciousness chimed perfectly with the 'acid heads' there. Looking for enlightenment, the New York 'trippers' joined his group, convincing others that Krishna consciousness was like a permanent high – although a discipline of no alcohol, sex, meat or drugs, many of the vices of the hippy generation, was to be strictly observed. The beat poet Allen Ginsberg soon became a convert, giving the movement credibility among the intellectual bohemians of New York. Ginsberg claimed that chanting 'Hare Krishna' would stabilize the consciousness of 'trippers' – similar, interestingly, to how Hoffman had originally viewed the use of LSD.

With the Beatles only just returned from India, the Swami sent devotees to London and to Apple to seduce the band. Harrison, particularly, was charmed and in August 1969 recorded the Hare Krishna chant on Apple records. It hit number 12 in the charts, suggesting that there was a growing acceptance of new ideas and spiritual cultures within both Britain and America.

India and Songwriting

Even though enlightenment had not been attained by the Beatles in India, the music and philosophy of the sub-continent had a key effect on their music, resulting in one of their most productive periods as songwriters. When they returned to England in March and April, they had more songs – some of them directly inspired by Maharishi's lectures – than could fit on a single album, and the subsequent recordings resulted in the eponymously-titled double album (also known as the *White Album*), plus a number of songs which later appeared on *Abbey Road*.

They tentatively began using traditional Indian instruments in 1965, and between 1966 and 1968 the Beatles recorded three songs written by George Harrison with a strong Indian influence. After hearing the name of Ravi Shankar on numerous occasions, Harrison went and bought one of his records: 'I put it on,' he said, 'and it hit a certain spot in me that I can't explain, but it seemed very familiar to me. The only way I could describe it was: my intellect didn't know what was going on and yet this other part of me identified with it.'[425]

Lennon wrote 'Child of Nature', later reworked as 'Jealous Guy' (but which exists today as a demo), and McCartney wrote 'Mother Nature's Son'. Both songs explored similar themes of the majesty and simplicity of nature, while at the same time linking it with the innocence of childhood, untarnished by the 'unnatural' world. Both songs indicate that Lennon and McCartney, as well as the other two Beatles, had felt that they had lost touch with themselves and with the world through their demanding lives as Beatles. As the above songs suggest, John and Paul attempted to reconnect to themselves and the world through the rediscovery of their inner child. Lennon had also written a song called 'India', of which only a demo exists, but which clearly indicates that Lennon and the other Beatles had gone to India in search of something. The song suggests this would be some kind of meaning to life.

Other songs included 'Dear Prudence' and 'Back in the USSR', as well as a song called 'Spiritual Regeneration', a kind of theme song for the Maharishi's programme. Some of Lennon's later compositions would also be inspired by his time in India. 'Across the Universe', for example, with its lyrics 'Ja Guru Deva', and 'Nothing's going to change my world, om', would attempt to capture the fruits of meditation, while describing the interconnectedness of the entire universe.

In his songs 'The Inner Light' and 'Within You, Without You', George Harrison attempted to describe the inner journey to wholeness and true maturity, in all its multifaceted and multi-dimensional grandeur. Harrison draws deeply from the major Hindu spiritual text *The Bhagavad Gita* and makes a conscious attempt to give the listener the ultimate reality — 'glimpse the truth' — which eastern spiritual philosophy refers to as 'Brahman'. Ronald Lee Zigler, in his essay 'Realising It's All Within Yourself', points out that Harrison, singing of the 'space between us all' in 'Within You Without You', is 'clearly identifying the reality of "reduced" awareness. From the perspective of expanded awareness of Brahman, "we are all one" and there is no "space between us all" — that perspective is part of Maya, illusion.'[426]

This notion of Brahman was also expressed in Lennon's line, 'Lay down all thought surrender to the Void', from 'Tomorrow Never Knows', while Lennon also refers to other instructions from *The Bhagavad Gita*, particularly the line, 'Ignorance and haste they mourn the dead', once again referring to the 'reduced' conscious mind. Through ignorance and the inability to grasp the bigger picture (Brahman), it cannot see that death is an impossibility, as the individual soul continues forever on a path of enlightenment, only coming in and out of physical existence. In other words, through the spiritual process of reincarnation, the individual realizes that life does not end with death. As Lennon indicates in the song, we play the 'game existence' to the 'end of the beginning'.[427]

Harrison had written 'Within You, Without You' before he had met the Maharishi, but clearly he had already been moving in a direction of self-awareness and an attempt to understand a universal consciousness sustained by universal love. The song berates those who lack awareness and make no attempt to change – a change that could bring about the salvation of the world. 'With our love we could save the world', Harrison would sing.

Change and impermanence would become major themes in Harrison's solo career, in which he ultimately grasps the nature of Maya and illusion, at least from a traditionally, eastern point-of-view. The future of world prosperity depends entirely on each individual's willingness to embrace Love. Though mostly influenced by the psychedelic movement, the song still gives a clear indication of the spiritual direction Harrison was heading, while the tone of the song also embraces a more eastern sensibility, in which it wanders and flows without any distinct form, almost like a meditation or mantra. By the time he had met the Maharishi, Harrison was, as were the other Beatles, ready for more spiritual instruction. Harrison's next Indian-inspired piece of music, 'The Inner Light', went deeper into the notions of meditation and self-fulfilment through inactivity, again another eastern concept, which Harrison had discovered in the Taoist holy book *Tao Te Ching*.

Much of Harrison's solo work would deal with his interest in spirituality, particularly that of an eastern inclination, and he was greatly inspired by the teaching of yogi Paramhansa Yogananda, who taught that: 'Indian music is a subjective, spiritual, and individualistic art, aiming not at symphonic brilliance but at personal harmony with God. The Sanskrit word for musician is *bhagavathar*, "he who sings the praises of God."'[428]

The White Album

The *White Album* was the start of the end for the band as a group of four tightly-knit individuals who had brought major happiness to the world, opening the floodgates for rock and pop musicians and songwriters. The Beatles had provided the world with a kind of spiritual healing following World War Two and during the Cold War, with its constant threat of nuclear wipe-out. The spiritual fabric that brought both the Beatles and the Sixties together overall was unravelling, and throughout the world it was certainly evident that the happiness of the Sixties was just an illusion, a dream that could only be hoped for. 'People were frightened about the Sixties coming to an end', says Beatle historian Philip Norman, and there was a neurotic feeling in the air, as if time was running out. The euphoria of the Sixties would soon be over.[429] The revolutions and distress throughout the western world indicated that the dream was certainly over, and that a new and much heavier and darker phase was beginning — one which had no place for a band like the Beatles, and one which was more and more affected by the self-consciousness that had emerged through the decade.

The Beatles had splintered into four mature and distinctly individual people who had lost their deeper spiritual connection with
each other and with the broader culture. As the Beatles' magic
waned, the music they would create after the Beatles – though significant in some senses – was not in any way as important or influential as that which they had made together as a band.

The *White Album*, however, was significant in that it captured the
essence of spiritual and cultural decay. It was the winter of their
career, symbolically expressed by the harshness of the sound and
the songs, as well as the sparse, white album cover, that seemed to
suggest both nothing and everything. In one sense, the plain white
cover was an empty canvas, with no indication of Beatle history
– while at the same time it was a blank canvas on which an end-
less number of possibilities could be projected. The cover in such
a sense represented the end of the Sixties, the end of the Beatles, of
the dream of peace, love and harmony, while simultaneously leaving open the possibilities of something more conscious and progressive for their individual futures, as well as that of society, as it
entered a new decade.

Once again, there was something intuitive about the Beatles even
at the point of their demise, which would parallel the demise of
the utopian dream that had looked so promising and which was
grasped, for a brief moment, during the later section of the era,
particularly in 1967, with the 'Summer of Love'. In some senses,
both the pop culture of the 1960s and the Beatles realized the need
for a positivity to counteract those otherwise negative forces. At
the same time, it was soon to be realized by the Beatles, and society itself, that it just couldn't last. It was an illusion, a dream from
which they and their generation were awakening. The period of
revolution signified this realization, with the Paris Revolution (May
1968), the Prague Spring (Jan-Aug 1968) and student demonstra-
tions worldwide.

Flower-power and the peace movements were genuine attempts
to counteract commercialism, the war and the mass technological

advancements that had sprung up after World War Two, pointing in an alternative direction, away from a focus on material greed and toward a world of unity, peace and spiritual evolution. The Beatles reflected this duality in society. Their Indian period began the end of a group of four individuals working as a cohesive and complementary unit, a perfect idea of how society itself could function[430] and the wonderful creations it could produce, but they were now, due to their own self-interests, pulling in opposing directions. The ideal symbolized in the Beatles was seen by the public, but beneath the surface the reality was much different.

The reality began to show, in fact, just before their sojourn in India, while they were in Bangor with the Maharishi and when their manager Brian Epstein died of a supposed drug-related incident. This was the first real tragedy of the Beatles since they had become public figures, the first of its original members to go. A quintessential member of the group that kept them together on a spiritual and managerial level was gone, escalating their own inevitable deterioration.

Epstein had metaphorically died once his significant role as the group's manager had been severely curtailed by their decision not to tour any longer. Although his personal life was fraught with difficulties, Epstein's death seemed to be so interconnected with his role as Beatles' manager that his life simply evaporated once his role was no longer important. The dependency and symbiosis of his life with the Beatles may suggest, keeping with the philosophical ideas they were exploring at the time, a life karmically linked to these four other individualities. This seems also to have been the case with Mal Evans, the Beatles' devoted roadie, who after the breakup of the Beatles lost all sense of purpose. He was, tragically, shot dead by a policeman when he had supposedly lost control one night and became dangerously violent.[431]

The violent death of Lennon and attack on Harrison were indications of the aggression that became associated with a group that had been full of life-affirming love and joy. Death, it seems, surrounded the group; and even the ever-blessed McCartney couldn't escape the clutches of the Grim Reaper, with strange conspiracies surrounding his 'death', many of which, as we have seen, gained more and more momentum over the years. The most deranged association in this regard comes from the rather dark connection made between the group and Charles Manson and his Family, who was convicted for the murder of a number of people at a house party in 1969, pinning the blame on the supposed subliminal messages in the Beatles' music (see Chapter 10).

India had been a huge influence in the lives of the four Beatles, inspiring them towards spiritual regeneration on many levels – an influence that was particularly lasting on George Harrison whilst providing other avenues of philosophical exploration and creative inspiration for their music (all four Beatles would continue the practice of meditation, for example, a practice which is still to this day promoted by McCartney and Starr).[432] However, India was, it turned out, only a brief though important stop on their road to self-discovery and spiritual awakening. They all clearly realized that though India had much to offer, it wasn't really where they belonged. Lennon would sum it up in lyrics from his song 'India'. 'I'm searching', he sings 'for an answer but I know I'll never find it here it's already in my mind', and 'I left my heart in England... I've got to follow my heart and my heart is going home.'

The Decadent Mysteries of the East

Although much of what the Beatles had learned from their association with the Maharishi had brought them to an awareness of spiritual ideas that had long been estranged to western thought, it had reintroduced to popular awareness the following notions and concepts: karma and reincarnation; that the material universe is an illusion; that the mind is the throne of all knowledge and understanding; and that peace, happiness and personal fulfilment could not be sought in the material world of Maya – the Hindu notion of material existence being an illusion – while only a true grasp of the inner life could bring about fulfilment and happiness.

The Beatles, though already on a path of spiritual awakening and self-knowledge as a result of the particular direction society had been moving, came to understand these ideas much more during the time they spent in India, and thus brought these concepts further into public awareness in the West. Some felt the Maharishi was responsible for a distortion of spiritual truths through eastern concepts and ideas, particularly as they were filtered through the Theosophical Society (an organization set up in the late nineteenth century, intent on bringing spiritual enlightenment to the western world, but whose spiritual ideologies were mostly influenced by eastern religions), or more accurately, through the personality of Helena Blavatsky (who claimed her books the *Secret Doctrine* and *Isis Unveiled* were inspired by eastern Masters called the Mahatmas). Whether this is accurate or not is not easy to say, but there is a belief that many of these ideas from the East were out of time for the development of modern western spiritual development.

Around 1875, Blavatsky wrote about Rosicrucian wisdom in her *Isis Unveiled*. According to Rudolf Steiner, much of this wisdom was confused, and later she came under the influence of a particular group of eastern, Tibeto-Indian occultists, who inspired her next book *The Secret Doctrine*, with its strongly anti-Christian bent. 'These occultists', says one writer:

> were the 'Mahatmas', whose teachings derived from a pre-Christian occult wisdom which held Lucifer higher than Christ, but also had a strongly materialistic and atheistic tinge. This 'occult materialism' did not deny the existence of higher beings (up to a point), or the human afterlife and reincarnation under the law of karma (indeed, the concept of karma entered western culture mostly through the Theosophical Society), but it did deny the existence of a theistic God and held that the higher realms consist only of refined, subtle matter.[433]

Again, according to Steiner the 'Mahatmas' sought revenge on the western world for suppressing eastern occultism and interference in and domination of the East. It has been said that the 'Mahatmas' who supposedly inspired Blavatsky despised western culture.[434] From this point-of-view, the Mahatmas were considered to be connected to secret brotherhoods in the East, who were working with secret brotherhoods in the West to prevent humanity's proper spiritual development, and to enslave them in a spiritually-dead Earth. It is thought that these Mahatmas also inspired the Russian Theosophist, Helena Roerich and her philosophy of Agni Yoga.[435]

Helena Roerich's husband, Nicholas Roerich, was a kind of New Age Buddhist, whom some viewed as being behind occult symbols that are 'hidden' in common-day American images (also used by the United Nations), and has been seen as a key figure behind the development of a 'slave' society, similar to that described by Aldous Huxley in his famous book *Brave New World* (1932). [436] He was also possibly a Soviet agent[437] who seemingly supported Karl Marx and the Russian Bolsheviks. The 'Mahatmas' appeared to be cooperating with Anglo-American secret societies in promoting the 'socialist experiment' in Russia.[438]

The following passage indicates how involved Roerich was in all this:

> The Tibetan Lamas and the Himalayan Mahatmas preach the identity of the communist ideas with Buddha's teachings. A.E Bystrov, the Soviet consul in Urumchi, who was befriended by Roerich, commented on his meeting with Roerich in April 1926 by noting that Roerich's aim was 'To ally Buddhism and Communism and to create the Great Eastern Union of Republics' and [that he] claimed that among Tibetan and Indian Buddhists 'there is a current belief that their liberation from the foreign yoke will come precisely from the Reds in Russia – the Northern Red Shambhala'. Mahatma Morya also repeatedly expressed support in statements such as 'Everything has changed – Lenin is with us', and 'Communism is necessary for evolution'. In the spring of 1926, Morya

had already drawn up a nine-point plan for negotiations with official bodies in Moscow, including declarations that Buddha's teachings were revolutionary and that Maitreya was the symbol of Communism.[439]

The anthroposophist Sergei O. Prokofieff claims that the 'Mahatmas' in question, who inspired Helena Roerich, were not the same Masters that inspired Blavatsky, but were black occultists 'who had illicitly appropriated their names and then tried – while deliberately misleading their followers – to attain their highly dubious occult political aims with the help of the occult movements which had already been initiated'. Prokofieff further claims that the messages received by Roerich were a distortion of eastern wisdom that encouraged a kind of 'occult materialism' that had 'insidious political goals', namely the creation of a One World Government with a One World secular religion (one might even suspect Lennon's song 'Imagine' may have been an anthem for such a world order).[440]

Many of Helena (and Nicholas) Roerich's ideas were later developed by individuals like Alice Bailey and her Lucis Trust organisation, which reportedly holds the spiritual being 'Lucifer' as the true wisdom of mankind, and which seems to have inspired contemporary individuals, like Benjamin Creme and his Share International Movement. The fact that Lucis Trust is today the spiritual/religious element of the United Nations, adopting Bailey's ideas into their 'Five Rays of Hope' campaign, which they began at the end of 2021, to 'do better'[441] – a campaign that chimes with another post Covid-19 globalist plan to 'Build Back Better',[442] – seems to support at least the possibility of Prokofieff's claims. This movement has been for some time preparing the way for the coming of the 'Maitreya Buddha', or the reappearance of 'Christ', as laid out in Bailey's book *Reappearance of the Christ*. The Theosophical Society, under the aegis of the mystic Annie Besant and the American journalist Henry Steel Olcott, had made claim to finding the reincarnated 'messiah' in the form of Jiddu Krishnamurti as a young boy, but he later, in adulthood, rejected this notion and eventually taught of the negative influence of leaders per se in the search for spiritual enlightenment.

The notions and teachings of these individuals seem to have a strong connection to the idea of the new 'Aquarian Age' (see Chapter 6), which was to be a time of great spiritual awakening and which the Sixties were supposed to encapsulate. There seems to be much misunderstanding of this Age, which did not, it would seem, at least from Rudolf Steiner's perspective, become a reality in the 1960s. In many ways, the 1960s did not in the end become the great spiritual awakening it was hoped to be. In fact, the Beatles' unsatisfactory association with India, as well as their disjointed White Album, appear to suggest that the promise of a 'Great Age' had been lost.

Though some, including his one-time followers, have exposed Maharishi as 'a fraud from the very beginning',[443] he is not necessarily linked to such people as the above-mentioned Roerich or Alice Bailey – yet it is interesting to read Benjamin Creme's tribute to Maharishi on his Share International website: 'Like the many other Gurus who have come from India, the Maharaishi has helped to prepare a huge group of people for the work of Maitreya.'[444] The point here is not to say that ideas coming from the East have always been negative for the West. However, some of these inspirations, like those emanating from the list of personalities above, as well as the misuse of psychotropic drugs (which have a strong eastern association, and which should be reserved for use by the shaman or those already spiritually enlightened),[445] are not necessarily the best practices for the western mind, whose path has been somewhat different. From the point-of-view of contemporary spiritual practises, such as those outlined by Rudolf Steiner, the western path is to engage with clear, precise and conscious thinking. The grounds for such practice are set out in Steiner's book The Philosophy of Freedom (1916), in which thinking in its highest form is described as an actual spiritual activity and not just a function of the brain, as our materialist view of science likes to believe. Such conscious thinking can be a path of spiritual growth and development.

What is clear regarding the Maharisihi, however, was his desire for self-promotion, material wealth, and his intention to use the Beatles in order to gain greater public awareness (which he certainly did), and to benefit from them financially. The Beatles, although immensely talented in artistic realms, were not always so discerning in other matters, particularly financial (with the exception of McCartney, though more so after the Beatles disbanded). They were also less discerning in associating with groups and movements, and were often at the mercy of those who wished to use them for their own ambitions, including individuals such as Timothy Leary, Alan Klein and the Maharishi too.

The Maharishi, together with the splintering of the group, the revolutions throughout the world, the murders by the Manson Family and the numerous deaths of pop's aristocracy – including Jim Morrison, Brian Jones, Jimi Hendrix, Brian Epstein, Janis Joplin and the tragic death at the Altamont rock show (discussed in Chapter 10) – all seemed to signal the end of an era; an era that seemed to have turned from the light to the dark. The Sixties' idea of freedom as self-realization had, by the end of the decade, given way to a sense of freedom based on egotism and self-importance (freedom as license, as the German idealist philosopher Hegel refers to it). Lennon's meeting with the Maharishi was ultimately the last straw in his realization that all was a smokescreen, and that the world they had lived in was indeed Maya, an illusion, a dream.

For Lennon, 'nothing is real' and as a result he succumbed to the reveries of heroin, which enabled him to ignore the sense of disillusionment of the 1960s, while the rest of the Beatles and Sixties' society had suddenly woken up to the reality. Lennon would sum-up the whole business of the Beatles, including their time with the Maharishi, in his song 'Nobody Loves You (When You're

Down and Out)', singing that 'everybody's hustling for a buck and a dime... All I can tell you is, it's all show biz'.

Despite some unfortunate episodes in their Indian period, the East gave the Beatles a language to express their experiences, and enabled them to cope with the illusion of being Beatles and the need to expand consciousness beyond what was 'normal'. Harrison would adopt the language of *The Bhagavad Gita* and Hinduism, mixed with western Christianity, for the rest of his life – something his Liverpool upbringing, swinging London or the consumer culture of America could not have done for him. Much of this was put into his *All Things Must Pass* album. George's interest in spiritual things, as he remarked to Hunter Davis, 'will last forever – reaching a blissful state is the most important thing'.[446] Harrison, however, would often fall prey to certain religious sects, particularly the Maharishi and the Hare Krishnas, who made good use of the hospitality offered to them by Apple Records by using it as a halfway house.

Though the end of the 1960s had turned dark and the Beatles had collapsed – their *Let It Be* album being evidence of it – they sought to bring some element of the decade's positivity back into the decaying era. The result was *Abbey Road* (which was released before *Let it Be*, but recorded after). Not an album necessarily inspired by the same sources as their earlier work, the four Beatles and producer Martin nevertheless made a concerted effort to leave the band and the 1960s on a positive note. They did what only they could have done, and exactly what they *should* have done, i.e. leave a silver lining in a very dark and cloudy sky. Interestingly, the Beatles had managed to do this out of their own forces – forces which they had individually and collectively garnered through their time as Beatles. Thus, the Beatles came into the Sixties and left with the same note of positivity – entering the decade somewhat unconsciously and leaving it with a positivity created out of their own conscious efforts. *Abbey Road* encouraged the culture to ask the very important question about whether, indeed, the 'love you make is equal to the love you take'.

A Step in the Right Direction

The Beatles had gone through a vast array of different experiences. They had begun their lives in the everyday, naively realistic consciousness that would prevail in the traumatized and paralyzed British society after the war; a consciousness that was guided primarily by an overly simplified idea of authoritarian politics in which the custodians of the nation took care of their citizens. In fact, a number of films in the late Sixties, particularly *Oh What a Lovely War* (1969), would challenge the idea that the leaders and rulers of the country actually had any real interest in or concern for the less privileged classes of their society. From such a perspective, these classes (the classes from which the Beatles themselves had emerged), were simply considered disposable pawns, used to further the aims and ambitions of the country's rulers.

However, the propaganda that had ensued during and after the war brought about a kind of religious fervour for the so-called custodians of the nation and individuals like Churchill (who history is beginning to view in a different light) as being tremendous benefactors of the people.[447]

The post-war consciousness that the individual members were born into was propped up by the conventional institutions of the time, of which the Church bodies, such as the Anglican Church and the Catholic Church, had a huge influence – maybe not on everyday consciousness as such, but in the hierarchical system propagated by the western ideologies of the time. This ideology tended to uphold the patriarchal systems of capitalism, out of which a new religion of consumer, self-centred culture arose. It was within this newly established consumer culture that the Beatles had seen their main aspirations and desires, focusing on the objectives of personal wealth and fame – although a certain rebellious unorthodoxy was also always present within their makeup.

By the time of Beatlemania, the Beatles had become disillusioned with the modern notions of success, and as a result their artistic, philosophical and personal outlook chimed with the search for personal salvation. The inward-looking psychedelic movement – a movement which, due to its dependency on the often unreliable, unpredictable LSD – was later rejected by the Beatles as being an unsatisfactory path towards personal enlightenment and realization. But if LSD had not been considered an authentic way to true enlightenment, it was certainly viewed by the Beatles as a necessary step, and above all gave them an understanding beyond what was traditionally handed down and often accepted unconsciously. The modernist composer and astrologer Dane Rudhyar would suggest the same, i.e. that although LSD and the attitude of the Sixties did not achieve any kind of transcendence, it did contribute to the disintegration of the rigid social structures of modern western society.[448]

J. Stillson Judah, in his book *Hare Krishna and The Counterculture*, stated that alternative religious movements, like the Krishna Consciousness movement that flourished in the 1960s, appealed to many of the post-war generation who desired, 'to rediscover a reality beyond the realm of logical validation of an established culture'.[449] They were 'seeking to validate an alternative style of life – a new culture and a new set of values – a new consciousness through meaningful shared experience in a religious context'.[450]

The search for such a philosophical basis on which one could conduct one's life was later found in the religious practices of the East, essentially Buddhism, Hinduism and the concepts of karma and reincarnation. 'The only thing that is important in life,' Harrison would realize, 'is karma; Samsara is the recurrence of all your lives and deaths'[451] – a step on the pathway to realizing something beyond the limitations of Maya and materialism. 'This actual world is an illusion. It's been created by worldliness and identification with objects',[452] said George's wife Pattie Boyd, who had been as interested in eastern culture as her husband. Their LSD period naturally led to a desire to pursue a spiritual life in a more natural and self-conscious manner, ultimately leading them to embrace Transcendental Meditation. This was a definite attempt to bridge the gap between East and West and deal with the question of East-West polarities. This approach brought to popular culture a greater understanding of the somewhat esoteric notions of karma and reincarnation, as well as an understanding of cosmic law and universal wisdom. 'I know,' said Pattie Boyd, considering the karmic connection between the Beatles:

> ... it was part of a pattern... it all follows a path, just like our path. John, Paul and George converged, then a little later Ringo. We were part of that action, which led to the next reaction. We were all just little cogs in an action that everyone is part of... you go on being reincarnated, till you reach the absolute truth. But heaven and hell are just a state of mind. Whatever it is you create it.[453]

Lennon would echo this sentiment when he indicated that he had no fear of dying, suggesting that 'death is getting out of one car and getting into another'.[454]

The notions of karma and reincarnation are again expressed in this idea of Pattie's: 'We were made John, Paul, George and Ringo because of what we did last time, it was all there for us, on a plate. We're reaping what we sowed last time, whatever it was.'[455] Even 'Strawberry Fields Forever' underlines the nihilistic view of Maya, in which Lennon declares 'nothing is real'. Lennon, however, would essentially reject that philosophy, although he would often continue to use the mystical language of the East, of Sufism and eastern mysticism. Harrison would do the same, but ultimately they would reject their earlier attempts to find salvation in drugs or eastern mysticism and would fundamentally exclaim a more Christian notion: 'The reason why we're all here,' suggests Harrison, 'is to achieve perfection, to become Christlike.'[456]

Chapter 10

The Dream Is Over:
Assassinations, Murders and Mind Control

Paint It Black

By the end of the decade, the Sixties' utopian dream of peace, love and hope had turned into a nightmare of death, violence and darkness, leaving an entire generation to wonder just how things had turned out so bad as, 'events around the globe foreshadowed a more sinister and chaotic world to come. Riots and an era of bloody strife, the murder of Sharon Tate and the Sixties' dream turned into a nightmare.'[457] Three events, particularly, dashed the hopes of the New Age. The first was the Manson (LaBianca/Tate) Murders, the second was the Rolling Stones' concert at Altamont, and the third was the breakup of the Beatles (the very symbol of Sixties' idealism).

Suddenly, right at the end of the Sixties the Beatles' announced their break up — 'the event', said one reporter, 'was so momentous that historians may view it as a landmark in the decline of the British Empire'.[458] Their 'magical quality', as Bob Stanley observed, their 'magic cloak of protection', seemed to vanish immediately as 'John was now coarse and self-pitying, Paul uptight and catty, George sat cross-legged behind his beard, and Ringo drank for England, while singing maudlin country from his barstool. They had always tried to tell us, and we finally had to face the truth: they were only human.'[459] Philip Norman had observed that people were frightened about the Sixties coming to an end, because everyone knew that the Sixties was something special. The Beatles' *Let It Be* is full of this sense of mourning.[460]

The Manson Murders

On 9 August 1969, a number of celebrity figures were murdered in a gruesome and horrific attack, by what were presented to the general public, as 'spaced out hippys', brainwashed by a 'messianic figure of darkness', who had been indoctrinated by the hippy culture of anarchy, rebellion, and the occult ideas of Aleister Crowley, as well as counterculture figures like Timothy Leary and Ken Kesey, whose Merry Pranksters had been emulated by Charles Manson's cult group, the Family, in their notion of 'free spiritedness'.

The media had covered the trial of Manson, presenting it as symbolic of how the 'Love' and 'Peace' ideology of the flower-power generation, with no guiding authorities, had been transformed into a 'Lord of the Flies' type scenario. The gruesome death of the young and beautiful Hollywood hopeful Sharon Tate, who was with child, and the murder of the LaBiancas, a supermarket executive and his wife living in Hollywood, Los Angeles, had horrified the public, who condemned not just Manson and his brainwashed cult followers, but the counterculture as a whole. Whatever sympathies had been with it and with the hippys prior to the murders, now soon vanished.

The Beatles, unfortunately, got caught up in the whole affair with Manson, who claimed that hidden messages had been fed to him through their music. This subject of subliminal recordings had, strangely enough, recently come into public consciousness in September of that year, just months before the Manson trial and the media's coverage of it, when the rumours of Paul McCartney's 'death' grabbed the attention of the international Press.

The notion that the Beatles had brainwashed Manson and the other murderers with songs from their *White Album*, and were thus in league with the Devil, was not, in some respects, too unimaginable, considering the controversies that had surrounded the Beatles throughout their career, particularly in America. Manson would claim that the Beatles' music had convinced him of the revolution to come, in which society would be turned upside down, 'Helter Skelter' like, and those in control would be ousted.

Manson saw the Beatles as the Four Horsemen of the Apocalypse, similar in the ways that others, such as Timothy Leary, had seen them in their prophetic roles, signalling an 'end of times'. In Manson's mind, the *White Album* track 'Helter Skelter' described Chapter 9 of the Book of Revelation, with the Beatles seen – by him – as the four angels who would wreak death upon a third part of mankind. Manson found scriptural basis for himself as a fifth Beatle, the angel of the bottomless pit, a role in which he was to prepare his disciples to kill. The song 'Revolution Number 9' was, for Manson, an order for him to rise up against elements of society. The word 'rise' was for this reason scrawled in blood across the LaBiancas' wall. The song 'Blackbird' was interpreted, again by Manson, as a 'racist doom' song, while 'Sexie Sadie' was, seemingly, a signal to Susan Atkins, aka Sadie Mae Glutz, one of Manson's girlfriends and disciples, to revolt and murder.

The Beatles' all-white cover of the *White Album* – according to Ed Sanders, author of the book on the Manson Murders, *The Family* (1971) – was symbolic to the Manson Family. Manson, he wrote, had a hypnotic rap about how blacks were arming themselves. He announced that black people would rise up, kill a few million whites, take over the reins of government and, through their 'super awareness' — in the words of the Family — would know that Charlie was 'where it was at', and 'nod' him into power.[461]

The Manson trial, one of the biggest in history and certainly the most media-focused, had a very strong impact on the public consciousness and, particularly, on how people viewed or reviewed the counterculture – many feeling that although 'love' and 'peace' are worthy concepts, these ideas could turn to anarchy without order. The Manson Murders, for this reason, presented an anarchistic picture of the flower-power children, whose misguided ideals soon descended into extreme anti-social behaviour. No one took Manson's connection to the Beatles seriously, and as such the band and their reputation didn't really suffer. However, Manson was perceived as a psychotic maniac and, whatever the motives behind the

Manson Murders, it was a very definite sign that the golden era of the Sixties had darkened.

The Rolling Stones and Altamont

A few months after the Manson Murders but before the trial had become a media sensation, the Rolling Stones, the second most popular band of the Sixties, and in many ways the symbol of the anti-establishment types behind the counterculture, were also involved in their own black day; another omen that the 'New Aquarian Age' was nothing more than an unrealizable pipedream.

On 6 December 1969, with the moon fully in Scorpio, an ominous sign in astrological terms, the Rolling Stones – in an attempt to remain relevant by following a trend of free concerts that many underground bands, like the Grateful Dead and Jefferson Airplane, performed – gave their own free concert in Altamont, California. The Stones, by trying to ingratiate themselves with the hippys, unfortunately encountered one of the darkest events of their career, casting a dark shadow over the Sixties for at least the next decade.

Very early on in their career, the Stones had set themselves up as the anti-Beatles, and so powerful was their PR that they began to believe it themselves, going so far as to encapsulate in their image and performance the notions that they were in fact in league with the devil. Jagger, always the businessman, saw a new fad in the occult, and began to connect himself to occult figures like the filmmaker Kenneth Anger. Their song 'Sympathy for the Devil' was inspired by the book the *Master and Margarita* (1967), and inspired Anger's film *Lucifer Rising* (1972). Jagger was seen branding the name Satan across his chest for the performance of the song in the band's *Sgt. Pepper's* inspired movie, *The Rolling Stones' Rock 'n' Roll Circus* (a disastrous film, from the Rolling Stones point-of-view, which only saw the light of day many years later).

Keith Richards, as well as Brian Jones and his girlfriend Anita Pallenberg, also dabbled with the occult and some forms of black magic. Richards would even claim, in a *Rolling Stone* interview, that 'witchcraft, magic and Satanism was something everyone should explore' and that he was an 'agent for Lucifer',[462] while his girl-friend Anita Pallenberg 'was obsessed with black magic'.[463] Marianne Faithfull, who was very much part of the Rolling Stones scene throughout the late Sixties, however, suggests that the interest in such things was only a naive fascination in 'the usual hippie stuff', and nothing more.[464]

By the time the Stones had taken to the stage, to an audience of nearly 500,000, the atmosphere was very dark. 'Half a million people together, with neither rules nor regulations as to how they must conduct themselves, can through sheer physical weight create terrible destruction... you felt that the next few seconds or minutes you could die... a bad dream but we were all in it', wrote one journalist.[465] By the time the band had got to 'Sympathy for the Devil', all hell had, literally, broken loose.

The Hells Angels, who were there in the capacity of security guards, were attacking the other bands and the audience, who had become extremely unsettled, while Jagger pleaded with the crowd and the Angels to 'be cool'. His words made little impression. One young black boy, Meredith Hunter, pulled a gun on a group of Hells Angels, who were bullying him. The Angels brought him to the ground and kicked and beat him until he was a lifeless corpse, while the band played 'Brown Sugar', a song of 'sadism, savagery, race hate/love, a song of redemption, a song that accepted the fear of night, blackness, chaos, the unknown, the fear that the mad-eyed Norsemen, transplanted from Odin drunk mead halls to California desert, were still seeking mad eyed to escape.'[466] According to researcher Mae Brussell, Altamont was nothing other than a 'ritualistic murder'.[467]

While the Stones were not held legally responsible for the death, there was a sense of immorality that lingered around the band and the whole affair, and when a film of the concert, which was a major source of the whole problem, was released sometime later, the Press came out with the condemning headline 'Making Murder Pay', describing the whole affair thus:

> It is touched by the epic opportunism and insensitivity with which so much of the rock phenomenon has been promoted, and written about, and with which I suspect the climatic concert at Altamont was conceived.[468]

The event was widely condemned, leading the writer Germaine Greer to voice the opinion that 'the rock revolution failed because it was corrupted. It was incorporated in the Capitalist system, which has power to absorb and exploit all tendencies including the tendencies towards its own overthrow.'[469]

Assassinations

For many years after the break-up of the Beatles, people had hoped that the golden age of the Sixties could be relived, at least for one last time, and that this could be done through a reforming of the Beatles. While the Beatles were still busy working out their own personal difficulties, the possibility of reforming was never entirely dismissed (in fact, according to some sources Lennon, the most hostile to the idea, had certainly been reconsidering it).[470] However, on 8 December 1980, the long hoped-for reunion was made an impossibility when John Lennon was shot outside his Dakota apartment in Manhattan, where he lived with his wife Yoko Ono.

For most people, the mainstream reporting of the events surrounding the murder of Lennon provided sufficient evidence to bring the whole situation to a conclusion. Lennon's murderer, Mark David Chapman – the official story goes – was simply a psychologically-disturbed 'lone nut', who wanted to achieve worldwide fame by killing someone famous.

Though most people accepted the plausibility of this theory – a convenient excuse to not present a logical and conclusive motive for a murder – there have been many researchers who have refused to accept this explanation. Interestingly, Lennon's son, Sean Lennon, believed 'it was in the best interests of the United States to have my dad killed, definitely'.[471] Mae Brussell, a friend of the Lennons and one of the first radio show researchers who had delved deeper into the assassinations of John and Robert Kennedy – which she felt had been given a superficial coverage – also felt that suspicious circumstances surrounded Lennon's murder.

Brussell, when discussing the 'lone nut' theory, said that single crimes of passion are easy to explain and easy to solve. However, when someone is gunned down – particularly someone like Lennon who is controversial, has political enemies, is hated by wealthy and well-organized religious movements, and is an open opponent of government policies at home and abroad – that kind of murder requires much more inquiry into the background of the assassin. The conclusions about the murder motive may turn out to be simple, yet in every political assassination since 1963 there were always more unanswered questions that led to a broader supposition of intention to kill by a group of people, rather than a single individual.[472]

Brussell covered the Lennon assassination six days after the tragic event, and though she didn't give any conclusive answers to its motive, she points out that there were many people who were upset with Lennon and his anti-war and anti-establishment stance. Lennon's 'Give Peace a Chance' campaign seemed to create great disturbance to those who wished for war both politically and financially, not to mention 'occult brotherhoods', who understood that war was a means to gain control over people and nations. 'Anybody who sings about love and harmony and life is dangerous to anyone singing about death', opined Brussell, while the writer Gore Vidal echoed these remarks, saying that 'Lennon was everything the American government hated'.[473]

According to government agents, Lennon wanted to awaken 'power' in the people, and had an intellectual force that other rock stars, like Mick Jagger – though superficially anti-establishment – didn't have.[474] Lennon thought that: 'Our society is run by insane people with insane objectives'[475] and, according to lawyer and one-time FBI field agent George Gordon Liddy, it was for these reasons that Lennon needed to be monitored.[476] FBI agent M. Wesley Swearingen confirmed this, saying that during the Seventies Lennon was not a threat until he started financing the people that the government were trying to put in jail.[477] Lennon was connected to political radicals like John Sinclair, Abbie Hoffman and Bobby Seal of the Black Panthers (an African-American revolutionary movement) as well as the broader counterculture. The government harassed anyone who was voicing dissent.[478]

British lawyer and journalist Fenton Bresler studied Lennon's murder for eight years, conducting unprecedented interviews and extracting a ream of previously unreleased government documents, which became the background for his book *Who Killed John Lennon?* Richard Nixon, his administration and other right-wing politicians (including ultra-conservative senator Strom Thurmond – who personally sent a memo to Attorney General John Mitchell on the subject of John Lennon) were, claims Bresler, fixated on what they saw as the 'Lennon problem'. To them, the politically outspoken singer-songwriter was an insidious subversive of the worst kind – the famous and beloved kind! Under the Freedom of Information Act, Bresler obtained U.S. government files on Lennon which showed that Lennon was under constant government surveillance, especially during the years 1971–72.[479] Some of the files relating to Secret Service investigations into Lennon's activities, which remain closed, continue to fuel suspicions of a cover-up. One page of Lennon's FBI file bears the handwritten, block-lettered, underlined words: 'ALL EXTREMISTS SHOULD BE CONSIDERED DANGEROUS'.[480]

According to Brussell, the new government were prepared to build up the Pentagon war machine and increase the potential for war against the USSR. Their first strikes would fall on small countries like El Salvador and Guatemala. Lennon was the only man (even without his fellow Beatles) who had the ability to draw out one million anti-war protestors in any given city within 24 hours, if he opposed those war policies. An example of Lennon's political power was witnessed when he got John Sinclair freed from prison. This happened only forty-eight hours after he played at a benefit gig to bring attention to what the organizers of the event felt was a very harsh and unfair ten-year sentence for cannabis possession.[481]

In his book *John Lennon – Life, Times, and Assassination,* author Phil Strongman takes a similar stance to Brussell and Bresler, claiming that the official story was a fabrication and that Mark David Chapman was a stooge. While any mention of Chapman's name is now accompanied by the phrase 'deranged fan', it seems he was anything but. He was no more or less an ardent Beatles/Lennon fan than anyone of his generation. His real rock hero was, seemingly, Todd Rundgren, 'a cynical studio craftsman who could not be further from Lennon in artistic sensibility',[482] while his announcement that he killed Lennon to promote the reading of *The Catcher in the Rye* seems utterly bizarre (Chapman never exhibited any feelings about the novel until shortly before the shooting). Chapman was not a 'loner' and was a normal social individual for most of his life[483] and a camp counsellor with the YMCA, who had a special rapport with children.[484]

Bresler, Brussell and Strongman all ardently believe that Chapman was a product of Secret Service mind-control experiments, a real life 'Manchurian Candidate'. According to Arthur O'Connor, the detective, who spent more time with Chapman immediately following the murder than anyone else, Chapman was not seeking the spotlight.[485] He stated that he, 'could have been used by somebody. I saw him the night of the murder. I studied him intensely. He looked as if he could have been programmed.' Bresler quotes O'Connor as saying, 'as far as you are trying to build up some kind of conspiracy, I would support you in that line. Like I said originally over the phone, if this gentleman [Chapman] wanted to get away with it, he could have got away with it. There was the subway across the road and no one around to stop him.'[486]

Other evidence also makes the notion of the 'lone nut' a difficult story to accept. Supposedly, eight or more gunshots were fired from Chapman's gun. This is unusual considering Chapman used a gun with five bullets in its chamber, which would have to mean that at least three other shots came from somewhere else. Chapman, it is reported, fired eight to ten shots from a five-shot revolver. There were four bullet holes in windows and bricks of the building, whilst three bullets hit Lennon's back and shoulder, and one bullet was found in his jacket.[487] Strongman doubts that Chapman fired the fatal shots. 'The bullets,' he says, 'slapped into Lennon's body so closely together that pathologists later had trouble marking out the different entry points. If all of these shots came from Chapman, it was a miraculous piece of shooting… In fact, if any of them came from him it was miraculous because Chapman was standing on Lennon's right and, as the autopsy report and death certificate later made clear, all Lennon's wounds were in the left side of his body.'[488]

There had to be another shooter involved, Strongman insists. He suggests that a CIA plant, who worked at the Dakota building, was the real killer. According to Strongman, the investigation around Lennon's murder was hopelessly inefficient. 'His [Chapman's] bizarre post-killing calm was not questioned, his behaviour was not checked with a drugs test, his "programmed" state [a word used about him by more than one police officer] was not investigated, his previous movements were not thoroughly looked into.'[489] Like Kennedy, Lennon's assassination is shrouded in mystery, and there is no clear motive for the killing, apart from the 'lone nut' theory, which gives no true rational explanation.

As with Lennon's assassination, George Harrison's attempted murder must also be considered with suspicion, considering that he too was attacked by another 'lone nut'. This happened, interestingly enough, just around the time that Harrison had become more politically involved, drawing people's attention to the hypocrisy of politics and government. 'The government,' he said, 'always gets in.' In 1992, Harrison had supported the Natural Law Party in a British

General Election, a party who had advocated to have 'conscious-ness' as the major force behind our society. He wanted people to become conscious in a spiritual sense, for Britain to become a kind of 'Platonic Republic'. Harrison saw a 'need to re-programming', according to a kind of cosmic intelligence. This was surely something that those in power are not interested in.[490]

Mind Control and the CIA

Chapman described his feeling at the time of the shooting as 'no emotion, no anger, dead silence in the brain'.[491] For Bresler, his unnatural tone sounded very familiar to other prominent assassins. Bresler was convinced that, like them, Chapman was a mind-controlled assassin, manipulated by some right-wing element. He speculates that Chapman was a 'Manchurian Candidate', brainwashed and pre-programmed to kill on command. When the moment had arrived, Chapman received his signal and performed his task.[492]

This does not seem all that far-fetched when one considers the numerous programmes the CIA had in operation for this very kind of thing. In April 1950, the CIA began work on 'PROJECT BLUEBIRD', their early attempt at 'behavioural modification' in individuals, more commonly known as mind control. Two years later, the agency had developed the project further into 'PROJECT ARTICHOKE'. According to a later CIA internal memorandum, PROJECT ARTICHOKE was intended to 'exploit operational lines, scientific methods and knowledge that can be utilised in altering the attitudes, beliefs, thought processes and behaviour patterns of agent personnel. This will include the application of tested psychiatric and psychological techniques including the use of hypnosis in conjunction with drugs.'[493] By April 1953, PROJECT ARTICHOKE had developed into what is widely known today as 'MK ULTRA'.

For over twenty years, through MK ULTRA, the CIA – in a cold and inhuman manner – sponsored the use of various forms of psychiatric and psychological methods, including the use of hypnotism and mind-altering substances and states to produce behavioural changes in individuals, using an unsuspecting public as guinea pigs to determine how possible and useful mind control actually was. From this point-of-view, the project was one of the most 'ahrimanic' forms of government control over people (while the use of LSD through the Love/Peace movement of the hippys tended to be of a more 'luciferic' nature).[494] Both of these terms, according to Rudolf Steiner, refer to esoteric forces (i.e. spiritual forces) that act on human consciousness.

The first, the ahrimanic, lacks all feeling and respect for the individual, acting upon a person as if they were a machine, a cog in the wheel of progress, that has no real validation in themselves. Bresler described the CIA's experiments on the human mind, in which at least two known cases of death occurred, as if it were 'just a piece of vegetable. Human dignity meant nothing. The sanctity of life itself was meaningless. One CIA report boasted of the agency's work "in effecting psychological entry and control of the individual".'[495]

The other force, the luciferic, moves the individual toward a feeling life in which they lose touch with reality. As a result, in effect they disassociate themselves from humanity as such, preferring the delusions of a fantasy world – one which LSD clearly induced.

Milton Kline, a New York psychologist and former president of the American Society for Clinical and Experimental Hypnosis, who had also appeared as a witness in the defence of Chapman,[496] believes 'that sophisticated techniques have now reached the stage where, if murder is desired, a killer, once programmed and "on hold", can be triggered into action by a phone call or by use of a particular book.'[497]

Richard Syrett, on *The Conspiracy Show*, tried to show that Chapman was a CIA Mind Control 'Manchurian candidate', and that Lennon was essentially a whistle-blower. The distinct possibility remains, in Strongman's opinion, that the Secret Service was certainly behind Chapman. Strongman claims that '*Catcher in the Rye* was part of Chapman's hypnotic programming, a trigger that could be "fired" at him by a few simple keywords [via] a cassette tape message, telex or telegram or even a mere telephone call'. Incidentally, John Hinckley also used *Catcher in the Rye* as the motive behind his crimes and, according to some, the book has been used by the British as post-hypnotic command for mind-controlled assassins since the 1950s.[498]

According to Brussell, mind-control assassins were to eliminate charismatic political leaders and personalities opposed to certain government policies, particularly those with an anti-war, anti-establishment stance, including John Lennon, John F. Kennedy and Martin Luther King.

The mind-control theory of individuals like Chapman goes much deeper than just random assassins. The Federal Government for example, says Brussell, has maintained active programmes to eliminate rock musicians and disrupt rock concerts. Senator Frank Church's Committee hearings in 1975 and the FBI's Huston Plan clearly document the intent to break up any gatherings of the 'new left', and there is hard evidence the CIA assigned agents to 'investigate the music industry'.

Brussell, in her radio show, discusses the impetus of a revolution happening in America around 1967, an impetus that followed from a new consciousness that evolved in the western world in 1966, with 'a leading role played by young people who were normally supposed to be passive', as Noam Chomsky saw it.[499] Brussell says there were revolutions in all areas of life in 1967, which impacted the sociological order. Essentially, Brussell claims the new attitudes and lifestyles upturned the capitalist system; the Vietnam War was big business and the hippys couldn't be allowed to get in the way of it. It is known that the FBI created an entire mission around infiltrating and discrediting the anti-war movement, known as 'COINTELPRO', whose aim was, 'to expose, disrupt, misdirect, discredit, or otherwise neutralise' any anti-war group, including hippys, socialists, the civil rights movement, and even Albert Einstein. The CIA had its own version of COINTELPRO, called 'CHAOS'.

As well as the mysterious deaths of rock musicians like Hendrix, Brian Jones, Janis Joplin and Jim Morrison, there is evidence pointing to others within the counterculture that had once been part of the establishment and were now seeking to infiltrate and destroy the new movement. This allegedly includes many rock groups that were associated with the Laurel Canyon region in California, most of whom had links to the military, including the Doors' front man Jim Morrison, Frank Zappa, Joni Mitchell, David Crosby, Stephen Stills, and bands like the Byrds, the Mamas and the Papas, Jefferson Airplane, The Monkees, not to mention a group of young actors known as the 'Young Turks' (which included Dennis Hopper, Jack Nicholson, Sharon Tate, Jane Fonda and Warren Beatty). All were vocal in their anti-establishment and anti-war views – a stance that artists and musicians often took to naturally, being seen as the conscience of society and at odds with the political motives of the ruling class (who were of course never in favour of dissent, criticism or opposition).

What is particularly interesting about this group from Laurel Canyon is that many of the key figures came not just from military backgrounds – Chapman came from a conservative military family, who had moved from Fort Worth, Texas, to Florida – but also from very wealthy, almost aristocratic, 'blue-blood' families. Terry Melcher, famed producer of the Byrds, for example, was the son of Doris Day, while David Crosby was from a family with a long line of generals, senators and other establishment types. Jim Morrison, one of the decade's most dissident voices, was the son of a leading military figure who was behind the Gulf of Tolkin incident. This affair had provided America with the justification for going to war in Vietnam. Others, like Sharon Tate, Dennis Hopper and Bruce Dern, also had strong links to the military and intelligence services. Dern and Hopper, with help from the actor Jack Nicholson, made a number of counterculture movies, including *Easy Rider* – which encouraged drug taking – as well as *The Trip*, a movie written by Nicholson, that attempted to capture the LSD experience.

In his book *Murder, Mystery, Mayhem: the Dark Heart of the Hippie Dream*, researcher David McGown alleges that these groups like the Byrds and individuals like Jim Morrison were part of an infiltration of the counterculture. He further alleges that Vito Paulekas, the original hippy, who massively influenced the scene in Los Angeles and who was connected by marriage to the Rockefellers (he was supposedly a cousin of 'Bobo' Rockefeller, who was married to Winthrope Rockefeller)[500] was some kind of secret agent whose task was to support and mould many of the groups in Laurel Canyon and Haight Ashbury and guide them towards a particular agenda (i.e., to control the counterculture and, through that, influence culture and society in a particular way). According to the author David Livingstone, in his book *Transhumanism: The History of a Dangerous Idea*, many of these individuals were in secret societies and cult organizations whilst others, like Vito Paulekas and Susan Atkins, had links to Anton LaVey's *Church of Satan*. Tate herself seems to have been connected to similar groups, particularly Alex Sanders' *Alexandrian Wicca*.[501]

McGown believes, like Brussell, that the hippys were infiltrated and exploited in order to undermine their influence. A certain CIA operation was possibly in place at Altamont. A *Washington Post* article on John Ellsworth – who had surreptitiously taken control of the Altamont concert, unbeknownst to the Rolling Stones – claims he had links to a number of groups, including the FBI, CIA and the Mafia,[502] while the Rolling Stones' tour manager claimed that Ellsworth had criminal connections, and FBI ones too.[503]

Brussell and researcher Miles Williams Mathis go as far as to declare that the Tate/LaBianca murders was a CIA operation. Mathis even gives convincing evidence that they were in fact staged events, and that any connections with the occult were simply to distract attention away from the Secret Service connections.[504] There is also the claim that the murders were not staged, but were the result of rival drug gangs in the area and a drug deal that went horribly wrong.[505] However, there is general agreement amongst these sources that the murders were then used by the media to under-mine the anti-war, hippy movement.

The details are too involved for this book to go into, but the crux of Brussell's and Mathis' argument is that Manson was a stooge to turn public opinion against the anti-war movement. When facts came out about the Tate murders, the hippys were blamed by the media, calling Manson, who was not present during the killings, an 'evil hippy genius', 'black magician', 'love and terror' cult leader, who 'mind-controlled' a group of vulnerable young people to kill Tate and her friends. Brussell and Mathis see the whole event as media brainwashing. According to this view, the media used the Beatles and their subliminal recordings to give the murders a motive, while at the same time attempting to discredit the Beatles and the whole impulse of the Sixties' 'Peace' and 'Love' movement.

As we look back, we can see that no other event so discredited and neutralized the hippy movement as the Tate murders. Due to the awful press Charles Manson and his followers gave the hippys, the movement was dead by early 1970. The entire anti-war move-ment was dealt a crushing blow by the Tate murders, since the Press used it to marginalize not only the hippys, but all protesters and 'malcontents'. The author Joan Didion wrote: 'Many people I know in Los Angeles believe the Sixties ended abruptly on August 9th, 1969; ended at the exact moment when word of the murders trav-elled like bushfire through the community.' This was a well-bought success for the Government, since they were able to spin the Viet-nam War out for five more years, spending countless billions and enriching the already wealthy via Pentagon contracts. The Vietnam War didn't end until eight months after Nixon's resignation in 1974. What a coincidence that the Tate murderers' leader should be the perfect patsy – a serial jailbird who didn't even want to be released from jail in 1967!

Charles Manson and the Manson Family, who had reportedly carried out the horrific murders of Sharon Tate – whose father, Paul Tate, was coincidentally a colonel in intelligence and had infiltrated the hippy movement in 1968 – have been portrayed as probably the most notorious murderers of the last century. However, there are other researchers who have come to the conclusion that Manson was in fact a patsy for a more nefarious element at work in society.[506]

The Beatles and Tavistock

Apart from attempts by the CIA to destroy the counterculture, there are many who believe that the counterculture itself was, if not created by elements of the Anglo-American intelligence services, then certainly steered by them with a purpose to effectively destroy the function of rational thought amongst the new post-war generation, and possibly the generations that would come after them: individuals like Ken Kesey, Charles Manson and Timothy Leary, with his crusade to destroy rational thought; some would even include the philosophers of the Frankfurt School, Gloria Steinem's *Ms* magazine, Jackson Pollock and the abstract expressionist art movement. As this line of thought goes, these individuals and movements were used to lead people to destroy their ability to think clearly – even to lead them towards the opinion that the very notion of 'truth' itself was a falsehood. There is no truth so don't bother trying to look for one![507] Such an approach would essentially make that and the following generations perfect subjects for manipulation who would accept, without question, certain deliberate ways of behaving that suited Government ideologies, namely those laid out in the literature of individuals like H.G. Wells and his books *The Open Conspiracy: Blue Prints for a World Revolution* (1928) and *The New World Order* (1940) and Aldous Huxley's book *Brave New World* (1932). Huxley's book suggests that the ruling oligarchies were aiming to manipulate culture in order for people to 'love their servitude'.[508]

According to Jan Irvin of gnosticmedia.com, while discussing his article 'Manufacturing the Deadhead: A product of social engineering'[509] with alternative media reporter James Corbett, Aldous

Huxley had purposely set out a means by which people could indeed be manipulated to be willingly enslaved. Huxley's relative, Julian Huxley, was closely connected to eugenics and Social Darwinism, in which the upper classes would enslave and rule the lower orders. According to Irvin and Corbett: 'If there is ever going to be a world government they will have to coerce a minority, even a majority into doing things they will not want to do',[510] while propaganda or public relations – as it was euphemistically called by Edward Bernays – encouraged the manipulation of people's thoughts and desires to get them to do things either favourable to Government policies or to private enterprise.[511]

Many individuals mentioned above were, incidentally, connected to Charles Manson, and it was Manson the 'chemical messiah', with John Phillips from the Mamas and Papas, who also had a strong military background and possible CIA connections, as did Terry Melcher, who would be instrumental in setting up the first hippy event, the Monterey Pop Festival, where many young people were introduced to LSD.

Writer and ex-MI5 serviceman John Coleman claims in his book, *The Committee of Three Hundred*, that the Beatles, in a similar manner to Charles Manson and Timothy Leary – along with others like Terence McKenna (over whom there is a question mark regarding whether or not he was a CIA/FBI agent)[512] and Robert Gordon Wasson (a key member of J.P. Morgan with links to the CIA, who published a *Life* magazine article in 1957 entitled 'Seeking the Magic Mushroom', bringing the culture of LSD to the mainstream public) – were part of a Government operation to bring about a so-called 'Dark Age' (possibly a false 'Aquarian Age'). The purpose was effectively to bring about the decline of western culture and a kind of willing submission, as Huxley describes in *Brave New World*, of a transformation of consciousness – but one towards slavery rather than freedom. The historian and mentor to former US president Bill Clinton, Carroll Quigley, in his book *Tragedy and Hope: A History of the World in Our Time* (1966), would point to such a decline in western civilization, which he felt had already come about and which had indeed been influenced by organizations such as the Bilderberg group and the Council on Foreign Relations. Another major influencer in this regard was Henry Luce, the founder of *Time, Fortune,* and *Life* magazines.[513] These magazines were intentionally set up by Luce, and his friend Briton Hadden, to promote Americanism across the globe. Luce's famous essay, published in *Time* magazine in February 1941, promoted the idea that the twentieth century was America's time to become the first global power and spread its ideas and ideologies around the world. *Life* magazine was intended as a popular magazine to lead the masses in this direction. It is certainly interesting that *Life* published articles on LSD, and by individuals like Wasson, who – according to the psychedelic researcher Robert Forte – had close connections with Luce.[514] Supposedly, the whole project was an attempt to steer the youth into a kind of Huxley-like 'Brave New World', where through the use of recreational drugs they would remain content and sedate and would be easily led by those in power, essentially handing over their sovereignty in exchange for a life of ease and contentment.[515]

Coleman suggests that the Beatles were controlled by the Tavistock Institution and that their music was used as a kind of brainwashing tool created by Theodor Adorno, a member of the so-called Frankfurt School, a group of Jewish intellectuals that fled Germany during the Third Reich, for America. There are many who see this school as bringing new concepts of liberalism to America and are greatly responsible for the greater personal and intellectual freedoms, who challenged the 'passive rationalism' of western society in favour of a critical rationalism, which encouraged individuals to question and challenge the mainstream notions of what was considered normal rational behaviour. Others, like David A. Noebel, however, feel they were part of a communist plot – as he accused the Beatles in 1965 – to destroy western values of democracy.

The Frankfurt School were essentially Marxists who believed that a social revolution had to begin within the cultural sphere before it could have any real political effect. From this point-of-view, there is some justification in thinking that there was a communist plot to infiltrate the sphere of culture before bringing about a full-scale Marxist revolution. Whether this is the case or not, what is clearly unsubstantiated is that the Beatles, either knowingly or unknowingly, were constructed by Government agencies to brainwash the population with their music, or with Adorno's music, which Coleman claims was based on an atonal system – a system which was essentially a distortion of modern western musical structures of tonality, and which had inherently destructive forces contained in it.

Many of Coleman's claims in his book are erroneous, while supporting evidence for many of his claims are mostly non-existent, as Col. Barry Turner points out in his critique of the work.[516] Coleman's suggestion that the Beatles' music is 'atonal' is nonsense, as although it has (at times) influences of non-western systems within it – as well as certain aspects of atonality – it accords very specifically to the western tradition of tonality. The musicologist Howard Goodall points out,[517] that the Beatles did a lot to re-popularize the tradition of western tonality in modern culture, which had been seriously challenged by many modern composers after the Second World War. Also, it is a complete impossibility that Adorno could have written music with four distinct personalities and styles, as was the case with the Beatles. Coleman's book and its unsupported accusations, if anything, could only lead to confusion – another case of cognitive dissonance.

While Coleman makes unsupported claims regarding the Beatles' music, the possibility, however, that the Beatles may have been used as part of some kind of social engineering is a lot more plausible. According to writer John Potash, in his book *Drugs as a Weapon Against Us*, Marshall McLuhan told John Lennon that the Beatles were created as a means of psychological warfare, to distract the masses – particularly in 1964 when the Warren Commission report came out to distract from the Kennedy assassination, and the attempts also to disrupt thinking through LSD.[518] He further alleges that the Beatles *were* part of the mass experimentation that contemporary society was being subjected to by the CIA, Britain's MI6 and the Tavistock Institute, utilizing extraordinarily powerful mind-altering psychedelic/psychotropic drugs. The Beatles' music was manipulated – mastered and changed – by the Tavistock Institute in London as part of MK Ultra Mind Control in order to get the younger generation to take drugs.

It seems unlikely that the CIA or Tavistock Institute created the Beatles and certainly they did not have anything to do with the music, but it is possible that certain elements controlled and steered the Beatles in certain ways. Leary, who some claim to have been a CIA asset, in particular had a huge impact on Lennon's psychedelic period – a period that nearly destroyed Lennon's mind with his attempt to destroy his ego – while the destructive effects on individuals like Brian Wilson and Jim Morrison were definitely the result of the acid-taking culture of the Sixties. According to psychedelic and entheogenic researcher Robert Forte, the LSD culture of the 1960s had been manipulated by individuals like Henry Luce to promote a society in which the masses would be dumbed down and controlled by a small group of elites. In this sense, individuals like Robert Gordon Wasson – who was actually a public relations specialist in the mould of Edward Bernays for J.P Morgan – had written his *Life* magazine article not in an attempt to educate the world on the benefits of psylocibin, but to steer the masses in a certain direction, mainly to distract and dumb them down.[519] Leary, Forte suggests, though influenced by these groups and the CIA, in fact ended up possibly as a renegade who saw other benefits to psychedelics, promoting a culture of individual exploration and conscious awareness:

> Question authority. That was the abiding theme through his whole life, it was about redirecting authority from institutions and leaders and gurus and redirect it back into the human psyche to take responsibility for yourself, to question authority and to empower individuals. That's the theme that continues, that's throughout his whole life, from his childhood all the way to the end of his life.[520]

It is possible that Lennon's supposed encounter with a 'UFO' during the Seventies was part of a US government policy of what was called 'perception management', likely connected to what has been called 'The Fourth World Agenda, the Battle of the Mind'. Researchers claimed that documents proved alien craft had visited earth, while the American Government made up a fake conspiracy-theory in order to keep secret new weapons they were developing. There were counter-intelligence operations to convince people that the UFOs were real.[521]

It's also possible that Lennon was duped in this respect, to spread these conspiracy ideas wider via his lyrics, such as, 'UFOs over New York and I ain't too surprised' (in his 'Nobody Told Me'). And on his album *Walls and Bridges*, he writes: 'On the 23th August 1974, I saw a UFO' (as with the *Yellow Submarine* album cover, the occult number '23' appears again).

This deception, what Rudolf Steiner referred to as the 'ahrimanic deception', fuelled the growing belief that governments lie to you through tactics of 'perception management' – the aim of which is to tell dramatic stories that capture public imagination, regardless of whether they are real or not, so long as they distract people. From this point-of-view, reality was just 'something to be played with'[522] and the whole LSD culture of the 1960s may have also been used to distort reality in such a manner.

It seems that Lennon became more political after meeting McLuhan in Canada. McLuhan was interested and convinced in conspiracy, and told Lennon he was a stooge, a useless fool of the secret societies who controlled the arts and sciences. Lennon was also aware that one of the 'big guns' in the CIA/Tavistock/MI6 arsenal, LSD, had been having an effect upon the population groups to which it had been funnelled so extensively – an effect that was most unexpected on the part of the social manipulators. (To a large extent, this effect was somewhat positive and beneficial.) Shortly before his death, Lennon had the audacity to blatantly 'out' the aforementioned consortium in a *Playboy* interview, indicating that he was aware of the extent to which he and other pop musicians had been set up to be used as dupes in massive social manipulation schemes.[523]

According to one account, the Beatles,

> ... were without any doubt 'used' by New World Order social manipulators (as were many other pop music groups) in an ongoing project designed to control the development of human society in the most fundamental ways. There are direct links which tie these activities to certain covert scientific projects of an extremely advanced, esoteric nature which were exploring the realms of (manipulation of) consciousness, time, thought and indeed 'reality' itself, which were being conducted during the same period of time on Long Island, N.Y.: activities which were part of the Phoenix/Montauk Project. In fact, we are talking about two sides of the same coin here. On one side, the covert, subtle manipulation and control of not only thought and human consciousness but of the most fundamental, subatomic, electromagnetic matrix of (perceived) reality itself, using newly-developed electromagnetic/radio frequency technologies of extraordinary, unheard-of power and potential. On the other side, directly and overtly shifting the paradigm, changing the basic concepts, widening the parameters, the envelope, changing the playing field and all the rules of play by which society defines itself within an exceptionally short period of time.[524]

If this were the case, it's possible that this deception had the effects that were required, particularly since the practice of deception – as the documentary film-maker Adam Curtis points out – has become more and more open, so that the public do not know what is real or unreal.[525] However, on a more positive note, as George Harrison pointed out in one of his final interviews, people are increasingly aware of what is happening in the world and are more open to different ideas, particularly of a spiritual and philosophical nature.[526]

Although there are many theories that the Beatles and the culture of freedom, love and peace of the Sixties was a Government-controlled thought programme, going hand-in-hand with a kind of

Social Darwinism – in which many of the key figures of the era were behind – much of the evidence to support this is confused. However, what seems clear is that the confusion is part of a wider challenge for humanity in its search for truth. From such a perspective, Rudolf Steiner points to two particular forces at work in the universe, which we mentioned earlier as the 'ahrimanic' and the 'luciferic', which constantly work to bring a sense of deception and confusion into the world – and particularly into the soul of each individual. It is the task of the human being to be alert to these forces and to use, to the best of one's ability, our own capacities of thinking, feeling, and will to counteract their affect. As Steiner suggests, 'consciousness of their presence and subtle influence helps catalyse right thought, right speech, and right action in one's life'. Lucifer and Ahriman, 'work into human beings through the presence of spiritual agents… inhabiting the human soul and working to overtake human consciousness and establish dominion over the Earth… Their keenly developed intelligence presents a force that human beings can only supersede with wisdom and the true power of love.'[527]

Conclusion

And in the End...
The Beatles' Legacy

The Healing Power of the Beatles

In addition to the obvious influence the Beatles had on music and culture in general, throughout the 1960s they brought a mercurial healing force to Europe and America, both suffering from the aftermath of two world wars. They also helped mend the dashed hopes that the post-war years brought with them through political scandals and assassinations. The Beatles were saviours of the dispossessed and hopeless, who were lost in traditionalism and conformity. Misfits could now find a place in the world; those without a 'gang' of their own found somewhere to belong.

The Beatles were a balancing effect to the civil unrest through the 1960s. Encouraging new ways of living and alternative lifestyles, they gave hope to a generation suffering from post-war depression, the threat of nuclear devastation and the emptiness of consumerism. The artistic success of four young working-class men was an example of what was now possible for the younger generation. The Beatles' sense of fun and joy eased the burdens that the bombed-out generation carried, dissolving the chill of the Cold War around them. Even in Russia, the Beatles gave a feeling of hope and warmth, though somewhat surreptitiously.

Their earlier connection to Germany and German youth, particularly Astrid Kirchherr, Klaus Voorman and the Exis, was a symbolic and spiritual healing of the rift between Britain/America and Germany. Astrid's artwork and style greatly influenced the Beatles' aesthetic, while their songs did a lot for the spread of the English language across other countries, like Russia and Japan, helping to re-establish friendly relations between East and West.

From a musical point-of-view, the band were in a unique position of writing their own material and not relying on 'paid professionals'. From this aspect, the group 'was able to capture adolescent spirit from first-hand experience. They were also able to write and record material that would not serve the sole purpose of becoming a radio hit.'[528] This gave a certain authenticity to their music and allowed the youth to feel a connection with the sound of the band, both personally and musically.

While the early records seemed to help unleash the sexual forces that were beginning to awaken in the youth culture of the day, they also provided a necessary energy that brought happiness, community and – from this perspective – a healing quality. The Beatles' scholar Ian MacDonald notes that 'treating the Beatles as icons can only be fruitful for young pop musicians because they coined almost every trend which has succeeded them'. To the Beatles we owe, as Howard Goodall suggests, 'the dramatic comeback of the western musical system'. And, because of the Beatles, 'the process of healing the damaging rift between popular and classical music' was able to take place.[529]

The 'harmony style' of the girl groups that the Beatles emulated, particularly in their earlier years, helped bring a sense of gender harmony to society – a balancing of male and female energies – that could only encourage a feminine perspective of life (and was thus, in a roundabout way, a positive influence on women's rights). Politically, the Beatles had brought greater awareness to the power of youth, and today young people have become a major demographic for politicians. Lennon's socialist ideologies and the open-minded politics of Harrison, and particularly his later interest in current affairs, were taken up by idealistic young people who had an affinity with politics. In eastern Europe and Russia, the Beatles represented 'freedom', and the young were drawn to the West as a result. Thus, the Beatles were as important in bringing down the Berlin Wall as any politician.

As we have seen, the esotericism of Huxley, theosophy, and even to some degree anthroposophy, can be found throughout the

Beatles' work. Their dabbling with psychedelic drugs and marijuana had a huge impact on the culture in its move towards mind-expansion and inner exploration. Although such experimentation left its casualties, it was very much through the lead of the Beatles that other Sixties' groups investigated the esoteric, mind-expansion and inner development, and reflecting such adventures in their music.

The Beatles' flirtation with occultists like Crowley, and the heavy music they produced on the *White Album*, led the way for an esoteric form of rock, with bands like Black Sabbath and Led Zeppelin helping bring an even greater awareness of esoteric ideas to popular culture. Although it may be argued that some of what these groups brought into popular consciousness was negative – notions of Satanism, Crowleyism and Black Magic – it should be noted that even the fact of bringing such esoteric ideas into culture meant that old stagnant traditions could be challenged and even destroyed. The next generation was able freely to decide what spiritual outlooks they might develop for themselves, and the path was open to explore and possibly find more positive esoteric and occult philosophies.

The Beatles attacked the phoney aspects of conventional and organized religion, and in doing so allowed many to find their own paths to the spirit – as much as each of the Beatles found theirs. In dealing with the subjects of reincarnation and karma, for example, they helped introduce mystical concepts, as well as spiritual practices like meditation, into popular western culture. This enabled the Sixties' and post-Sixties' generation the possibility to challenge the rigid views of orthodox religion and to create a fuller and deeper picture of their own humanity, of the spiritual worlds and the relationship that exists between life and death. The Beatles were thus role models for many on their own spiritual journeys. Individuals found courage through the Beatles' music, through the (often simple but sometimes complex) philosophical and spiritual themes of their lyrics, through the Beatles' myths and journeys (Beatlemania,

LSD, eastern mysticism and meditation), and also through the expression of Love and Christ-consciousness that permeated the Beatles' world.

John, Paul, George and Ringo

John's solo works would continue to embrace religious and mystical concepts of God and Love, which enabled the broader culture to explore such matters as a counterbalance to the increasing consumerism that the post-war society had developed. Like many of his Beatles' records, John's solo songs, such as 'Love', 'Mind Games' and 'Number 9 Dream', as well as 'Imagine' and even 'Woman' (which captured a dreamlike, ethereal quality of the archetypal woman and her cosmic significance), were tinged with a mystical, esoteric quality, often replacing the simple pop themes of the period. Many of John's other songs would become vehicles to vent his inner demons, sometimes through the process of Primal Scream Therapy, once again bringing to mass culture the notion of inner healing and development.

John's solo career would continue to shift between spiritual ideas, enlightenment, expressions of his own inner anxieties, as well as political themes. Songs like 'Mind Games' would look deeper into the psychological barriers that prevent us achieving any kind of real connection with each other, while 'Imagine' asked the listener to think about a world with no boundaries, no possessions, and above all no concepts of reward and punishment – no 'Heaven' or 'Hell'. (Some would challenge John's view of a world without Heaven or Hell, feeling that he was calling for a secular world of universal brotherhood which had no place for spiritual development or development of the human race – in other words, cut off from our true home and purpose of life here on Earth.)

John's political leanings were mixed with a spiritual intuition, though often one clouded in 'dreaminess'. John constantly tells us of his dreamy nature — ' I was dreaming of the past', 'you may say

I'm a dreamer', 'so long ago, was it in a dream?', 'nothing is real' – which would certainly suggest that he viewed the brotherhood of man in such a way. However, at the same time many of his interviews suggested that it is only through one's own inner struggles and inner connections that true brotherhood, and a true Philadelphia, would come about.

John's dealing with peace and love, as well as social and spiritual revolution, tended to be viewed as having greater sincerity and conviction. Thus he convinced the world that he was prepared to put himself on the line for his thoughts – to even ridicule himself for the sake of peace. The effect of 'God', 'Give Me Some Truth', 'Power to the People', 'Woman is the N****r of the World', 'Working Class Hero', as well as the album *Sometime in New York City*, had a certain grit to them that inspired the working-class socialism of later British punk (as did his earnest habit of bearing his soul). On the other hand, the 'love is all you need' anthem, as well as his call for universal brotherhood in 'Imagine' and 'Across the Universe', had a sincerity that would inspire pop music themes for future generations.

While Paul's 'Pipes of Peace 'and 'Ebony and Ivory' were considered social candy-floss – sentimental but unrealistic themes of peace and racial harmony – this attitude could also be a sign of modern culture's cynicism. 'Peace and harmony' is a simple concept, and one that Paul continues to promote. However, Paul did not delve into any spiritual or strong social commentary in his music, particularly in his solo work – although some songs capture a sense of humanity and deep empathy, such as 'Eleanor Rigby', 'Blackbird' and 'Hey Jude'.

Paul's strength is mostly the melodic aspects of his music – music purely for music's sake, or simply for the joy of song. He can clearly paint a picture, like 'Penny Lane' or 'Ob-la Di-Ob-La-Da', and in this way it is easier for the public to identify with these images, often seeing them as representations of their own lives. But it could be said that the pictures are somewhat superficial; there is no scratching under the surface, there is no hidden meaning, although they do capture an immediacy of life. As a lyricist, this was Paul's gift to the Beatles, while musically it was the celebration of the melody and arrangement. McCartney, more than any of the other Beatles, brings a sense of harmony through his music, which is easy to sing along to and best sung in groups. 'Hey Jude' is the prime example of the camaraderie of everyone singing out the coda together, as demonstrated on *The Frost Show*, while 'Let It Be' is the perfect anthem for peace (see the whole crowd singing along at the Live Aid concert in 1985, as a perfect end to that event).

As his 'The Song We Were Singing' suggests, despite however complex or philosophical he or the other Beatles became, Paul was the one who 'always came back to the song we were singing'. This he did exceptionally, filling the world with hundreds of melodies over a career that spans more than fifty years. Paul writes simply to bring joy through music, and in this way he changed the world on a deeper, spiritual and humanitarian level – his music, not his ideologies or his convictions, wielded tremendous power. He is simply the most successful songwriter ever.

It was George within whom the dichotomy between spiritual searching and materialistic comfort was most evident within the Beatles. Harrison, however, probably more than the others, went through the most radical transformation. The most concerned about wealth and money, fame and being a pure rock 'n' roller, he underwent a profound transformation in the mid-Sixties, and moved further away from the conventions within which he had grown up. He embraced much of the thinking and attitudes of the East, and even adopted Indian and eastern music and culture as a way of life. He became a devotee of Hare Krishna and did a lot to introduce mystical concepts into mainstream western culture. He also opened up people to real music of spiritual enlightenment and, although he has often been criticised for being preachy and dogmatic,[530] he was committed, for the rest of his life, and in most of the music that he made, to bring people a spiritual message. His songs often took the form of the Sufi poets, who speak of God or the Divine in terms of 'lover' and 'beloved' – filling romantic love with a deep spiritual urgency.

George was the Beatle who made it okay to be religious and to believe in the Lord and a life beyond our material world. His themes of transcendentalism have done as much for the Indian influences of yoga, Krishna-consciousness and Buddhism in the West as the mystical writers of the Sixties or the Indian swamis who came to the West to promote their belief systems. Harrison's themes of spirituality and esotericism have also inspired two generations to make journeys to the East.

George's solo music has not lasted the test of time in the way Lennon's and McCartney's have – and certainly not as much as the Beatles' – although sadly the need for such spiritual sentiments are more in need today than ever before. Harrison was often outspoken about the development of modern culture and the shaky path he felt humanity was going down, singing that 'someone turned out the spiritual light'. In terms of the manipulation of culture and society by the powers-that-be, Harrison expressed his feelings quite clearly. Particularly straightforward are the lyrics to his song 'Brainwashed' in 2002, in which he openly criticizes modern culture and mass media for holding the human mind to ransom.

Although Harrison's association with rather unorthodox and often unusual spiritual groups didn't help people take up his spiritual message in the way that he intended, he gave society a much-needed alternative to mass-consumerism. The beautiful music that often accompanied his spiritual message also brought something spiritually significant to the world, expanding the musical palette beyond what was conventional for pop culture. However, George's music could sometimes be too challenging for a popular music audience, which has meant that his message of love and transcendence has been lost to some (unlike, for example, John's 'Imagine' which still resonates with millions today). George, it seems, was indifferent to whether his message was received or not, and was prepared to let people drown in their own ignorance. In his Beatles' music, this attitude was always betrayed – *just leave me alone and think it out for yourself.*

Ringo, although essential to the makeup of the Beatles, was possibly less philosophically inclined and complicated. Contributing less than the others in terms of artistic input (at least in the area of composition and production), he was invaluable as a drummer as well as for his more down-to-earth easy-goingness, endearing him to many fans. Ringo kept the group grounded. He didn't seem to worry about his fortune, and didn't ask deep existential questions about how fame had changed him or people's relationship with him; he simply accepted it. Ringo remained primarily in that state of acceptance, although his easy-goingness would end up getting him into trouble, particularly with alcohol, with which he battled for many years. However, it should be noted that Ringo was instrumental in bringing the spiritual music of the composer John Tavener to the world.

Ringo never explicitly presented any spiritual direction, religious or political conviction, except for the simplicity of the Sixties' message, which he still holds to this day — 'peace and love'. But in many ways, it is this message that the Sixties and the Beatles attempted to encapsulate and disseminate to the world. What could be more effective than this simple heart gesture of 'peace and love'? This message is in essence no different to that to be found in the Gospel of Saint John:

'*Little children, let us not love in word or talk but in deed and in truth.*'[531]

Notes

See Bibliography on p. 269 for full publishing details.

1 Christopher Sandford, *McCartney*, pp. 29, 36-37.
2 Mark Lewisohn, *The Beatles: Tune In*, p. 57.
3 Ibid.
4 Lewisohn, p. 61. See also *Amazing Journey: The Story of the Who.*
5 Sandford, p. 23.
6 Tony Judt, *Postwar*, p. 300.
7 *The Century: America's Time.*
8 Tim Riley, *Lennon*, pp. 3-4.
9 George Harrison quoted in Mark Lewisohn, *The Beatles: Tune In*, p. 49.
10 Lewisohn, *The Beatles: Tune In*, pp. 47-52.
11 Michael Seth Starr, *Ringo: With a Little Help*, p. 1.
12 This was a more common term for the time and was later of course replaced by 'African-American'.
13 Hanif Kureishi and Jon Savage, *Book of Pop*, pp. 60-63.
14 Films like Howard Hawks' *Sergeant York* (1941).
15 Riley, *Lennon* p. 36.
16 Riley, *Lennon* p. 38.
17 Riley, *Lennon* pp. 33-40.
18 Riley, *Lennon* pp. 25-26.
19 Riley, *Lennon* p. 26.
20 Marc Shapiro, *All Things Must Pass*, p. 18.
21 Ibid.
22 Ibid.
23 Sandford, p. 31.
24 Sandford, p. 32.
25 Michael Seth Starr, *Ringo: With a Little Help*, p. 15.
26 Philip Norman, *Paul McCartney*, p. 30.
27 Norman, *Paul McCartney*, p. 30.
28 Oldham, *Stonefree*, Kindle ed.
29 Shapiro, p. 16.
30 David Livingstone, *Transhumanism: The History of a Dangerous Idea*, p. 59.

31 Sandford, p. 22.

32 Lewisohn, p. 61.

33 Norman, *Paul McCartney*, p. 33.

34 Gary Lachman, *Politics and the Occult*, p. XIII.

35 Allison Taich, 'Beatlemania: The Defiance of a Generation'.

36 Taich.

37 Philip Norman, *Paul McCartney*, p. 51.

38 Norman, *Paul McCartney*, p. 55.

39 *Anthology.*

40 Norman, *Paul McCartney*, p. 53.

41 Norman, *Paul McCartney*, p. 56.

42 Sandford, p. 28.

43 Shapiro, p. 25.

44 'Vintage Rock', Issue 30, July/ August 2017, p. 79.

45 *All You Need Is Love,* Documentary.

46 Ibid.

47 Norman, *Paul McCartney*, p. 58.

48 Shapiro, p. 25.

49 Norman, *Paul McCartney,* p. 59.

50 Starr, p. 19.

51 Ibid.

52 Shapiro, p. 26.

53 Starr, p. 24.

54 *Anthology.*

55 An expression used by Paul McCartney to describe his rock 'n' roll heroes and quoted in Mark Lewisohn's *The Beatles: Tune In*, p. 3. Lennon also used the expression in a 1969 interview, quoted in Lewisohn, p. 87.

56 *The Century: America's Time.*

57 Norman, *Paul McCartney*, p. 54.

58 *The Century: America's Time.*

59 *Anthology.*

60 Lewisohn, p. 86.

61 Lewisohn, p. 87.

62 http://m.imdb.com/name/nm0006168/quotes

63 *Anthology.*

64 Derek Taylor – *All You Need Is Love.*

65 Taich.

66 'Vintage Rock', p. 18.

67 'Vintage Rock,' p. 21.

68 *Stuart Sutcliffe, The Lost Beatle.*

69 Turner, *Beatles '66*, p. 77.

70 Dustin Garlitz, 'A Reflection on the Dionysian Spirit of Music in Nietzsche's *The Birth of Tragedy*', University of South Florida, 2006, p. 3.

71 Ruth Padel, *I'm A Man: Sex, Gods and Rock 'N' Roll*, Faber and Faber, 2000, p. 186.

72 Hunter Davies, *The Beatles: The Authorized Biography*. UK: Heinemann Publishing, 1968, p. 277.

73 Davies.

74 Ross Langager, 'With Our Love, We Can Save the World: The Beatles Within and Without the Late '60s Zeitgeist', *Pop Matters*, 2009. https://www.popmatters.com/115776-with-our-love-we-can-save-the-world-the-beatles-within-and-without-t-2496121406.html

75 Davies, *The Beatles: The Authorized Biography*, pp. 287-288.

76 Leslie Woodhead, *How the Beatles Rocked the Kremlin*, London, BBC, 2009.

77 Jon Savage, *Book of Pop*, Faber and Faber, 1995, pp. 196-197.

78 Damon Paul McGregor, 'Nietzsche, Unconscious Processes, and Non-Linear Individuation', 2011, pp 15-16https://digitalcommons.lsu.edu/gradschool_theses/265. See also Henri Bortoft, *The Wholeness of Nature: Goethe's Way Toward a Science of Conscious Participation in Nature*, Lindisfarne Books, 1996.

79 Li-Da Kruger, *The 60s: The Beatles Decade-1962-1964*, UK, 2006.

80 Davies, *The Beatles: The Authorized Biography,* p. 299.

81 Tony Palmer, *All You Need Is Love*, London, LWT, 1977.

82 Savage, *The Faber Book of Pop,* p. 195.

83 Nick Jones, *Melody Maker*, 3 July 1965.

84 Savage, *The Faber Book of Pop*, p. 177.

85 Dave Lambert, *Magical Mystery Tour Memories*, UK. Wienerworld Limited, 2008.

86 John 15: 1-17.

87 https://www.britannica.com/topic/Dionysus

88 Nietzsche, *The Birth of Tragedy: Out of the Spirit of Music*, Penguin Classics, 1993, p. 10.

89 Ross S. Kraemer, 'Ecstasy and Possession: The Attraction of Women to the Cult of Dionysus', *The Harvard Theological Review*, Vol.72, No.1/2 (Jan – Apr., 1979), Cambridge University Press 1979, p. 5.

90 Charles Kovacs, *Christianity and the Ancient Mysteries: Reflections on Rudolf Steiner's Christianity as Mystical Fact*, Floris Press, 2017, p. 31.

91 Bob Stanley, *Yeah Yeah Yeah: The Story of Modern Pop*. Faber and Faber, 2014, p. 126.

92 Savage, *The Faber Book of Pop*, p. 177.

93 Ron Howard, *The Beatles: Eight Days a Week – The Touring Years*. UK, Apple Corps, 2016.

94 Allison Taich, Popmatters: 'Beatlemania: The Defiance of a Generation', Nov 2009, https://www.popmatters.com/115702-beatlemania-the-defiance-of-a-generation-2496119961.html

95 Taich, 'Beatlemania: The Defiance of a Generation'.

96 Italics mine.

97 Cited in Taich, 'Beatlemania: The Defiance of a Generation'.

98 Padel, *I'm A Man: Sex, Gods and Rock 'N' Roll*, p. 295.

99 Padel, *I'm A Man: Sex, Gods and Rock 'N' Roll*, pp. 229-230.

100 Dustin Garlitz. 'A Reflection on the Dionysian Spirit of Music in Nietzsche's *The Birth of Tragedy*', University of South Florida, 2006, p. 6.

101 Elizabeth Hess, 'The Women', *Village Voice* (November 8, 1994), p. 91, cited in Taich, 'Beatlemania: The Defiance of a Generation', 2009.

102 Padel, *I'm A Man: Sex, Gods and Rock 'N' Roll*, p. 27.

103 Davies, *The Beatles: The Authorized Biography*, pp. 290-291.

104 Garlitz, 'A Reflection on the Dionysian Spirit of Music in Nietzsche's *The Birth of Tragedy*,' pp3-4.

105 Bertrand Russell, *A History of Western Philosophy*, Simon and Schuster, 1967, p. 16.

106 Andy Peebles, 'John Lennon: The Final Interview', 6 December 1980.

107 Barbara Bradby, 'She Told Me What to Say', The Beatles and Girl Group Discourse', *Popular Music and Society*, Volume 28, Issue 3, 2005, pp. 359-390.

108 Firth and McRobbie, cited in Bradby, 'She Told Me What to Say', The Beatles and Girl Group Discourse', p. 383.

109 Susan Douglas, *Where the Girls Are: Growing Up Female with the Mass Media*. New York, Three Rivers Press, 1994, pp. 113-121.

110 Susan Niditch, *'My Brother Esau is a Hairy Man': Hair and Identity in Ancient Israel*, Oxford Scholarship Online, 2008.

111 Rudolf Steiner, *The Universal Human, The Evolution of the Individuality*, Lectures 1909 and 1916, Munich and Bern, Translation edited by Christopher Bamford and Sabine H. Seile, https://wn.rsarchive.org/Lectures/Dates/19091207p02.html

112 Palmer, *All You Need Is Love.*

113 Nietzsche, *The Birth of Tragedy,* p. 24.

114 Genesis 25:25, KJV: 'And the first came out red, all over like a hairy garment; and they called his name Esau.'

115 Steiner, *The Universal Human,* (Lectures).

116 Steve Turner, *Beatles 66: The Revolutionary Year.* Eco Publishing, 2016, p. 120.

117 Rudolf Steiner, *An Outline of Occult Science.* Rudolf Steiner Press, 2011, p. 39-60.

118 Diane Long Hoeveler, *Blake's Erotic Apocalypse: An Androgynous Ideal in Blake and Shelley.* University of Illinois, 1976, p. 21.

119 Hiebel, p. 107.

120 Garlitz, 'A Reflection on the Dionysian Spirit of Music in Nietzsche's *The Birth of Tragedy*', p. 3.

121 Turner, *Beatles '66,* p. 3.

122 Davies, pp. 436-437.

123 Rudolf Steiner, *Occult Science.*

124 Lana Cooper 'The Magical Mystery Four: The Beatles As a Successful System of Archetypes.'

125 See Nik Cohn's *Wop Bop a Loo Bop.*

126 John points to this fact in an interview in 1971. https://www.youtube.com/watch?v=J9wapICXiPg

127 Cooper.

128 Joshua Wolf Shenk, The Power of Two: https://www.theatlantic.com/magazine/archive/2014/07/the-power-of-two/372289/

129 Hiebel, pp. 99-123.

130 Ibid.

131 Friedrich Nietzsche, *The Birth of Tragedy*, translated by Walter Kaufmann (New York: Random House 2000).

132 Lori L. Dilican. *Nietzsche: Interpretation of the Primordial,* Florida Atlantic University. https://www.fau.edu/athenenoctua/pdfs/Lori%20Dilican.pdf

133 Wolf Shenk.

134 Lori L. Dilican.

135 Hiebel, 2008, p. 107.

136 Cited in Wolf Shenk, The Power of Two: https://www.theatlantic.com/magazine/archive/2014/07/the-power-of-two/372289/

137 Hiebel, p. 110.

138 Hiebel, 2008, pp. 99-123.

139 The lyric is from the chorus section of McCartney's song 'Penny Lane'.

140 *The Anthology*, 1995.

141 Cited in Hiebel, p. 115.

142 Ibid.

143 Ibid.

144 Hiebel, p. 118.

145 Ibid.

146 Hiebel, p. 104.

147 Luke 17:21.

148 *Anthology.*

149 Lewisohn, *The Beatles: Tune In*, p. 160.

150 *George Harrison: The Quiet Beatle.*

151 Schneider, p. 101.

152 Lewisohn, photo caption of George in Hamburg, *The Beatles: Tune In*.

153 For more on this subject see Steiner's lectures *The Renewal of the Social Organism*, SteinerBooks, 1985 and *The Threefold Social Order*, GA 23.

154 *The Beatles: All You Need is Love.*

155 Schneider, p. 101.

156 Schneider, p. 102.

157 Long, Herbert S. (1948) *Study of the Doctrine of Metempsychosis in Greece, from Pythagoras to Plato*. Princeton, New Jersey.

158 Cooper.

159 Cooper.

160 Cooper.

161 Creg Heisler, *Spirit led Preaching: The Holy Spirit's Role in Sermon Preparation and Delivery*, xii. See also *The Holy Spirit and His Gifts* Dr. Anthony Landon, p. 16.

162 'Vintage Rock', p. 41.

163 Ibid.

164 *The Brian Epstein Story.*

165 https://www.theguardian.com/music/2016/mar/09/paul-mccartney-george- martin-beatle-producer-tribute Wednesday 9 March 2016, 23.44 GMT.

166 Malcolm, 'Five 'Revolver'-era Songs That Prove George Martin's Impact on the Music World.'

167 *Stuart Sutcliffe: The Lost Beatle.*

168 Ibid.

169 Philip Norman, *Shout*, p215.

170 *Rolling Stone,* http://www.rd.com/culture/paul-mccartney-quotes/. *Also* Richard Kaczynski, *The Life of Aleister Crowley*, i.

171 *Inside John Lennon* Documentary, 2003.

172 Lewisohn, *The Beatles: Tune In.*

173 http://beyondthefold.chieftain.com/mobile/2199264-123/beatles-songs-music-lennon Published: 4 February 2014; Last modified: February 27, 2014.

174 http://beyondthefold.chieftain.com/mobile/2199264-123/beatles-songs-music-lennon.

175 Davies, p. 445.

176 http://beyondthefold.chieftain.com/mobile/2199264-123/beatles-songs-music-lennon.

177 https://www.thespec.com/entertainment/music/2012/10/05/beatlemania-it-began-50-years-ago-today.html. Last Accessed 23/7/22.

178 *Anthology.*

179 truthcontest.com.

180 http://beyondthefold.chieftain.com/mobile/2199264-123/beatles-songs-music-lennon.

181 See Rudolf Steiner's *The Reappearance of Christ in the Etheric* lecture cycle.

182 Jesaiah Ben-Aharon, *The Spiritual Event of the Twentieth Century, An Imagination: The Occult Significance of the 12 Years, 1933-45 in the Light of Spiritual Science*, pp. 55-58.

183 Turner, *Beatles '66*, p. 1.

184 Maureen Cleave, *Evening Standard*, 4 March 1966.

185 Schneider, pp. 177-183.

186 Ibid.

187 http://www.rollingstone.com/music/features/when-john-lennons-jesus-controversy-turned-ugly-w431153, 29 July 2016.

188 Maureen Cleave, *Evening Standard*, 4 March 1966.

189 Jordan Runtagh http://www.rollingstone.com/music/features/when-john-lennons-jesus- controversy-turned-ugly-w431153, 29 July 29 2016.

190 Ibid.

191 *The Beatles Diary.*

192 *Book of Pop*, p. 279.

193 Runtagh, Jordan. 'When John Lennon's "Bigger than Jesus" Controversy Turned Ugly', *Rolling Stone*, 29 July 2016.

194 Ibid.

195 Philip Norman, *Shout!*, p. 280.

196 Ibid.

197 Ibid.

198 Ibid.

199 Turner, *Beatles '66*, p. 106.

200 Turner, *Beatles '66*, pp. 92-93.

201 Runtagh.

202 Ibid.

203 Ibid.

204 *Anthology*.

205 *Book of Pop*, p. 279.

206 Jordan.

207 *The Beatles Diary*.

208 Ibid.

209 Jordan.

210 Turner, *Beatles '66*, p. 22.

211 Jay Spangler, *The Beatles Ultimate Experience*. John Lennon Interview: London *Evening Standard*, 'More Popular Than Jesus', 3/4/1966 www. beatlesinterviews. org.

212 Stanley, p. 127.

213 Turner, *Beatles '66*, pp. 93-94.

214 '48 Hours with Paul McCartney' during the 1989-1990 World Tour.

215 *Inside John Lennon*.

216 Turner, *Beatles '66*, p. 88.

217 *Book of Pop*, p. 283.

218 *Book of Pop*, pp. 279 and 284.

219 Davies, p. 410.

220 Glenn Frankel. 'If John Lennon Were a Painting...' *Washington Post*, Oct. 26, 2008.

221 *Inside John Lennon*.

222 BBC Radio 4's *Sunday Programme*, Ken Seymour of the Canadian Broadcasting Corporation https://www.smh.com.au/world/give-christ-a-chance-lennon-20080713-3ek4.html. Last accessed 1/8/2022.

223 Turner, *The Beatles '66*, p. 93.

224 *The Century: America's Time*.

225 *Feed Your Head*.

226 *The Century: America's Time.*

227 Ibid.

228 *Book of Pop*, p. 267.

229 Ibid.

230 Gary Lachman, *Turn Off Your Mind*, p. 8-9.

231 Lachman, *Turn Off Your Mind*, p. 15.

232 Turner, *Beatles '66*, p. 131.

233 Lachman, *Turn Off Your Mind*, p. 75.

234 Lachman, *Turn Off Your Mind*, p. 78.

235 Turner, *Beatles '66*, p. 125.

236 http://www.carygrant.net/autobiography/autobiography14.html

237 *The Beatles in India*, http://thebeatlesinindia.com

238 Quoted in Turner, *Beatles '66*, p. 117.

239 Lachman, *Turn Off Your Mind*, p. xvi.

240 Turner, *Beatles '66*, p. 4-5.

241 *Book of Pop*, p. 271.

242 *Hoffman's Potion.*

243 Padel, p. 348-349.

244 Rivers, *Love and the Evolution of Consciousness*, p. 24.

245 Plato *The Symposium,* 1952, p164 quoted in Rivers, p. 25.

246 Rivers, p. 25.

247 Jacob M. Held, 'All You Need Is Love: Hegel, Love and Community', *The Beatles and Philosophy*, p. 27.

248 Held, p. 30.

249 Held, p. 27-32.

250 Held, p. 35.

251 Rivers, p. 23.

252 Ibid.

253 http://www.clashmusic.com/features/12-things-you-never-knew-about-jimi-hendrix- 5/3/2010,

254 https://blog.oup.com/2017/01/bob-dylan-christianity/ 21 Jan 2017.

255 *Turn Off Your Mind*, p. 29.

256 Robert Arp in his essay 'All My Loving: Paul McCartney's Philosophy of Love', *The Beatles and Philosophy*, p. 38-39.

257 Jody Rosen, 'Everything You Know About Sgt. Pepper's Is Wrong'.

258 Davies, p. 410.

259 Ibid.

260 Jesper Sorensen, *A Cognitive Theory of Magic*, p. 89.

261 Paul Allan Mirecki, *Magic and Ritual in the Ancient World*, p. 144.

262 Jere O'Neill Surber, 'I'd Love to Turn You On', *The Beatles and Philosophy*.

263 See Steiner.

264 *Anthology*, p. 273.

265 Rudolf Steiner, *World History in the Light of Anthroposophy*, p. 109.

266 Coleridge, *The Eolian Harp*.

267 *Anthology*.

268 Turner, *Beatles 66*, p. 115.

269 Lachman, *Turn Off Your Mind*, p. 145-146.

270 Lachman, *Turn Off Your Mind*, p. 149.

271 Lachman, *Turn Off Your Mind*, p. xvi.

272 Turner, *Beatles '66*, p. 117.

273 Victoria Woollaston, 'Uploading Our Minds to Computers By 2045', *Mail Online*, 19 June 2013.

274 Rivers, p. 32.

275 Ibid.

276 Steiner, June 1915, 'Preparing for the Sixth Epoch.' Lecture, Dusseldorf.

277 Peter Nathan, 'Jerusalem: Center of the Earth? Part 2: The Unforeseen Endgame'. Summer, 2004 http://www.vision.org/visionmedia/ history-middle-east-jerusalem/604.aspx.

278 https://www.youtube.com/watch?v=miVoRC5eP8U. Mar 14, 2011, 'Is Ours the Age of Aquarius or Antichrist?' Terry Boardman, Limerick, February 2011.

279 Ibid.

280 Turner, *Beatles '66*.

281 See Rudolf Steiner's books *An Occult Science* and *Theosophy*.

282 *The US Vs. John Lennon*.

283 Rivers, p. 34.

284 Frost Interview.

285 Ibid.

286 Ibid.

287 Turner, *Beatles '66*, p. 65.

288 'The Beatle Mysteries, Sgt Pepper, and Solar Worship: An Interview with the Number Nine Site'
https://sagesigmaunbounddotcom.wordpress.com/2016/07/04/the-beatle-mysteries-sgt-pepper-and-solar-worship-an-interview-with-the-number-nine-site/

289   Ibid.

290   Marcus Grail, *The History of Rock 'n' Roll in 10 Songs*.

291   See note 288.

292   *All You Need Is Love.*

293   *The Vintage News* https://www.thevintagenews.com/2016/09/30/priority-beatles-brought-soviet-union-destroyed-communism/ Last accessed on 30/7/2022.

294   *All You Need Is Love.*

295   https://www.scribd.com/document/159177915/The-Beatles-Illuminatis

296   https://thenumbernineblog.wordpress.com/2016/06/20/ive-opened-up-the- doors/ Last accessed on 30/7/2022.

297   https://sagesigmaunbound.com/2016/07/04/the-beatle-mysteries-sgt-pepper-and-solar-worship-an-interview-with-the-number-nine-site/

298   https://midnight-rant.com/the-cult-of-twenty-three/

299   Ibid.

300   See Plato's book *The Phaedo*. Also http://www.comparativereligion.com/reincarnation3.html

301   https://news.wttw.com/sites/default/files/article/file-attachments/Revolver%20Book%20Excerpt.pdf

302   Jessy Krupa, *Yesterday... and Today.*

303   The Beatles: 'Yesterday and Today' album discussion with Candy Leonard. See also Beatles' historian Richard Potter's interview on *Deep: Beatles Album Covers Explained,* published 12 April 2017 https://www.youtube.com/ watch?v=PpjhgFhqtV0

304   Savage, p. 110.

305   Savage, p. 130.

306   Turner, *Beatles '66*, p. 122-123.

307   Norman, *Shout!*, p. 279.

308   https://sagesigmaunbound.com/2016/07/04/the-beatle-mysteries-sgt-pepper-and-solar-worship-an-interview-with-the-number-nine-site/

309   Nov. 15 1991 interview with *Goldmine* magazine, https://news.wttw.com/sites/default/files/article/file-attachments/Revolver%20Book%20Excerpt.pdf

310   https://iblp.org/questions/what-umbrella-protection. Last accessed 14/7/22.

311   https://www.youtube.com/watch?v=7LPn_yKT1Ag. Last accessed 14/7/22.

312   A number of different researches have interpreted many modern pop artists from an occult perspective. The following articles maybe of interest to the reader: https://www.illuminaticelebrities.com/rihanna/rihanna-

umbrella-masonic-video/ Last accessed 14/7/22. https://vigilantcitizen. com/musicbusiness/lady-gaga-the-illuminati-puppet/. Last accessed 14/7/22. https://www.culledculture.com/the-lions-of-like-a-virgin/. Last accessed 14/7/22.

313 Du Noyer, *Conversations with McCartney*, pp. 69-70.

314 See *The Beatles Anthology*, 1995.

315 John Kruth, *This Bird Has Flown: The Enduring Beauty of Rubber Soul*, Fifty Years On. Backbeat Books, 2015.

316 Norman, *Paul McCartney*, p. 265.

317 Richard White, *Come Together: Lennon and McCartney in the Seventies*, p. 52.

318 *Time* declared in its Sep. 22 1967, Olivia B. Waxman, 'The Story Behind Sgt. Pepper's Lonely Hearts Club Band Cover'. 30 March 2017. http:// time.com/4713080/sgt-Pepper's-album-photo/

319 *The Mammoth Book of The Beatles*, p. 126.

320 Turner, *Beatles' 66*, p. 112.

321 http://www.theartstory.org/artist-blake-peter.htm

322 Turner, *Beatles '66*, p. 4.

323 http://www.theartstory.org/artist-blake-peter.htm

324 Goodall, *50 Years of Sgt Pepper's*.

325 Marianne Faithfull, *Faithfull*, p. 25-26.

326 Livingstone, p237-238. See also http://www.thelasttuesdaysociety.org/ listings/ event/michael-hollingshead-man-who-turned-world-lsd/#. Wd9uCltSxQI

327 https://medium.com/cuepoint/devil-music-a-history-of-the-occult-in- rock- roll-3e671a821ba5. See also *The Occult Arts of Music: An Esoteric Survey from Pythagoras to Pop Culture* by David Huckvale.

328 Artist Jann Haworth talks about the fashion and style featured on the Beatles' iconic 'Sgt. Pepper's' album cover, Andrew Nodell, *Los Angeles Times*, 2 June 2017.

329 Robert Lake, 'With A Little Help from Their (Mostly White) Friends: Searching for Invisible Members of Sgt. Pepper's Lonely Hearts Club Band.'

330 https://www.beatlesbible.com/features/working-titles/

331 Bill Gibron, 'Yin and Yang the Beatles: *A Hard Day's Night* vs. *Help!*'

332 Tomberg, *The Wandering Fool & Three Lectures on Hermeticism: Love and its Symbols, Early Studies on the Tarot*.

333 Bebergal, *Season of the Witch*, p. 59.

334 Ibid.

335 Hieronimus, p. 127.

336 Hieronimus, p. 37.

337 Hieronimus, p. 19.

338 Hieronimus, p. 303.

339 *Anthology.*

340 Savage, *1966.*

341 Bebergal, *Season of the Witch: How the Occult Saved Rock and Roll.*

342 *Love Is All You Need.*

343 Terry Boardman, *Mapping the Millennium*, pp. 106-107 and 174-175. See also Boardman's article 'The Idea of the Threefold Society at the Dawn of the Millennium', http://threeman.org/?p=1393. Also http://the-number-23. blogspot.ie/2007/02/religion-sects-and-occult.html

344 Clare Kennedy, *Paradox, Aphorisms and Desire in Novalis and Derrida*, p. 88.

345 Krerowicz, p. 76.

346 Du Noyer, *Conversations with McCartney*, p. 79.

347 http://www.institute4learning.com/2012/08/07/the-stages-of-life-according-to-rudolf-steiner/

348 http://www.whizzpast.com/cover-story-11-fascinating-facts-about-the-beatles-abbey-road-album-cover/

349 https://www.beatlesbible.com/features/paul-is-dead/. Last accessed 31/7/22.

350 http://hoaxes.org/archive/permalink/paul_is_dead. Last accessed 31/7/22.

351 Glenn, Alan (November 11, 2009). '"Paul is dead" (said Fred).' *Michigan Today*. University of Michigan.

352 Norman, *Paul McCartney*, p. 404.

353 Norman, *Paul McCartney* p. 406.

354 *Anthology.*

355 Brian Moriarty, 'Game Developers Conference,' San Jose, CA 1999. https://www.youtube.com/watch?v=BQLoRUS-ypM. Last accessed 31/7/22.

356 Richard White, *Come Together: Lennon and McCartney in the Seventies*, p. 52.

357 Hunter Davies, *John Lennon Letters*, p. 86.

358 Youtube, https://www.youtube.com/watch?v=aQJg0H6QrTU. Last accessed 31/7/22.

359 Kollerstrom, *The Life and Death of Paul McCartney*, p. 11.

360 Kollerstrom, p. 57.

361 Kollerstrom, pp. 57-62.

362 Kollerstrom, p. 34.

363 Kollerstrom, p. 118.

364 Kollerstrom, p. 17.

365 onabbeyroad.com/ringo4.htm

366 3 April 1964 ,Twickenham Film Studios, London, Star Parade, Tyne Tees TV, aired 9 April 1964. https://www.youtube.com/watch?v=j9e6zHA6eOY

367 Kollerstrom, p. 147.

368 Sandford, p. 30.

369 Sandford, p. 40.

370 'Did Paul McCartney ACTUALLY die in 1966? Let's find out through vocal analysis!'
https://www.youtube.com/watch?v=8nARWOoxGfA&t=1s, published 14 Jan. 2022.

371 Turner, *Beatles '66*, pp. 100-103.

372 http://www.allaboutvision.com/conditions/eye-color-hazel.htm). See also *Our Twelve Senses: How Healthy Senses Refresh the Soul* by Albert Soesman, Hawthorn Press, 2014.

373 *Book of Pop*, p. 288.

374 https://www.beatlesbible.com/features/paul-is-dead/. Last accessed 31/7/22.

375 Turner, *Beatles '66*, p. 61.

376 Sandford, p. 19.

377 http://www.pophistorydig.com/topics/paul-is-dead-saga-1969-1970/

378 Sandford, pp. 127-128.

379 Adam Curtis, *Hypernormalization*.

380 http://plasticmacca.blogspot.ie/. Last accessed 31/7/22.

381 Kollerstrom, p. 16.

382 Turner, *Beatles '66*, pp. 2-3.

383 *John Lennon The Final Interview*, BBC Radio 1, 6 December 1980.

384 Turner, *Beatles '66*, p. 5.

385 Turner, *Beatles '66*, p. 17.

386 'The Beatles Album Cover that Started a Decade-Long Conspiracy Theory', *Mail*-online, 9 August 2009.

387 Norman, *Paul McCartney*, p. 405.

388 Kollerstrom, p. 74.

389 http://www.triumphpc.com/mersey-beat/beatles/neilaspinall2.shtml. Last visited 7/7/2022.

390 http://beaconfilms2011.blogspot.com/2013/03/iamaphoney-neil-aspinall-and-apple.html

391 http://beaconfilms2011.blogspot.com/2013/03/iamaphoney-neil-aspinall-and-apple.html

392 https://www.theguardian.com/theguardian/2012/oct/23/beatles-magical-mystery-tour-1969.
Accessed 1/7/2022.

393 https://www.youtube.com/watch?v=BQLoRUS-ypM&t=10s. Accessed 1/7/2022.

394 https://truthscrambler.com/2021/11/12/the-two-jesus-children-rudolf-steiner/. Accessed 1/7/2022.

395 *Anthology.*

396 Norman, *Paul McCartney*, p. 29.

397 Paul is Dead: The Rotten Apple, https://www.youtube.com/watch?v=3Qs5IjQuQ3M&t=1s. Accessed 1/7/2022.

398 https://www.rollingstone.com/culture/culture-lists/the-27-club-a-brief-history-17853/. Accessed 1/7/2022.

399 Rudolf Steiner, 'Social and Anti-Social Forces in the Human Being', Lecture, 12 December 1918.

400 Kollerstrom, p. 13 and p. 21

401 www.plasticmacca.com. Accessed 1/7/2022.

402 https://tmhome.com/experiences/interview-lennon-and-harrison-on-meditation/. Last accessed 1/8/2022.

403 Mary Swift, 'How The Beatles Learned Transcendental Meditation and What They Thought About It' https://tmhome.com/experiences/interview-lennon-and-harrison-on-meditation/ Last accessed 1/8/2022.

404 Turner, *Beatles '66*, p. 52.

405 https://www.open.ac.uk/researchprojects/makingbritain/content/ayana-deva-angadi. Last accessed 15/7/22.

406 http://www.earcandymag.com/beatles-abracadabrabook-india.htm. Last accessed 15/7/22.

407 http://thebeatlesinindia.com/stories/beatles-maharishi-meditation/. Last accessed 16/7/22.

408 *Anthology.*

409 Saltzman, *The Beatles in India.*

410 The School had been considered a cult by a number of governments, particularly in Belgium where it is classed as a cult: https://forum.culteducation.com/read.php?12,63254 (Last accessed 15/7/22.) Some of

its branches in the UK have been found guilty by the Townsend Report of child abuse https://www.youtube.com/watch?v=Cnv1tTcm6t4 (Last accessed 15/7/22.)

411 Ibid.

412 Saltzman, *The Beatles in India*.

413 Frost Interview.

414 Saltzman, *The Beatles in India*.

415 Davies, p. 439.

416 Barry Miles, *McCartney: Many Years from Now*.

417 George Harrison, *The Frost Show*.

418 *Anthology*.

419 Cynthia Lennon, *John*, Audio Book.

420 Jann S. Wenner, *Lennon Remembers*.

421 *Anthology*.

422 https://www.theguardian.com/music/2015/dec/09/indian-retreat-where-the-beatles-learned-to-meditate-is-opened-to-the-public (Last accessed 16/7/22.)

423 Ibid.

424 Bill Harry, *Encyclopedia of The Beatles*, p. 428.

425 George Harrison, *Billboard*, December 1992.

426 Ronald Lee Zigler, 'Realizing It's All Within Yourself', *The Beatles and Philosophy*, p. 145.

427 Zigler, p. 144.

428 Simon Leng, *While My Guitar Gently Weeps: The Songs of George Harrison*, p. 192.

429 The Beatles Decade (Part 5).

430 See Hegel's notion of society. Stephen Houlgate's *Freedom, Truth and History: An Introduction to Hegel's Philosophy* is a good introduction.

431 https://rockandrollroadmap.com/places/death-sites/los-angeles-area-death-sites/mal-evans-death-site-roadie-assistant-and-friend-of-the-beatles/ (Last accessed 15/7/22.)

432 'Surviving Beatles Unite to Promote Meditation,' March 4, 2009, http://edition.cnn.com/2009/SHOWBIZ/Music/03/04/mccartney.meditation.concert/index.html?iref=nextin (Last accessed 16/7/22.)

433 Robert S. Mason, *The Advent of Ahriman*. http://www.anthroposophie.net/Ahriman/ahriman_old.htm (Last accessed 16/7/22.)

434 http://www.anthroposophie.net/Ahriman/ahriman.htm (Last accessed 16/7/22.)

435 http://wn.rsarchive.org/Lectures/GA094/English/ SGP1978/19060530p01.html a different approach to yoga and meditation (Last accessed 16/7/22.)

436 Roerich seemed to have a strong mystical presence, which he used to gain favour in political circles, something which Rudolf Steiner felt was as a kind of 'black magic' influence, as its effect was to interfere with an individual's freedom to make choices. Also, the use of symbols to exert influence ,which Steiner also viewed as a kind of 'black magic', as it by-passed an individual's rational and conscious mind which is the modern means of achieving spiritual awakening. For more on this see *The Secret Mysteries of America.*

437 Lachman, *Politics and the Occult*, p. 151.

438 http://www.anthroposophie.net/Ahriman/ahriman.htm (Last accessed 31/7/22.)

439 Isrun Engelhardt. 'The Strange Case of the "Buddha from Space".' http:// himalaya.socanth.cam.ac.uk/collections/journals/ret/pdf/ret_42_02.pdf (Last accessed 16/7/22.)

440 Sergei O. Prokofieff *The East in the Light of the West: Parts 1-3*. Temple Lodge Publishing, 2010.

441 https://www.lucistrust.org/blog_wgun/five_rays_of_hope_stream_from_ the_un (Last accessed on 1/8/2022.)

442 https://www.undrr.org/terminology/build-back-better (Last accessed on 1/8/2022). See also https://www.un.org/en/coronavirus/building-back-better-requires-transforming-development-model-latin-america-and-caribbean (Last accessed on 1/8/2022) and https://www.gov.uk/government/publications/build-back-better-our-plan-for-growth (Last accessed on 1/8/2022).

443 https://medium.com/@transcendentaldeception/maharishi-fraud-voodoo-science-open-letter-to-david-lynch-part-2-47485aaaf918 (Last accessed 16/7/22). http://minet.org/www.trancenet.net/secrets/soma/ index.shtml (Last accessed 16/7/22).

444 https://www.share-international.org/magazine/old_issues/2008/ march_08.htm#tribute (Last accessed 31/7/22.)

445 Manly P. Hall, 'Effects of Stimulants and Narcotic Drugs on the Human Psyche'.

446 Davies, p. 453.

447 See Pat Buchanan's book *Churchill, Hitler and the Unnecessary War: How Britain Lost Its Empire and the West Lost the World*. See also Richard Overy's *The Bombing War.*

448 Dane Rudhyar, *The Magic of Tone and the Art of* Music, 1982, Shambhala Press.

449 J. Stillson Judah, *Hare Krishna and The Counterculture.* John Wiley and Sons, New York, 1974, p. 78.

450 Judah, p. 108.

451 Davies, p. 445.

452 Davies, p. 446.

453 Davies, pp. 445-446.

454 *Inside John Lennon.*

455 Davies, p. 446.

456 Davies, p. 446.

457 *The 60s, The Beatles Decade-Episode 5: The Party Is Over.*

458 *George Harrison: Living in the Material World.*

459 Stanley, pp. 128-129.

460 *The 60s, The Beatles Decade-Episode 5: The Party Is Over.*

461 Quoted in the *Book of Pop,* pp. 337-338.

462 *Turn Off Your Mind,* p. 294.

463 Lachman, *Turn Off Your Mind,* p. 294.

464 Faithfull, p. 242.

465 *Book of Pop,* pp. 348-350.

466 *Book of Pop,* p. 359.

467 'Monterey Pop to Altamont OPERATION CHAOS, The CIA's War Against the Sixties Counterculture', November 1976.

468 Vincent Canby, *New York Times,* quoted in Selvin, pp. 303-304.

469 Germaine Greer, *Oz,* November 1969.

470 Hieronimus, p. 328.

471 *John Lennon: A Conspiracy of Silence* https://www.youtube.com/watch?v=vZGQA0nqScI&t=53s Last accessed 22/11/22.

472 Ibid.

473 Mae Brussell, 'John Lennon Investigation', Broadcast 473, 28/12/80.

474 Ibid.

475 Ibid.

476 Ibid.

477 Ibid.

478 Ibid.

479 Bresler, p. 8.

480 Bresler, p. 59.

481 *US Verses John Lennon.*

482 Bresler, p. 93.

483 Bresler, p. 96.

484 Bresler, p. 87.

485 Bresler, pp. 13-14.

486 Bresler, p. 15.

487 *John Lennon: A Conspiracy of Silence.*

488 Ibid.

489 Tony Rennell, 'Was Lennon's Murderer a CIA Hitman', *Mail*-online, 4 December 2010.

490 VH1 interview. https://www.youtube.com/watch?v=cjWTFlg2Er0

491 http://johnlennon.bizhat.com/the_assassination_of_john_lennon.htm

492 Bresler, pp. 32-54.

493 Bresler, p. 36.

494 Rudolf Steiner, 'The Balance in the World and Man, Lucifer and Ahriman', Lecture, 3 January 2001. Also Steiner, 'The Influence of Lucifer and Ahriman', GA 191, Nov. 1919. https://rsarchive.org/Lectures/GA191/English/AP1993/InLuAr_index.html

495 Ibid.

496 Bresler, p. 44.

497 Ibid.

498 Brussell, Broadcast 473- 28/12/80, 'John Lennon Investigation'.

499 *US Vs. John Lennon.*

500 David McGowan, 'Inside The LC: The Strange but Mostly True Story of Laurel Canyon and the Birth of the Hippie Generation', Part 8, *Illuminati News Presents* (*The Center for an Informed America*), 24 July 2008.

501 Ibid.

502 Sam Cutler, *You Can't Always Get What You Want, My Life With The Rolling Stones...*, Chapter 47.

503 Peter Fornatale, *50 Licks: Myths and Stories from Half a Century of the Rolling Stone*s, p. 117.

504 http://mileswmathis.com/2014.html.

505 Nikolas Schreck, *The Manson File.* https://www.youtube.com/watch?v=kAEVK_L2K4I. Last accessed 20/7/22.

506 For more on the Manson Murders the reader is directed to the work of Nikolas Schreck, https://www.youtube.com/watch?v=kAEVK_L2K4I. Last accessed 20/7/22.

507 Corbett Report, '5 People You Wouldn't Believe Worked for the CIA', published 11 Oct. 2017, https://www.youtube.com/watch?v=6FpyED4uJwQ. See also http://www.gnosticmedia.com/ and http://www.openculture.com/2013/01/ken_kesey_talks_about_the_meaning_of_the_acid_tests_ in_a_classic_ interview.html. Also Frances Stonor Saunders, *Independent*, 'Moden Art was a CIA Weapon', http://www.independent.co.uk/news/world/ modern-art-was-cia-weapon-1578808.html. 21 Oct. 1995. Also http://www.constantinereport.com/timothy-leary-and-the-cia/

508 Aldous Huxley, Berkley Interview, 1962 https://www.youtube.com/watch?v=xj_0HANY5o4. Last accessed 22/11/22.

509 http://www.gnosticmedia.com/manufactu...

510 Corbett Report, series 672, https://www.corbettreport.com/interview-672- jan-irvin-on-the-cia-mk-ultra-and-the-creation-of-the-drug-culture/

511 C.I.A., MK-ULTRA & The 60's Counterculture, published on 17 Oct. 2013. https://www.youtube.com/watch?v=mdY1G5c3uJU http://www.gnosticmedia.com/manufacturing-the-deadhead-a-product-of-social-engineering-by-joe-atwill-and-jan-irvin/. See also Adam Curtis, *Century of Self.*

512 Logomedia NEW MKULTRA DISCOVERY: Terence McKenna admited that he was a 'deep background' and 'PR' agent (CIA or FBI). Last accessed 19/7/22.

513 https://history.state.gov/milestones/1937-1945/internationalism. Last accessed 22/11/22.

514 https://poddtoppen.se/podcast/1169842000/last-born-in-the-wilderness/robert-forte-the-records-of-gordon-wasson-the-secret-origins-of-the-psychedelic-movement. Last accessed 22/11/22.

515 Ibid.

516 Col. Barry Turner, 'Committee of 300 John Coleman – Critique'. https://www.youtube.com/watch?v=W5KWHr-yFuk&t=923s Published on Apr 13, 2012. Last accessed 22/11/22.

517 *Great Composers of the 20th Century, The Beatles.*

518 John Potash, 2014, *Drugs as a Weapon Against Us.*

519 https://poddtoppen.se/podcast/1169842000/last-born-in-the-wilderness/robert-forte-the-records-of-gordon-wasson-the-secret-origins-of-the-psychedelic-movement.

520 Ibid.

521 http://www.gnosticmedia.com/manufacturing-the-deadhead-a-product-of-social-engineering-by-joe-atwill-and-jan-irvin/

522 Robert Perry, *Associated Press and Newsweek* reporter, interviewed in Curtis' *Hypernormalization*.

523 NewsHawk Inc.

524 Ibid.

525 Curtis, *Hypernormalization*. See also http://www.gnosticmedia.com/manufacturing-the-deadhead-a-product-of-social-engineering-by-joe-atwill- and-jan-irvin/

526 John Fugelsang Interveiw with George Harrison, VH1, 1997.

527 Ibid.

528 Rivers, *Love and the Evolution of Consciousness*, 2016, p. 52.

529 *Great Composers of the 20th Century*.

530 See Ian MacDonald's, *Revolution in the Head*.

531 John 3:18.

Bibliography

Barnard, Stephen. 1986. *Rock: An Illustrated History*. New York: Schirmer Books

Barnes, Richard. 1979. *Mods!* London: Plexus

Baur, Michael and Steven. 2006. *The Beatles and Philosophy*. Open Court

Betrock, Alan. 1983. *Girl Groups: The Story of a Sound.* New York: Deliah Books, Putman Publishing Group, New York

Bebergal, Peter. 2015. *Season of the Witch: How the Occult Saved Rock and Roll*. Penguin

Ben-Aharon, Jesaiah. 1993. *The Spiritual Event of the Twentieth Century, An Imagination: The Occult Significance of the 12 Years, 1933-45 in the Light of Spiritual Science*. Temple Lodge

Block Avital and Umansky, Lauri. 2005. *Impossible to Hold: Women and Culture in the 1960s*. New York: NYU Press

Blaney, John. 2005. *John Lennon: Listen to This Book*. Paper Jukebox

Boyd, Pattie. 2007. *Wonderful Today*. Harmony Books

Bradby, Barbara. 2005. 'She Told Me What to Say: The Beatles and the Girl Group Discourse', *Popular Music and Society*, Vol. 28, No. 3

Bresler, Fenton. 1989. *Who Killed John Lennon?* Sedgwick and Jackson

Campbell, Michael. 2005. *Popular Music in America: The Beat Goes On.* Belmont

Clayson, Alan. 1995. *Beat Merchants: The Origins, History, Impact and Rock Legacy of the 1960's British Pop Groups*. London: Blandford Press

Davis, Hunter. 2009. *The Beatles*. Edbury Press

Downes, Julia (ed.). 2012. *Women Make Noise: Girl Bands from Motown to the Modern*. Twickenham, UK: Supernova Books

Doggett, Peter. 2011. *You Never Give Me Your Money*. Harper Paperbacks

Doggett, Peter. 2007. *There's A Riot Going On, Revolutionaries, Rock Stars, and the Rise and Fall of the '60s*, Canongate, New York

Dougals, Susan. 1994. *Where the Girls Are: Growing Up Female With The Mass Media*. New York: Times Books, Random House

DuNoyer, Paul. 2006. *John Lennon: We All Shine On. The Stories Behind Every John Lennon Song 1970-1980*. London: Carlton Books

DuNoyer, Paul. 2015. *Conversations with McCartney*. Hodder and Stoughton

Egan, Sean. 2009. *The Mammoth Book of the Beatles*. Philadelphia, London: Running Press

Emerson, Ken. 2006. *Always Magic in the Air: The Bomp and Brilliance of the Brill Building Era*. London: Forth Estate

Estulin, Daniel. *Tavistock Institute: Social Engineering the Masses*. Trine Day, 2015

Everett, Walter. 2001. *The Beatles as Musicians: The Quarrymen Through Rubber Soul*. London: Oxford University Press

Foster, Mo. 2000. *Play Like Elvis! How British Musicians Bought The American Dream*. Cornwall: MPG Books, Bodmin

Gaar, Gillian. 2002. *She's a Rebel: The History of Women in Rock and Roll.* Expanded second edition, New York: Seal Press

Garlitz, Dustin 'A Reflection on the Dionysian Spirit of Music in Nietzsche's *The Birth of Tragedy*,' (University of South Florida, 2006), 3. Online at: http://www.philosophyofmusic.org/nietzsche_music_garlitz_2006.pdf

Gluck, Sherna, Berger. 1988. *Rosiethe Riveter: Women, the War and Social Change*. New York: Meridian Press

Gordy, Berry. 2013. *To Be Loved: The Music, Magic, Memories of Motown*, Rosetta Books

Grieg, Charlotte. 1989. *Will You Still Love Me Tomorrow?: Girl Groups from the 50s On*. London: Virago

Heisler, Creg. 2007. *Spirit-Led Preaching: The Holy Spirit's Role in Sermon Preparation and Delivery*, Broadman and Holman Publishers, Nashville, USA

Hieronimus, Dr. Robert R.. 2002. *Inside the Yellow Submarine*. Krause Publication

Hewitt, Paolo. 2009. *The Sharper World: A Mod Anthology*. London: Helter Skelter Publishing

Hoeveler, Diane Long *Blake's Erotic Apocalypse: An Androgynous Ideal in Blake and Shelley* (Champaign, IL: University of Illinois Press, 1976), 21.

Houlgate, Stephen. 1991. *Freedom, Truth and History: An Introduction to Hegel's Philosophy*. Routledge, Judt, Tony. 2010. *Postwar: A History of Europe Since 1945*. London: Vintage.

King, Carole. 2013. *A Natural Woman*. London, Virago Press

Kollerstrom, Nicholas. 2015. *The Life and Death of Paul McCartney*. Moon Rock Books

Krerowicz, Aaron. 2014. *The Beatles and the Avant-Garde*, AK Books

Kureishi, Hanif, and Savage, Jon. 1995. *Pop*. London: Faber and Faber

Lachman, Gary. 2001. *Turn Off Your Mind*. The Disinformation Company

Lachman, Gary. 2008. *Politics and the Occult: The Left, The Right and The Radically Unseen*, Quest Books

Landon, Dr Anthony. 2011. *The Holy Spirit and His Gifts*. West Bow Press

Lee, Martin A., and Shalin, Bruce. 1994. *Acid Dreams: The Complete Social History of the CIA, the Sixties and Beyond*. Grove Press

Leng, Simon. 2006. *While My Guitar Gently Weeps: The Songs of George Harrison*. Hal Leonard

Lennon, Cynthia. 2005. *John*. Audio Book

Lewisohn, Mark. 2013. *The Beatles: Tune In*. Little Brown

Livingstone, David. 2015. *Transhumanism: The History Of A Dangerous Idea*, Sabilillah Publications

MacDonald, Ian. 2008. *Revolution in the Head: The Beatles Records and the Sixties*. Third Revised Edition, London: Vintage Books

MacLeod, Sean. 2015. *Leaders of the Pack: Girl Groups of the 1960s and their Influence on Popular Culture*, London, New York, Rowman and Littlefield

McRobbie, Angela (ed.). 1982. *Zoot Suits and Second Hand Dresses: An Anthology of Fashion and Music*. London: Macmillan

Miles, Barry. 1998. *Paul McCartney: Many Years from Now*. New York: Owl Books

Miles, Barry. 2009. *The British Invasion*. Sterling, New/London

Mirecki, Paul Allan. 2002. *Magic and Ritual in the Ancient World*. Abe Books

Norman, Philip. 2008. *John Lennon: The Life*. New York: Harper Collins

Norman, Philip. 2011. *Shout!: The Beatles in Their Generation*. New York: Simon and Schuster

Norman, Philip. 2013. *Mick Jagger*. Harper Press

Norman, Philip. 2016. *Paul McCartney*. Weidenfeld and Nicolson, UK

Oldham, Andrew Loog. 2000. *Stoned*. London: Vintage Press

Oldham, Andrew Loog. *Stonefree*, Kindle edition

Padel, Ruth. 2000. *I Am a Man: Sex Gods and Rock and Roll*. London: Faber and Faber

Philo, Simon. 2015. *The British Invasion: The Crosscurrents of Musical Influence*. London, New York, Rowman and Littlefield

Ribowsky, Mark. 2006. *He's a Rebel: Phil Spector, Rock and Roll's Legendary Producer*. Cambridge, MA: Da Capo Press

Richards, Keith. 2011. *Life*. Back Bay Books. Reprint Edition

Riley, Tim. 2005. Fever: *How Rock 'n' Roll Transformed Gender in America*. New York: Picador

Riley, Tim. 2011. *Lennon: The Man, the Myth and the Music*. Hyperion

Rivers, Karen L. 2016. *Love and the Evolution of Consciousness*. Lindisfarne Books

Selvin, Joel. 2016. *Altamont: The Rolling Stones, The Hells Angels, and The Inside Story of Rock's Darkest Day*. Harper Collins

Sanchez, Tony. 1979. *Up and Down with the Rolling Stones: My Rollercoaster Ride with Keith Richards*. W. Morrow

Sandford, Christopher. 2006. *McCartney*. London: Arrow Books

Salewicz, Chris. 2002. *Mick and Keith*. London: Orion

Savage, Jon. 2015. *1966*. Faber and Faber

Seddon, Richard. 2001. *The End of the Millennium and Beyond*. Temple Lodge

Shapiro, Marc. 2005. *All Things Must Pass: The Life of George Harrison*. Virgin Books

Shaw, Arnold. 1987. *The Rockin' 50s: The Decade that Transformed The Pop Music Scene*, Da Capo Press, New York

Shepherd, John, Horn, David and Oliver, Paul (eds.). 2003

Continuum Encyclopedia of Popular Music of the World. Part 1 Vol 1 Media Industry and Society. New York: *Continuum*

Spitz, Bob. 2005. *The Beatles: The Biography*. Boston: Little Brown

Stanley, Bob. 2013. *Yeah, Yeah, Yeah: The Story of Modern Pop*. London: Faber and Faber

Starr, Michael Seth. 2015. *Ringo: With a Little Help*. Backbeat Books.

Steiner, Rudolf. *The Universal Human, The Evolution of the Individuality*, Lectures 1909 and 1916 Munich and Bern. Translation edited by Christopher Bamford and Sabine H. Seile, Anthroposohpical Press.

Steiner, Rudolf. 1906. *The Occult Basis of Music*, GA 283

Steiner, Rudolf. 1919. *The Threefold Social Order*. GA 23https://steinerlibrary. org/Books/23/AP1972/Chapter_01.html Last Accessed 11/11/22

Steiner, Rudolf. 1920. 'Polarities in the Evolution of Mankind' (GA 197) lecture of 24 June in Stuttgart

Steiner, Rudolf. 1966. *The Threefold Social Order*, Translation by Frederick C. Heckel, Anthroposophic Press, Inc. New York

Steiner, Rudolf (a). 1969. *Occult Science: An Outline*. Rudolf Steiner Press, London

Steiner, Rudolf (b). 1961. *The Study of Man*, GA 293

Steiner, Rudolf. 1977. *World History in the Light of Anthroposophy*, Rudolf Steiner Press, London

Steiner, Rudolf. 1983. *The Inner Nature of Music and the Experience of Tone*

Steiner, Rudolf. 1992. *The Philosophy of Freedom*. Translated by Ritta Stebbing. Rudolf Steiner Press, Bristol

Steiner, Rudolf. 1994. *Theosophy*. Steiner Books

Steiner, Rudolf. 1998. *Anthroposophical Leading Thoughts: Anthroposophy as a Path of Knowledge*, Rudolf Steiner Press, London

Steiner, Rudolf. 2003. *Science: An Introductory Reader*. Sophia Books, Rudolf Steiner Press, UK.

Steiner, Rudolf. (2004). *The Social Future* (Schmidt Number: S-3886, Online Since 30 November, The Social Question As A Cultural Question, A Question of Equity and a Question of Economics [New English edition, translation completely revised by Henry B. Monges]

Strass, Laurie (ed.). *She's So Fine: Reflections of Whiteness, Femininity, Adolescence and Class, 1960s Music*. Surrey, UK and Burlington, USA: Ashgate, 2011

Soesman, Albert. 2014. *Our Twelve Senses: How Healty Senses Refresh the Soul*. Hawthorn Press

Sorensen, Jesper. 2006. *A Cognitive Theory of Magic*. Rowman and Littlefield

Taylor, Steve. 2004. *The A to X of Alternative Music*. London: Bloomsbury

Turner, Steve. 2009. *The Beatles: A Hard Day's Write, The Stories Behind Every Song*. New York: MJF Books

Turner, Steve. 2016. *Beatles '66*. Harper Collins Press

Warwick, Jacqueline. 2007. *Girl Groups: Girl Culture, Popular Music and Identity in the 1960's*. London, New York: Routledge

Whiteley, Sheila. 2000. *Women and Popular Music: Sexuality, Identity and Subjectivity*. New York: Routledge

Williams, Nicholas M. 1998. *Ideology and Utopia in the Poetry of William Blake*. Cambridge University Press

Wilson, Brian. 1996. *Wouldn't It Be Nice: My Own Story: Brian Wilson, The Creative Genius Behind the Beach Boys*. London, New York, Bloomsbury

Wilson, Mary. 1999. *Dreamgirl: My Life as a Supreme*. New York: Cooper Square Press

Wilson, Mary. 1999. *Supreme Faith*. New York: Cooper Square Press

Woodhead, Leslie. 2013. *How the Beatles' Rocked the Kremlin*. Bloomsbury

Womack, Kenneth. 2007. *Long and Winding Roads: The Evolving Artistry of the Beatles*, Bloomsbury, New York and London

Magazines and Articles:

Atwill, Joe and Irvin, Jan. 2013. 'Manufacturing the Deadhead: A Product of Social Engineering', https://logosmedia.com/2013/05/manufacturing-the-deadhead-a-product-of-social-engineering-by-joe-atwill-and-jan-irvin/

Boysen, Ryan. 2015. 'Cloak and Dropper: The Twisted History of the CIA and LSD', *Alternet*

Cooper, Lana. 'The Magical Mystery Four: The Beatles As a Successful System of Archetypes.' Popmusicmatters.com

Ellen, Barbara. 2016. 'Was '66 Pop's Greatest Year?, The Beach Boys: Pet Sounds', *The Observer*

Gibron, Bill. 'Yin and Yang the Beatles: *A Hard Day's Night* vs. *Help!*' Popmusicmatters.com

Irvin, Jan. 2015. 'Spies in Academic Clothing: The Untold Story of MKULTRA and the Counterculture', 13 May

Krupa, Jessy. 'Yesterday... and Today.' Popmusicmatters.com

Lake, Robert. 2017. 'With A Little Help from Their (Mostly White) Friends: Searching for Invisible Members of Sgt. Pepper's Lonely Hearts Club Band.' In J.Austin (Editor). *Spinning Popular Culture as Public Pedagogy*. Rotterdam, The Netherlands. Sense Publishers

Brussell, Mae. 1976 'Monterey Pop to Altamont OPERATION CHAOS, The CIA's War Against the Sixties Counter-Culture', November. http://www.whale.to/b/brussell1.html

Noebel, David A. 1965. 'Communisim, Hypnotism, and The Beatles.' A Christian Crusade Publication

O' Hagan, Sean. 2016. 'Was 66 Pop's Greatest Year?, The Beatles: Revolver,' The Observer, 31 Jan.

Riebling, Mark. 2010. 'Was Timothy Leary a CIA Agent?' *American Resistance to Empire*, Jan. 23

Rosen, Jody. 2007. 'Everything You Know About Sgt. Pepper's Is Wrong', Slate.com

Runtagh, Jordan. 2016. 'When John Lennon's "Bigger than Jesus" Controversy Turned Ugly.' *Rolling Stone*, 29 July

Documentaries, Films, Television and Radio Interviews:

Aspinall, Neil and Chipperfield, Chips. 2000. *Anthology: The* Beatles, Apple Corps, UK

Braudy, Leo. 2001. *Walk On By: The Story of Popular Music*, BBC, UK

Byers, Michiko. 2003. *Inside John Lennon.* Multicom Entertainment, USA

Cole, Steve. 2005. *Stuart Sutcliffe: The Lost Beatle*. BBC, UK

Cowley, Elizabeth. 1966. *A Whole Scene Going*, January, BBC, UK

Crowder, Paul and Lerner, Murray. 2007. *Amazing Journey: The Story of the Who*, Spitfire Pictures, UK

Curtis, Adam. 2016. *Hypernormalization*. BBC, UK

Curtis, Adam. 2009. *It Felt Like a Kiss*. BBC, UK

Curtis, Adam. 2002. *The Century of Self*. BBC, UK

Fleischman, Stephen. 1966. *Anatomy of Pop: The Music Explosion*, ABC Documentary, USA

Goodall, Howard. 2004. *Great Composers of the 20th Century*. Channel 4, UK

Haworth, Don. 1965. *Liverpool: The Singing City*. BBC. UK

Harrel, Rod. 2010. *A Conspiracy of Silence: The Murder of John Lennon*. Orthicon Ghost Production, independent release, UK

Howard, Ron. 2016. *Eight Days a Week*. Studio Canal, UK

Knowles, Christopher. 2001. *The Secret History of Rock & Roll*, Frozen Television, USA

Kruger, Li-Da and Oremland, Paul. 2006. *The 60s, The Beatles Decade*. UK

Lester, Richard. 1965. *Help!* Shenson Films, United Artists, USA

Lester, Richard. 1964. *A Hard Day's Night*, United Artists, USA

Lambert, Dave. 2008. *Magical Mystery Tour Memories*, Wienerworld Ltd, UK

Leaf, David and Scheinfeld, John. 2006. *The US Vs. John Lennon*. Lionsgate, USA

Lindsay-Hogg, Michael. 1970. *Let it Be*. Apple Corps, UK

Littlefield, Connie. 2002. *Hoffman's Potion*. Conceptafilm, National Film Board of Canada, Canada

Manday, Charlie and Raven, Abbe. 1999. *The Century: America's Time*. ABC News, USA

Marquand, Richard. 1998. *The Brian Epstein Story*. A & E Television Networks, USA

McGinn, Stephen and Piper, John. 2015.*The Nations Favourite Beatles Number 1*. Shiver Productions, ITV, UK

Moriarty, Brian. 1999. 'Game Developers Conference.' San Jose, CA

O' Dell, Dennis. 1967. *Magical Mystery Tour*. Apple Corps, UK

Oppenheim, David. 1967. *Inside Pop: The Rock Revolution* CBS News special, 25 April. USA

Palmer, Tony. 1977. *All You Need Is Love: The Story of Popular Music*. UK

Peebles, Andy. 1980. 'John Lennon The Final Interview,' BBC Radio 1, December 6th. BBC, UK

Prism Films. 2007. *The Byrds: Under Review*, Prism Films, Chrome Dreams Media, UK

Santilli, Ray. 2002. *George Harrison: The Quiet Beatle*

Scorsese, Martin. 2011. *Living in the Material World*, Grove Street Pictures. USA

Tickell, Paul. 2016. Arena: *1966-50 Years Ago Today*, BBC

Woodhead, Leslie. 2009. *How the Beatles' Rocked the Kremlin*, BBC Four, UK

Books to challenge  *your perception of reality*

A message from Clairview

We are an independent publishing company with a focus on cutting-edge, non-fiction books. Our innovative list covers current affairs and politics, health, the arts, history, science and spirituality. But regardless of subject, our books have a common link: they all question conventional thinking, dogmas and received wisdom.

Despite being a small company, our list features some big names, such as Booker Prize winner Ben Okri, literary giant Gore Vidal, world leader Mikhail Gorbachev, modern artist Joseph Beuys and natural childbirth pioneer Michel Odent.

So, check out our full catalogue online at
www.clairviewbooks.com
and join our emailing list for news on new titles.

office@clairviewbooks.com

CLAIRVIEW